formatio

TRADITION. EXPERIENCE.
TRANSFORMATION.

Formatio books from InterVarsity Press follow the rich tradition of the church in the journey of spiritual formation. These books are not merely about being informed, but about being transformed by Christ and conformed to his image. Formatio stands in InterVarsity Press's evangelical publishing tradition by integrating God's Word with spiritual practice and by prompting readers to move from inward change to outward witness. InterVarsity Press uses the chambered nautilus for Formatio, a symbol of spiritual formation because of its continual spiral journey outward as it moves from its center. We believe that each of us is made with a deep desire to be in God's presence. Formatio books help us to fulfill our deepest desires and to become our true selves in light of God's grace.

ANCIENT CHRISTIAN
Devotional

A Year of Weekly Readings

LECTIONARY
CYCLE
C

General Editor Thomas C. Oden

Edited by Cindy Crosby

IVP Books

An imprint of InterVarsity Press
Downers Grove, Illinois

InterVarsity Press
P.O. Box 1400, Downers Grove, IL 60515-1426
ivpress.com
email@ivpress.com

InterVarsity Press® is the book-publishing division of InterVarsity Christian Fellowship/USA®, a movement
of students and faculty active on campus at hundreds of universities, colleges and schools of nursing in the
United States of America, and a member movement of the International Fellowship of Evangelical Students.
For information about local and regional activities, visit intervarsity.org.

The Scripture quotations quoted herein are from the Revised Standard Version of the Bible, copyright
1946, 1952, 1971 by the Division of Christian Education of the National Council of the Churches of Christ in
the U.S.A. Used by permission. All rights reserved.

Design: Cindy Kiple
Images: Scala/Art Resource, New York. View of the apse. St. Vitale, Ravenna, Italy.

ISBN 978-0-8308-3528-7

Printed in the United States of America ∞

Library of Congress Cataloging-in-Publication Data

Ancient Christian devotional: a year of weekly readings / edited by
Cindy Crosby; general editor, Thomas C. Oden.
    p. cm.
  Includes bibliographical references and index.
  ISBN 978-0-8308-3431-0 (pbk.: alk. paper)
  1. Bible—Devotional literature. I. Crosby, Cindy, 1961- II. Oden,
Thomas C.
  BS491.5.A52 2007
  242'.3—dc22

                                           2006101569

P	18	17	16	15	14	13	12	11	10	9	8	7	6	5	4
Y	31	30	29	28	27	26	25	24	23	22	21	20	19		

CONTENTS

Welcome to the
ANCIENT CHRISTIAN
DEVOTIONAL

Listen carefully to me. Procure books [of the Bible]
that will be medicines for the soul. . . . Don't simply dive into them.
Swim in them. Keep them constantly in your mind.

JOHN CHRYSOSTOM,
HOMILIES ON COLOSSIANS 9

Many Christians today lack grounding in the riches of church history. We may find ourselves "rootless and drifting in a barren secular and ecclesiastical landscape."* The church fathers offer us context and tradition that will help us establish the roots we need. They do so by taking us deeper into the rich resources of Scripture, helping us to read holy writings with ancient eyes.

This devotional combines excerpts from the writings of the church fathers as found in The Ancient Christian Commentary on Scripture with a simple structure of daily reading and prayer. It is designed to allow you to work through the material at your own pace. You can read a little each day, or, if you like to have a longer time of prayer once a week, it would work nicely in that format as well.

There are fifty-two weeks of readings, which follow the liturgical year. The date range with each week indicates the Sunday associated with the reading. The year begins with the readings for the first Sunday in Advent, four Sundays before Christmas. Depending on where Easter falls in a given year, you may need to adjust your reading. The readings for the first Sunday of Lent begin in Week 13 and go through Week 18. Easter is in Week 19. Six weeks of Easter readings then follow. If Easter was early and you skipped some readings, you might at this point go back and pick them up. Pentecost is in Week 26. In Week 27 we then pick up the dating of the entries. You will also find a special week of readings in Week 48 for All Saints' Day, which is celebrated November first or the first Sunday in November.

Each week you will find the following elements.

THEME

An overview of the week's theme, drawing together the texts of the week. (The texts follow the Revised Common Lectionary Cycle C.)

OPENING PRAYER

A simple prayer taken from early church sources, which you can pray daily.

READINGS

Each week you will find an Old Testament, Epistle and Gospel reading, in keeping with the long tradition of the church lectionary cycles (depending on the liturgical cycle, some readings may differ slightly).

PSALM OF RESPONSE

The psalm can be used for prayer and meditation. It is there to help you offer words of petition and praise to God. You may want to pray through it daily.

REFLECTIONS FROM THE CHURCH FATHERS

These quotes offer insight on the Scripture passage. Read a few of these quotes each day, and stop when you feel stirred to pray or ponder. Give yourself time to reflect before God on what you are learning. You may want to journal your thoughts.

CLOSING PRAYER

This simple prayer drawn from ancient sources is designed to be used daily to close your time with God.

If you want to spend ten or fifteen minutes with this material each day, a suggested structure for your time would be to read the opening prayer, the psalm, one of the Scripture texts, two or three of the Reflections from the Church Fathers, and the closing prayer. Feel free to write in the book to note the sections you have completed as you go.

Don't worry about getting through the material on any particular schedule. Allow God to speak to you. Listen. Rest. This book should not be a source of guilt but a resource of grace. May your reading draw you to dig deep into the riches of God's Word.

> The Word of God is in your heart. The Word digs in this soil so that the spring may gush out. (Origen)

*Robert Wilken, as quoted in Christopher Hall, *Reading Scripture with the Church Fathers* (Downers Grove, Ill.: InterVarsity Press, 1998).

Walk in Love

THEME

Our God is a God of justice and righteousness (Jer 33:14-16). During the Advent season, we are reminded that we are called to learn his ways and walk in the paths of humility and love (Ps 25:1-9). As we look to his return (Lk 21:25-36), we pray and give thanks, desiring to become holy as he is holy (1 Thess 3:9-13).

OPENING PRAYER: *First Sunday in Advent*

Incline, O Lord, thy merciful ears, and illuminate the darkness of our hearts by the light of thy visitation; through Jesus Christ our Lord. Amen. *The Gelasian Sacramentary*

OLD TESTAMENT READING: *Jeremiah 33:14-16*

REFLECTIONS FROM THE CHURCH FATHERS

The Promise Springs Forth. LEO THE GREAT: But the majesty of the Son of God, in which he is equal with the Father in its garb of a slave's humility, feared no diminution, required no augmentation. And the very effect of his mercy, which he expended on the restitution of humanity, he was able to bring about solely by the power of his Godhead, thus rescuing the creature that was made in the image of God from the yoke of his cruel oppressor. But because the devil had not shown himself so violent in his attack on the first man as to bring him over to his side without the consent of his free will, the voluntary sin and hostile desires of humanity had to be destroyed in such a way that the standard of justice should not stand in the way of the gift of grace. And therefore in the general ruin of the entire human race there was but one remedy in the secret of the divine plan which could help the fallen, and that was that one of the sons of Adam should be born free and innocent of original transgression, to prevail for the rest both by his example and his merits. Still further, because this was not permitted by natural generation, and because there could be no offspring from our faulty stock without seed, of which the Scripture says, "Who can make a clean thing conceived of an unclean seed? Is it not you who are alone?" David's Lord was made David's Son and sprang from the fruit of the promised branch—One without fault, the twofold nature coming together into one person, that by one and the same conception and birth might spring our Lord Jesus Christ, in whom was present both true Godhead for the performance of mighty works and true humanity for the endurance of sufferings. *Sermon 27.3.*

PSALM OF RESPONSE: *Psalm 25:1-9*

NEW TESTAMENT READING: *1 Thessalonians 3:9-13*

REFLECTIONS FROM THE CHURCH FATHERS

The Truth of Faith Pastorally Taught. AUGUSTINE: But every discourse on this topic, where one's goal is that what is said may not only be believed but also understood and known, is burdensome for those still spiritually immature. These the apostle says are carnal, needing to be nourished with milk, as they do not have the strength to perceive such things and are more easily frustrated than fed. *Tractates on John 98.5.1.*

Their Grace Is One. ATHANASIUS: For one and the same grace is from the Father in the Son, as the light of the sun and the sun's radiance is one, and as the sun's illumination is effected through the radiance. So too when Paul prays for the Thessalonians, in saying, "Now God himself our Father, and the Lord Jesus Christ, may he direct our way to you," he has guarded the unity of the Father and of the Son. For he has not said, "May they direct," as if a double grace were given from two sources . . . but "may he direct," to show that the Father gives grace through the Son. *Discourses Against the Arians 3.25.11.*

The Unrestrained Overflowing of Love. CHRYSOSTOM: This is proof of superabundant love, that he not only prays for them by himself but even inserts his prayer in his epistles. Paul's prayers demonstrate a fervent soul unable to restrain his love. The mention of his prayers also proves that Paul and Silvanus's failure to visit them was not voluntary or the result of indolence. It is as though Paul said, May God himself shorten the trials that constantly distract us, so that we may come directly to you. "And the Lord make you to increase and abound." Do you see the unrestrained madness of love that is shown by these words? *Homilies on Thessalonians 4.*

GOSPEL READING: *Luke 21:25-36*

REFLECTIONS FROM THE CHURCH FATHERS

Signs in the Heavens When People Fall into Unbelief. AMBROSE: This is a true sequence of prophecy and a fresh cause of mystery, because the Jews will be led captive a second time to Babylon and Assyria. Those throughout the world who have denied Christ will be captive. A hostile army will trample visible Jerusalem as the sword kills Jews. All Judea will be put to the spiritual sword, the two-edged sword, by the nations that will believe. There will be different signs in the sun, moon and the stars. . . . When very many fall away from religion, a cloud of unbelief will darken bright faith, because for me that heavenly Sun is either diminished or increased by my faith. If very many gaze on the rays of the worldly sun, the sun seems bright or pale in proportion to the capacity of the viewer, so the spiritual light is imparted to each according to the devotion of the believer. In its monthly courses, the moon, opposite the earth, wanes when it is in the sun's quarter. When the vices of the flesh obstruct the heavenly Light, the holy church also cannot borrow the brightness of the divine Light from the rays of Christ. In the persecutions, love of this life alone certainly very often shuts out the light of God. *Exposition of the Gospel of Luke 10.3-37.*

Drunkenness Weakens Soul and Body. ORIGEN: Drunkenness is therefore destructive in all things. It is the only thing that weakens the soul together with the body. According to the apostle, it can happen that when the body "is weak," the spirit is "much stronger," and when "the exterior person is destroyed, the interior person is renewed." In the illness of drunkenness, the body and the soul are destroyed at the same time. The spirit is corrupted equally with the flesh. All the members are weakened: the feet and the hands. The tongue is loosened. Darkness covers the eyes. Forgetfulness covers the mind so that one does not know himself nor does he perceive he is a person. Drunkenness of the body has that shamefulness. *Homilies on Leviticus 7.5-6.*

Adversity a Sign That the Kingdom Is at Hand. CYPRIAN: Beloved brothers and sisters, whoever serves as a soldier of God stationed in the camp of heaven already hopes for the divine things. He should recognize himself so that we should have no fear or dread at the storms and whirlwinds of the world. Through the encouragement of his provident voice, the Lord predicted that these things would come when he was instructing, teaching, preparing and strengthening the people of his church to endure everything to come. Christ foretold and prophesied that wars, famine, earthquakes and epidemics would arise in the various places. So that an unexpected and new fear of destructive agencies might not shake us, he forewarned that adversity would increase in the last times. *On Mortality 2.*

CLOSING PRAYER

Grant us, O Lord, not to mind earthly things but to love things heavenly; and even now, while we are placed among things that are passing away, to cleave to those that shall abide through Jesus Christ our Lord. *The Leonine Sacramentary*

Prepare the Way

THEME

The prophets foretold the coming of Christ (Mal 3:1-4), as did Zechariah (Lk 1:68-79) and John the Baptist, who prepared the way for the Lord (Lk 3:1-6). Until Christ returns again, we strive to become more like him (Phil 1:3-11).

OPENING PRAYER: *Second Sunday in Advent*

Cleanse us, O Lord, from our secret faults, and mercifully absolve us from our presumptuous sins, that we may receive thy holy things with a pure mind; through Jesus Christ our Lord. *The Leonine Sacramentary*

OLD TESTAMENT READING: *Malachi 3:1-4*

REFLECTIONS FROM THE CHURCH FATHERS

First and Second Advents Foretold. AUGUSTINE: Speaking further of Christ in the same vein, Malachi says, "Behold, I send my angel, and he shall prepare the way before my face. And presently the Lord, whom you seek, and the angel of the testament whom you desire, shall come into the temple. Behold, he comes, says the Lord of hosts. And who shall be able to think of the day of his coming? And who shall stand to see him?" In this text he foretells both comings of Christ, the first and the second—the first where he says, "And presently the Lord shall come into his temple." This refers to Christ's body, of which he himself said in the Gospel, "Destroy this temple, and in three days I will raise it up." His second coming is foretold in these words: "'Behold, he comes,' says the Lord of hosts. 'And who shall be able to think of the day of his coming? And who shall stand to see him?'" *City of God 18.35.2.*

John Is Elijah to Prepare the Way. IRENAEUS: And that we may not have to ask, of what God was the Word made flesh? He does himself previously teach us, saying, "There was a man sent from God, whose name was John. The same came as a witness, that he might bear witness of that light. He was not that light but came that he might testify of the light." By what God, then, was John, the forerunner who testifies of the light, sent into the world? Truly it was by him of whom Gabriel is the angel, who also announced glad tidings of his birth: that God who also had promised by the prophets that he would send his messenger before the face of his Son, who should prepare his way, that is, that he should bear witness of that light in the spirit and power of Elijah. *Against Heresies 3.11.4.*

Judgment by Fire. CHRYSOSTOM: The same Christ who did all this will hereafter stand before us as our judge. Certainly the prophets did not pass over this but foretold it. Some saw him in that very form in which he would stand before us; others predicted this only in words. *Demonstration Against the Pagans 11.1-3.*

Consuming Fire of Salvation. ORIGEN: The divine word says that our God is a "consuming fire" and that "he draws rivers of fire before him." He even enters in as "a refiner's fire and as a fuller's herb" to purify his own people. But when he is said to be a "consuming fire," we inquire what are the things that are appropriate to be consumed by God. And we assert that it is wickedness, and the works which result from it. *Against Celsus 4.13.*

RESPONSE: *Luke 1:68-79 (the Song of Zechariah)*

NEW TESTAMENT READING: *Philippians 1:3-11*

REFLECTIONS FROM THE CHURCH FATHERS

God Who Begins a Good Work in Us Will Complete It. CHRYSOS-TOM: See how he teaches them to be modest. Having just given them a superb testimonial, in order that they should not feel down and out as human beings are so apt to feel, he immediately teaches them to refer both the past and the future—everything—to Christ, who will bring to completion what he has begun in them. He does not take away anything from their achievement, for he has said, "I rejoice because of your fellowship," obviously pointing to their own very high level of accountability. But he does not imply that the achievement was theirs alone. Rather it was primarily God's work in them. *Homily on Philippians 2.1.6.*

The Grounds of Paul's Confidence. AMBROSIASTER: Paul had always found the Philippians to be immovable in their devotion to God. He knew how straight and unwearied their course was. He knew they were worthy to share in his own joy. People who share the same faith have good reason to rejoice together in the hope of future immortality and glory. *Epistle to the Philippians 1.7.*

How His Chains Confirm His Testimony. CHRYSOSTOM: His chains are without doubt a "confirmation of the gospel." How? Because if he had refused the bonds, he would have been seen as a deceiver. But the one who endures everything, including persecution and imprisonment, shows that he does not suffer them for any human reason but on account of God, who rights the balance. . . . See how absolutely he turns everything on its head. For what others might view as a weakness or reproach, this he calls *confirmation. Homily on Philippians 2.1.7.*

Discerning What Is Useful. AMBROSIASTER: He wishes, with God's assistance, to pour into them pure Christian doctrine, that their faith will be firm and that they will see clearly all the vast implications of their faith. He wants them to be able to distinguish what is useful from what is useless. He prays that they may adorn the teaching of the Lord with works of righteousness, producing the fruit of immortality to bring about an abundance of good things. This will be the glory of the apostle to the Gentiles. *Epistle to the Philippians 1.11.*

God Glorified by the Fruits of Righteousness. THEODORET OF CYR: Enjoy these gifts! Keep your faith uncontaminated! Present the fruit of righteousness to God, so that God will be celebrated by all. *Epistle to the Philippians 1.11.*

GOSPEL READING: *Luke 3:1-6*

REFLECTIONS FROM THE CHURCH FATHERS

Setting the Stage for Salvation History. GREGORY THE GREAT: It is apparent, then, that Judea, which lay divided among so many kings, had reached the end of its sovereignty. It was also appropriate to indicate not only under which kings but also under which high priests this occurred. Since John the Baptist preached one who was at once both king and priest, the Evangelist Luke indicated the time of his preaching by referring to both the kingship and the high priesthood. *Forty Gospel Homilies 6.*

Repent to Prepare for John's Baptism. ORIGEN: The precursor of Christ—the voice of one crying in the wilderness—preaches in the desert of the soul that has known no peace. Not only then, but even now, a bright and burning lamp first comes and preaches the baptism of repentance for the forgiveness of sins. Then the true Light follows, as John himself said: "He must increase, but I must decrease." The word came in the desert and spread in all the countryside around the Jordan. *Homilies on the Gospel of Luke 21.3.14.*

Prepare by Making Ready to Receive Christ. CYRIL OF ALEXANDRIA: John, being chosen for the apostleship, was also the last of the holy prophets. For this reason, as the Lord has not come yet, he says, "Prepare the way of the Lord." What is the meaning of "Prepare the way of the Lord"? It means, Make ready for the reception of whatever Christ may wish to do. Withdraw your hearts from the shadow of the law, discard vague figures and no longer think perversely. Make the paths of our God straight. For every path that leads to good is straight and smooth and easy, but the one that is crooked leads down to wickedness those that walk in it. *Commentary on Luke, Homily 6.*

No Barriers to the Coming of Truth. PRUDENTIUS:
As messenger of God, who was about to come,
He faithfully observed this law, constructing well,
That every hill might low become and rough ways plain,
Lest when the truth should glide from heaven down to earth
It then would find a barrier to its swift approach.
Hymns for Every Day 7.51-55.

☙ CLOSING PRAYER

O God, the Author and Giver of true blessedness, guide us into the path of the undefiled, that, seeking the testimonies of thy law with pious hearts, we may continually love what thou command and desire that whereunto they lead; through Jesus Christ our Lord. *The Gelasian Sacramentary*

Rejoice!

THEME

We should rejoice! The Lord promises us he will renew us with love and eventually bring us home to be with him (Zeph 3:14-20). We need not be anxious or afraid; rather, we can give thanks for our salvation and the strength that God gives us (Is 12:2-6). We are promised "the peace of God, which passes all understanding" (Phil 4:4-7) even as we prepare our hearts during Advent for the good news—Christ's coming (Lk 3:7-18).

OPENING PRAYER: *Third Sunday in Advent*

O God, make us children of quietness and heirs of peace. *Clement of Rome*

OLD TESTAMENT READING: *Zephaniah 3:14-20*

REFLECTIONS FROM THE CHURCH FATHERS

The Joy of the Lord's Redemption. THEODORE OF MOPSUESTIA:
Live now in utter delight, O Jerusalem, living in complete happiness and satisfaction; for God has removed all your lawless deeds and of necessity has rescued you from the power of the foe to whom you were subjected in paying the penalty of punishment. The Lord will now be in your midst, showing his kingship by his care for you, so that trouble will no longer be able to approach you. *Commentary on Zephaniah 3.11-15.*

Rejoice in Salvation Through Christ. CYRIL OF ALEXANDRIA: As far as the deeper meaning of the passage is concerned, it clearly commands Jerusalem to rejoice exceedingly, to be especially glad, to cheer up wholeheartedly as its trespasses are wiped out, evidently through Christ. The spiritual and holy Zion—that is, the church, the holy multitude of the believers—is justified in Christ and only in him. By him and through him we are also saved as we escape from the harm of the invisible enemies, for we have a Mediator who was incarnated in our form, the king of all, that is, the Word of God the Father. Thanks to him, we do not see evil anymore, for we have been delivered from the powers of evil. He [the Word] is the armor of good will, the peace, the wall, the one who bestows incorruption. *Commentary on Zephaniah 43.*

The Prophecy About Redemption. THEODORET OF CYR: I am aware that some commentators understood this text to apply to the return from Babylon and the renovation of Jerusalem, and I do not contradict their words: the prophecy applies also to what happened at that time. But you can find a more exact outcome after the incarnation of our Savior: then it was that he healed the oppressed in heart in the washing of regeneration, then it was that he renewed human nature, loving us so much as to give his life for us. After all, "greater love than this no one can show than for one to lay down one's life for one's friend," and again, "God so loved the world as to give his only-begotten Son so that everyone believing in him might not be lost but have eternal life." *Commentary on Zephaniah 3:16-18.*

RESPONSE: *Isaiah 12:2-6*

NEW TESTAMENT READING: *Philippians 4:4-7*

REFLECTIONS FROM THE CHURCH FATHERS

Forbearance Defined. MARIUS VICTORINUS: Forbearance is individual patience that observes due measure without straining beyond its station. When we live among strangers and live in a way commensurate with our lowliness, God will lift us up. So it is here; we do well to recognize our lowliness. "Therefore let your moderation," he says, "be known to all." Why does he tell us this? So that we may make a pleasing show here? No, but so that when Christ comes he may raise up our lowliness and exalt our moderation. *Epistle to the Philippians 4.4-5.*

Let Others See, That They May Profit. **AMBROSIASTER:** Paul wants all to profit by good examples. When their forbearance becomes apparent as their regular way of life, their works will shine forth. There will be nothing lacking in those who imitate their virtue. They will be blessed not only from doing good deeds but also by inspiring good deeds in others. *Epistle to the Philippians 4.7.1.*

How This Peace Passes All Understanding. **CHRYSOSTOM:** "The peace of God," which he imparted to us, "passes all understanding." For who could have expected and who could have hoped for such benefits? It transcends every human intellect and all speech. For his enemies, for those who hated him, for the apostates—for all these he did not refuse to give his only begotten Son, so as to make peace with them. . . . The peace which will preserve us is the one of which Christ says, "My peace I leave with you; my peace I give you." For this peace passes all human understanding. How? When he sees that we should be at peace with enemies, with the unrighteous, with those who display contentiousness and hostility toward us, how does this not pass human understanding? *Homily on Philippians 15.4.4-7.*

GOSPEL READING: *Luke 3:7-18*

REFLECTIONS FROM THE CHURCH FATHERS

John's Call to Repent Is for Everyone. **ORIGEN:** To you who are coming to baptism, Scripture says, "Bear fruits that befit repentance." Do you want to know what fruits befit repentance? Love is a fruit of the Spirit. Joy is a fruit of the Spirit. So are peace, patience, kindness, goodness, faith, gentleness, self-control, and the others of this sort. If we have all of these virtues, we have produced "fruits that befit repentance." . . . John, the last of the prophets, prophesies the expulsion of the first nation and the call of the Gentiles. To those who were boasting about Abraham he says, "Do not begin to say to yourselves, 'We have Abraham for a father.' " And again he speaks about the Gentiles, "For I tell you, God is able from these stones to raise up children to Abraham." From what stones? Surely he was not pointing to irrational, material stones but to people who were uncomprehending and sometimes hard. *Homilies on the Gospel of Luke 22.6, 8-9.*

Repentance Requires Almsgiving. AUGUSTINE: In a word, therefore, let us all listen and seriously reflect what great merit there is in having fed Christ when he was hungry—and what sort of a crime it is to have ignored Christ when he was hungry. Repentance for our sins does indeed change us for the better. But even repentance will not appear to be of much use to us if works of mercy do not accompany it. Truth bears witness to this through John, who said to those who came to him, "Bear fruits that befit repentance." And so those who have not produced such fruits have no reason to suppose that by a barren repentance they will earn pardon for their sins. *Sermon 389.6.27.*

Gehenna for All Who Do Not Produce Good Works. GREGORY THE GREAT: The tree is the entire human race in this world. The axe is our Redeemer. His humanity is like the axe's handle and iron head. It is his divinity that cuts. The axe is now laid at the root of the tree because, although he is waiting patiently, what he will do is nonetheless apparent. Every tree that does not bear good fruit will be cut down and thrown into the fire. Every wicked person, refusing to bear the fruit of good works in this life, will find the conflagration of Gehenna all the more swiftly prepared for him or her. *Forty Gospel Homilies 6.*

The Axe Is God's Wrath, but a Remnant Is Saved. CYRIL OF ALEX-
ANDRIA: What he means by the axe in this passage is the sharp wrath
which God the Father brought on the Jews for their wickedness toward
Christ and brazen violence. . . . John does not say, however, that the axe
was laid into the root, but at the root, that is, near the root. The
branches were cut off, but the plant was not dug up by its root. Thus
the remnant of Israel was saved and did not perish utterly. *Commentary
on Luke, Homily 7.*

Fire Refers to the Fiery Tongues at Pentecost. CYRIL OF JERUSA-
LEM: John, filled with the Holy Spirit from his mother's womb, was
sanctified for the purpose of baptizing the Lord. John himself did not
impart the Spirit but preached the glad tidings of him who does. He
says, "I indeed baptize you with water, for repentance. But he who is
coming after me, he will baptize you with the Holy Spirit and with fire."
Why fire? Because the descent of the Holy Spirit was in fiery tongues.
Concerning this the Lord says with joy, "I have come to cast fire on the
earth, and how I wish that it would be kindled!" *Catechetical Lecture
17.8.*

CLOSING PRAYER

O Lord, my God, grant us your peace; already, indeed, you have made
us rich in all things! Give us the peace of being at rest, that sabbath
peace, the peace which knows no end. *Augustine*

Restoration

◌ THEME

The prophets foretold the birth of Christ (Mic 5:2-5a), who would "be great to the ends of the earth." We look to God for restoration and salvation (Ps 80:1-7) through the ultimate sacrifice of his Son, Jesus Christ (Heb 10:5-10), whose birth through the virgin Mary was prophesied by Elizabeth (Lk 1:39-55) and which we anticipate during this Advent season.

◌ OPENING PRAYER: *Fourth Sunday in Advent*

We praise you, Father, invisible, giver of immortality. You are the source of life and light, the source of all grace and truth; you love us all, and you love the poor, you seek reconciliation with all and draw them all to you by sending your dear Son to visit them, who now lives and reigns with you, Father, and the Holy Spirit, one God forever and ever. Amen. *Serapion*

◌ OLD TESTAMENT READING: *Micah 5:2-5a*

REFLECTIONS FROM THE CHURCH FATHERS

Eternal but Born in a Temporal Place. CYRIL OF JERUSALEM: It is enough for piety for you to know, as we have said, that God has one only Son, one naturally begotten, who did not begin to be when he was born in Bethlehem but is before all ages. For listen to the prophet

Micah: "And you, Bethlehem, house of Ephratha, are little to be among the thousands of Judah. From you shall come forth for me a leader who shall feed my people Israel; and his goings forth are from the beginning, from the days of eternity." Therefore do not fix your attention on him as coming from Bethlehem simply but worship him as begotten eternally of the Father. Admit no one who speaks of a beginning of the Son in time, but acknowledge his timeless beginning, the Father. *Catechetical Lecture 11.20.*

Christ's Human Birth Defended. AUGUSTINE: According to prophecy, Christ was born in Bethlehem of Judah, at the time, as I said, when Herod was king in Judea. At Rome, the republic had given way to the entire empire, and the emperor Caesar Augustus had established a worldwide peace. Christ was born a visible man of a virgin mother, but he was a hidden God because God was his Father. So the prophet had foretold: "Behold, the virgin shall be with child and shall bring forth a son; and they shall call his name Emmanuel, which is interpreted, God with us." To prove that he was God, Christ worked many miracles, some of which—as many as seemed necessary to establish his claim—are recorded in the Gospels. Of these miracles the very first was the marvelous manner of his birth. *City of God 18.96.*

Herod Feared an Earthly Rival. LEO THE GREAT: Evidently the Hebrew leaders understood the prophecy in a carnal manner, just as Herod did, and reckoned that Christ's kingdom would be like the powers in this world. They hoped for a temporal leader, while Herod feared an earthly rival. "Herod, you are trapped in a useless fear. In vain do you attempt to rage against the child you suspect. Your realm does not encompass Christ, nor does the Lord of the world care about the meager limits within which you wield the rod of your power. He whom you do not wish to see reign in Judea reigns everywhere. You yourself would reign more happily if you would submit to his rule. Why not turn into honest service that which you resolve to do in falsehood and guile? Go with the wise men and worship the true king in humble adoration. But more inclined as you are toward the Jewish blindness, you do not imitate the faith of these Gentiles. You turn your perverse heart to cruel wiles. Yet you are not going to kill the one you fear, nor will you harm those whom you eliminate." *Sermon 34.2.*

PSALM OF RESPONSE: *Psalm 80:1-7*

NEW TESTAMENT READING: *Hebrews 10:5-10*

REFLECTIONS FROM THE CHURCH FATHERS

The Old Testament and the Prediction of Christ. PHOTIUS: Christ spoke "while coming into the world," not "after he had entered it." But manifestly he was already entering it when he promised David and maintained that he would seat one from the fruit of his loins on his throne until the age would come. Therefore, "while entering into the world because of the promises made to David, he also says this through him, since 'you did not wish for sacrifice and offering, neither were you well pleased' with the rites in the law." . . . And he calls the book the whole Old Testament. For the chief thing and the most noteworthy supposition of the Old Testament are the predictions about Christ. *Fragments on the Epistle to the Hebrews 10.5-9.*

The Abolition of Sacrifice. CHRYSOSTOM: Here he does not blame those who offer, showing that it is not because of their wickednesses that he does not accept them, as he says elsewhere, but because the thing itself has been convicted for the future and shown to have no strength or any suitableness to the times. *On the Epistle to the Hebrews 18.1.*

GOSPEL READING: *Luke 1:39-55*

REFLECTIONS FROM THE CHURCH FATHERS

Elizabeth Heralds Christ as God. PRUDENTIUS:
Believe what says the angel who was sent
From the Father's throne, or if your stolid ear
Catch not the voice from heaven, be wise and hear
The cry of aged woman, now with child.
O wondrous faith! The babe in senile womb
Greets through his mother's lips the Virgin's Son,
Our Lord; the child unborn makes known the cry
of the Child bestowed on us, for speechless yet,
He caused that mouth to herald Christ as God.
The Divinity of Christ 585-93.

Christ the Fruit of the Faithful. AMBROSE: You see that Mary did not doubt but believed and therefore obtained the fruit of faith. "Blessed . . . are you who have believed." But you also are blessed who have heard and believed. For a soul that has believed has both conceived and bears the Word of God and declares his works. Let the soul of Mary be in each of you, so that it magnifies the Lord. Let the spirit of Mary be in each of you, so that it rejoices in God. She is the one mother of Christ according to the flesh, yet Christ is the Fruit of all according to faith. Every soul receives the Word of God, provided that, undefiled and unstained by vices, it guards its purity with inviolate modesty. *Exposition of the Gospel of Luke 2.26.*

The Lord Is Magnified in Our Image of Him. ORIGEN: We ask how a soul can magnify the Lord. The Lord can undergo neither increase nor loss. He is what he is. Thus, why does Mary now say, "My soul magnifies the Lord?" . . . My soul is not directly an image of God. It was created as the image of an Image that already existed. . . . Each one of us shapes his soul into the image of Christ and makes either a larger or a smaller image of him. The image is either dingy and dirty or it is clean and bright and corresponds to the form of the original. Therefore, when I make the image of the Image—that is, my soul—large and magnify it by work, thought and speech, then the Lord himself is magnified in my soul, because it is an image of him. *Homilies on the Gospel of Luke 8.1-3.*

CLOSING PRAYER

Let us pray to the Lord without duplicity, in tune with one another, entreating him with sighs and tears, as befits people in our position—placed as we are between the many, lamenting that they have fallen away, and the faithful remnant that fears it may do the same itself; between the weak, laid low in large number, and the few still standing firm. Let us pray that peace may very soon be restored to us, help reach us in our dangers, to draw us from our dark retreats, and God's gracious promises to his servants find fulfillment. May we see the church restored and our salvation secured; after the rain, fair weather; after the darkness, light; after these storms and tempests, a gentle calm. Let us ask him to help us, because he loves us as a father loves his children, and to give us the tokens of his divine power that are usual with him. So will our persecutors be stopped from blaspheming, those who have fallen away repent to some purpose and the firm, unwavering faith of the steadfast be crowned with glory. *Cyprian*

Celebrate His Birth

THEME

For to us a child is born, to us a son is given (Is 9:2-7). In Bethlehem, Jesus is born of the virgin Mary; an event heralded by angels and marveled at by shepherds (Lk 2:1-20). The Lord reigns! Let us celebrate his birth and applaud his marvelous works (Ps 96). Christ is our blessed hope, who redeems us from sin and offers salvation to all who follow him (Tit 2:11-14).

OPENING PRAYER: *Christmas*

God's compassion for us is all the more wonderful because Christ died not for the righteous or the holy but for the wicked and the sinful, and, though the divine nature could not be touched by the sting of death, he took to himself, through his birth as one of us, something he could offer on our behalf. *Leo the Great*

OLD TESTAMENT READING: *Isaiah 9:2-7*

REFLECTIONS FROM THE CHURCH FATHERS

God's Grace. AMBROSE: Hence he was in the shadow of life, whereas sinners are in the shadow of death. According to Isaiah, the people who sinned sat in the shadow of death. For these a light arose, not by the merits of their virtues but by the grace of God. . . . No one can say that he can acquire more by his own efforts than what is granted to him by

the generosity of God. *On Paradise 5.29.*

Christ the Light. LEO THE GREAT: Although he filled all things with his invisible majesty, Christ came, nevertheless, to those who had not known him, as if from a very remote and deep seclusion. At that time, he took away the blindness of ignorance, as it has been written: "For those sitting in darkness and in the shadow of death, a light has risen." *Sermon 25.3.*

Both God and Human. AUGUSTINE: We read, "A child is born to us," because we see him in the nature of a servant, which he had because the Virgin conceived and brought forth a son. However, because it was the Word of God who became flesh in order to dwell among us, and because he remains what he was (that is, really God hidden in the flesh), we use the words of the angel Gabriel and call "his name Emmanuel." He is properly called God with us to avoid thinking of God as one person and the humanity [in Christ] as another. *Sermon 187.4.*

On His Shoulders. JUSTIN MARTYR: "A child is born to us, and a son is given to us, and the government is on his shoulders." This signifies the power of the cross, which, at his crucifixion, he placed on his shoulders. *First Apology 35.*

Christ's Names Point to His Divinity. CHRYSOSTOM: Come now, and let me show you that the Son is called God. "Behold, the virgin shall be with child and shall give birth to a son, and they shall call his name Immanuel, which means, 'God is with us.'" Did you see how both the name Lord is given to the Father and the name God is given to the Son? In the psalm, the sacred writer said, "Let them know that *Lord* is your name. Here Isaiah says, "They shall call his name Immanuel." And again, he says, "A child is born to us, and a son is given to us; and his name shall be called Angel of Great Counsel, God the Strong, the Mighty One." *Against the Anomoeans 5.15.*

The Throne of David. BEDE: Isaiah said, "His government will be increased, and there will be no end to peace on the throne of David and his kingdom, to confirm and strengthen it in right judgment and justice." He did not say "to acquire the glory of worldly riches" or "to have victory over many peoples and cities" or "to conquer the powerful," but "to confirm it in right judgment and justice." For it is through this that the church is strengthened and the kingdom of Christ is extended both within each of the faithful and throughout the entire world. *Exposition of the Gospel of Luke 1.1-33.*

PSALM OF RESPONSE: *Psalm 96*

NEW TESTAMENT READING: *Titus 2:11-14*

REFLECTIONS FROM THE CHURCH FATHERS

Two Comings. CYRIL OF JERUSALEM: For Paul has also shown us that there are these two comings, in his epistle to Titus where he says, "The grace of God our Savior has appeared unto all men, teaching us that, denying ungodliness and worldly lusts, we should live soberly, righteously and godly in this present world; looking for that blessed hope and the glorious appearing of the great God and our Savior Jesus Christ." You note how he acknowledges with thanksgiving the first coming and that we look for a second. . . . So our Lord Jesus Christ comes from heaven and comes with glory at the last day to bring this world to its close. *Catechetical Lectures 15.2-3.*

Life with God the Goal. BASIL THE GREAT: Therefore, the common Director of our lives, the great Teacher, the Spirit of truth, wisely and cleverly set forth the rewards, in order that, rising above the present labors, we might press on in spirit to the enjoyment of eternal blessings. "Blessed is the man who has not walked in the counsel of the ungodly." What is most truly good, therefore, is principally and primarily the most blessed. And that is God. So Paul also, when about to make mention of Christ, said, "according to the manifestation of our blessed God and Savior Jesus Christ." For, truly blessed is Goodness itself toward which all things look, which all things desire, and unchangeable nature, lordly dignity, calm existence; a happy way of life, in which there is no alteration, which no change touches, a flowing fount, abundant grace, inexhaustible treasure. *Homilies on the Psalms 10.3.*

For One and All at the Same Time. CHRYSOSTOM: "That he might purify to himself a people of his own." Considering the desperate condition of human nature and the ineffably tender solicitude of Christ, in what he delivered us from and what he freely gave us, and kindled by the yearning of affection toward him, this is a remarkably tender expression. Thus the prophets often appropriate to themselves him who is God of all, as in the words, "O God, you are my God, early will I seek you." Moreover, this language teaches that each individual justly owes a great debt of gratitude to Christ, as if he had come for that person's sake alone. For he would not have grudged this his condescension even if it were only for one person. The measure of his love to each is as great as to the whole world. *Commentary on Galatians, Galatians 2:20.*

GOSPEL READING: *Luke 2:1-20*

REFLECTIONS FROM THE CHURCH FATHERS

Heavenly Light in an Earthly Inn. AMBROSE: He is brought forth from the womb but flashes from heaven. He lies in an earthly inn but is alive with heavenly light. *Exposition of the Gospel of Luke 2.42-43.*

The Lord of Creation Has No Place to Be Born. JEROME: The Lord is born on earth, and he does not have even a cell in which to be born, for there was no room for him in the inn. The entire human race had a place, and the Lord about to be born on earth had none. He found no room among people. He found no room in Plato, none in Aristotle, but in a manger, among beasts of burden and brute animals, and among the simple, too, and the innocent. For that reason the Lord says in the Gospel: "The foxes have dens, and the birds of the air have nests, but the Son of Man has nowhere to lay his head." *Homilies on the Psalms 44.*

Heaven and Earth Are Joined in the Birth of Christ. JOHN THE MONK: Heaven and earth are united today, for Christ is born! Today God has come on earth, and humankind gone up to heaven. Today, for the sake of humankind, the invisible one is seen in the flesh. Therefore let us glorify him and cry aloud: glory to God in the highest, and on earth peace bestowed by your coming, Savior: glory to you! *Stichera of the Nativity of the Lord.*

Shepherds First Proclaimers of the Gospel. BEDE: The shepherds did not keep silent about the hidden mysteries that they had come to know by divine influence. They told whomever they could. Spiritual shepherds in the church are appointed especially for this, that they may proclaim the mysteries of the Word of God and that they may show to their listeners that the marvels which they have learned in the Scriptures are to be marveled at. *Homilies on the Gospels 1.7.*

CLOSING PRAYER

Christ is born: glorify him. Christ comes from heaven: go out to meet him. Christ descends to earth: let us be raised on high. *Gregory of Nazianzus*

Wise Men

THEME

During Epiphany, we remember the coming of the wise men from the east to honor the Savior's birth (Mt 2:1-12). As the prophets foretold, Christ, the light of the world, has penetrated the darkness (Is 60:1-6), bringing justice and peace (Ps 72:1-7, 10-14). Because of God's grace and Christ's birth, death and resurrection, we are offered salvation from sin (Eph 3:1-12).

OPENING PRAYER: *The Epiphany*

Almighty and everlasting God, you have revealed the incarnation of your Son by the bright shining of a star, which the wise men saw, and offered costly gifts in adoration; let the star of your justice always shine in our hearts, that we may give as our treasure all that we are and all that we possess, to your service; through Jesus Christ our Lord. *The Gelasian Sacramentary*

OLD TESTAMENT READING: *Isaiah 60:1-6*

REFLECTIONS FROM THE CHURCH FATHERS

Easter Exultation in New Jerusalem. JOHN OF DAMASCUS: Shine, shine, O new Jerusalem, for the glory of the Lord has shone on you. Rejoice and be glad, O Zion! And you, O immaculate, O Mother of God, exult with Job in the resurrection of your Son. Christ is risen, and he has crushed death and raised the dead: rejoice, therefore, O nations of the earth! Shine, shine, O new Jerusalem, for the glory of the Lord has risen over you. Cry out now and rejoice, O Zion; and you, the pure one, the Mother of God, exult in the resurrection of the one to whom you gave birth. On this day, the whole creation rejoices and exults, for Christ is risen and hades despoiled. *The Canon of Pascha, Ninth Ode.*

Christ Shares His Glory with Us. CYRIL OF ALEXANDRIA: Christ made our poverty his own, and we see in Christ the strange and rare paradox of lordship in servant's form and divine glory in human abasement. That which was under the yoke in terms of the limitations of manhood was crowned with royal dignities, and that which was humble was raised to the most supreme excellence. The Only-Begotten, however, did not become man only to remain in the limits of that emptying. The point was that he who was God by nature should, in the act of self-emptying, assume everything that went along with it. This was how he would be revealed as ennobling the nature of humanity in himself by making it participate in his own sacred and divine honors. We shall find that even the saints call the Son of God the "glory" of God the Father, and King and Lord, even when he became a man. Isaiah, for example, says in one place . . . "Shine forth, Jerusalem, for your light has come, and the glory of the Lord has risen on you. Behold, darkness and gloom may cover the earth, but over you the Lord shall be made manifest, and his glory shall be seen on you." *On the Unity of Christ.*

Divine Light Becomes the Outward Lifestyle. METHODIUS: It is the church whose children shall come to it with all speed after the resurrection, running to it from all quarters. The church rejoices, receiving the light that never goes down and clothed with the brightness of the Word as with a robe. For with what other more precious or honorable ornament was it becoming that the queen should be adorned, to be led as a bride to the Lord, when she had received a garment of light and therefore was called by the Father? Come then, let us go forward in our discourse and look on this marvelous woman as on virgins prepared for a marriage, pure and undefiled, perfect and radiating a permanent beauty, lacking nothing of the brightness of light; and instead of a dress, clothed with light itself; and instead of precious stones, her head adorned with shining stars. *Symposium, or Banquet of the Ten Virgins 8.5.*

PSALM OF RESPONSE: *Psalm 72:1-7, 10-14*

NEW TESTAMENT READING: *Ephesians 3:1-12*

REFLECTIONS FROM THE CHURCH FATHERS

The Disjointed Sentence Has a Simple Meaning. JEROME: After a diligent search I have found nothing that answers to his prior clause. . . . For he does not say, "For this reason I, Paul, have done this or that or have taught this or that." Instead, leaving the thought in suspense, he goes on to other matters. Perhaps we ought to pardon him for what he himself has admitted when he said, "if unschooled in speech, at least not in knowledge," and look for order in his meaning rather than in his words. This can be rendered as follows: "I, Paul, in the chains of Jesus Christ and in chains for you Gentiles, have learned the mystery so that I may hand it on to you." *Epistle to the Ephesians 2.3-1.*

Grace Given by the Working of God's Power. MARIUS VICTORINUS: Everywhere Paul reminds us that we receive God's gifts not by our own merit but by grace. Grace belongs to the giver, not to the recipient. And by adding "according to the working of his power," he also ascribes this to God, so that "if I do any work, it is God's power. For it is not my power that works in me but God's." *Epistle to the Ephesians 1.3.7-8.*

Paul's Humility. CHRYSOSTOM: Those who visit a doctor do not complete their journey simply by arriving there. They must also learn the remedy and apply the medicines. We too, having reached this

point, need to do the same, by learning the great humility of Paul. . . .
Paul demonstrates humility when he calls himself a blasphemer and a
persecutor. He describes himself as a dreadful offender on account of
his former sins, which had now been canceled . . . hence as "the least
of all the saints." He did not say "of the apostles" but of the saints who
come after the apostles. *Homily on Ephesians 7.3.8-11.*

GOSPEL READING: *Matthew 2:1-12*

REFLECTIONS FROM THE CHURCH FATHERS

Herod and Christ. PETER CHRYSOLOGUS: What does this mean,
that it was in the time of a very malevolent king that God descended to
earth, divinity entered into flesh, a heavenly union occurred with an
earthly body? What does this mean? How could it happen that a tyrant
could then be driven out by one who was not a king, who would free
his people, renew the face of the earth and restore freedom? Herod, an
apostate, had wrongly invaded the kingdom of the Jews, taken away
their liberty, profaned their holy places, disrupted the established order, abolished whatever there was of discipline and religious worship.
It was fitting therefore that God's own aid would come to succor that
holy race without any human help. Rightly did God emancipate the
race that no human hand could free. In just this way will Christ come
again, to undo the antichrist, free the world, restore the original land of
paradise, uphold the liberty of the world and take away all its slavery.
Sermon 156.5.

A Cradle the World Cannot Hold. CHROMATIUS: For immediately
the magi fell to their knees and adored the one born as Lord. There in
his very cradle they venerated him with offerings of gifts, though Jesus
was merely a whimpering infant. They perceived one thing with the
eyes of their bodies but another with the eyes of the mind. The lowliness of the body he assumed was discerned, but the glory of his divinity

is now made manifest. A boy he is, but it is God who is adored. How inexpressible is the mystery of his divine honor! The invisible and eternal nature did not hesitate to take on the weaknesses of the flesh on our behalf. The Son of God, who is God of the universe, is born a human being in the flesh. He permits himself to be placed in a manger, and the heavens are within the manger. He is kept in a cradle, a cradle that the world cannot hold. He is heard in the voice of a crying infant. This is the same one for whose voice the whole world would tremble in the hour of his passion. Thus he is the one, the God of glory and the Lord of majesty, whom as a tiny infant the magi recognize. It is he who while a child was truly God and King eternal. *Tractate on Matthew 5.1.*

CLOSING PRAYER

Lord, I pray that you may be a lamp for me in the darkness. Touch my soul and kindle a fire within it, that it may burn brightly and give light to my life. Thus my body may truly become your temple, lit by your perpetual flame burning on the altar of my heart. And may the light within me shine on my brethren that it may drive away the darkness of ignorance and sin from them also. Thus let us be lights to the world, manifesting the bright beauty of your gospel to all around us. *Columbanus*

Mercy

⌁ THEME
Because the Lord loves us and knows us by name, we need not be worried or fearful (Is 43:1-7). God is all-powerful and blesses us with strength and peace (Ps 29) and with the gift of the Holy Spirit (Acts 8:14-17). Through Christ's baptism (Lk 3:15-17, 21-22) we can better understand the plan God has for our own salvation.

⌁ **OPENING PRAYER:** *First Sunday After Epiphany*
Be present, O Lord, to our prayers, and protect us by day as well as by night, that in all successive changes of time we may ever be strengthened by Thine unchangeableness; through Jesus Christ our Lord. Amen. *The Leonine Sacramentary*

⌁ **OLD TESTAMENT READING:** *Isaiah 43:1-7*

REFLECTIONS FROM THE CHURCH FATHERS

God Redeems His Creation. **PROCOPIUS OF GAZA:** "You are mine." For we are said to have been Christ's, even before the separation from God that occurred when we as sinners went out of the garden, though by nature we were always God's. But he has made us once more to be his own through the Holy Spirit making us strong through every trial. Rivers, water and flames denote the many channels of temptation. For it is written, "All who wish to live godly lives in Christ Jesus will be persecuted." And Christ says to those who believed in him, "You will have sorrow in the world." *Commentary on Isaiah 43.1-13.*

The Virtues of the Wayfarer. AMBROSE: We are wayfarers in this life. Many are walking along this way. All need to make a good passage. The Lord Jesus is walking with one who is making a good passage. Thus we read, "When you pass through the waters, I will be with you, and the rivers shall not cover you or fire burn your garments when you shall walk through." But one who keeps a fire pent up in his body, the fire of lust, the fire of immoderate desire, does not pass through but burns the covering of his soul. A good name is more excellent than money, and above heaps of silver is good favor. Faith itself redounds to itself, sufficiently rich and more than rich in its possession. There is nothing that is not the possession of the wise person except what is contrary to virtue. Wherever he goes, he finds all things to be his. The whole world is his possession, since he uses it all as his own. *Letter 15.*

Grace to Keep Our Head Above Water. GREGORY THE GREAT: For the rivers overflow those whom the active business of this world confounds with perturbation of mind. But one who is sustained in mind by the grace of the Holy Spirit passes through the waters and yet is not swamped by the rivers, because in the midst of crowds of people he so proceeds along his way as not to sink the head of his mind beneath the active business of the world. *Letter 7.4.*

Material and Spiritual Refreshment. DIDACHE: You, almighty Master, created all things for your name's sake and gave food and drink to people to enjoy, that they might give you thanks, but to us you have graciously given spiritual food and drink and eternal life through your servant. Above all we give thanks because you are mighty; to you be the glory forever. *The Didache 10.3-4.*

PSALM OF RESPONSE: *Psalm 29*

NEW TESTAMENT READING: *Acts 8:14-17*

REFLECTIONS FROM THE CHURCH FATHERS

The Spirit Manifests Himself. AUGUSTINE: For the Holy Spirit was at that time given in such sort that he even visibly showed himself to have been given. For those who received him spoke with the tongues of all nations, to signify that the church among the nations was to speak in the tongues of all. So then they received the Holy Ghost, and he appeared evidently to be in them. *Sermon 49 (99).10.*

The Triune Baptismal Formula. ORIGEN: From all of which we learn that the person of the Holy Spirit is of so great authority and dignity that saving baptism is not complete except when performed with the authority of the whole most excellent Trinity, that is, by the naming of Father, Son and Holy Spirit. *On First Principles 1.3.2.*

The Baptism by Philip Need Not Be Repeated. CYPRIAN: The Samaritan believers had come to the true faith and had been baptized by Philip the deacon, whom these very apostles had sent, within the one church to which alone it has been granted to give the grace of baptism and to loose sins. Since they had already obtained the lawful baptism of the church, it would have been wrong to baptize them any more. Peter and John supplied only what they lacked. *Letter 73.9.*

GOSPEL READING: *Luke 3:15-17, 21-22*

REFLECTIONS FROM THE CHURCH FATHERS

Fire Refers to the Fiery Tongues at Pentecost. CYRIL OF JERUSALEM: John, filled with the Holy Spirit from his mother's womb, was sanctified for the purpose of baptizing the Lord. John himself did not impart the Spirit but preached the glad tidings of him who does. He says, "I indeed baptize you with water, for repentance. But he who is

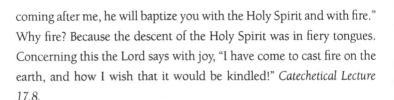

coming after me, he will baptize you with the Holy Spirit and with fire." Why fire? Because the descent of the Holy Spirit was in fiery tongues. Concerning this the Lord says with joy, "I have come to cast fire on the earth, and how I wish that it would be kindled!" *Catechetical Lecture 17.8.*

The Mystery of the Trinity Present at Jesus' Baptism. AMBROSE: Now let us consider the mystery of the Trinity. We say, "one God," but we confess the Father, and we confess the Son. For although it is written, "You shall love the Lord your God and serve him alone," the Son denied that he is alone, saying, "I am not alone, for the Father is with me." Nor is he alone now, for the Father bears witness that he is present. The Holy Spirit is present because the Trinity can never be separated from itself. Then "heaven was opened, the Holy Spirit descended in bodily shape like a dove." *Exposition of the Gospel of Luke 2.92.*

The Holy Spirit Vital to Jesus' Ministry. GREGORY OF NAZIANZUS: Christ is born; the Spirit is his forerunner. Christ is baptized; the Spirit bears him witness. Christ is tempted. The Spirit leads him up. Christ performs miracles. The Spirit accompanies him. Christ ascends. The Spirit fills his place. *Oration 31.29, On the Holy Spirit.*

Jesus Is Baptized for Our Sin, Not His. CYPRIAN: From the first moment of his descent from the glories of heaven to earthly things, he did not disdain to put on man's flesh although he was the Son of God. Although he himself was not a sinner, he did not disdain to bear the sins of others. Having put aside his immortality for a time, he suffered himself to become mortal, in order that though innocent he might be slain for the salvation of the guilty. The Lord was baptized by his servant, and he, although destined to grant the remission of sins, did not disdain to have his body cleansed with the water of regeneration. *The Good of Patience 6.*

CLOSING PRAYER

Maker of all, the Lord
   And ruler in the height,
Thy care does robe the day in peace,
   Thou give sleep by night.
Let rest refresh our limbs
   For toil, though wearied now,
And let our troubled minds be calm,
   And smooth the anxious brow.
We sing our thanks, for day
   Is gone and night appears;
Our vows and prayers in contrite hope
   Are lifted to thine ears.

Ambrose

Spiritual Gifts

⊰ THEME

God rejoices and delights in us (Is 62:1-5); his steadfast love offers us
refuge in the shadow of his wings (Ps 36:5-10). Christ showed his
power while on earth, working many signs and miracles, including one
at the wedding at Cana (Jn 2:1-11). God gives each of us spiritual gifts
to use in his service (1 Cor 12:1-11).

⊰ OPENING PRAYER: *Second Sunday After Epiphany*

Most high God, our loving Father, infinite in majesty, we humbly beseech thee for all thy servants everywhere, that thou would give us a
pure mind, perfect love, sincerity in conduct, purity in heart, strength
in action, courage in distress, self-command in character. May our
prayers ascend to thy gracious ears and thy loving benediction descend
on us all, that we may in all things be protected under the shadow of
thy wings. Grant us pardon of our sins; perfect our work; accept our
prayers; protect us by thine own name, O God of Jacob; send us thy
saving help from thy holy place; and strengthen us out of Zion. Remember all thy people everywhere; give us all the grace of devotion to
thy will; fulfill our desires with good gifts; and crown us with thy
mercy. When we serve thee with faithful devotion, pardon our sins and
correct us with fatherly tenderness. Grant that, being delivered from all
adversity, and both here and eternally justified, we may praise thee forever and ever, saying Holy, holy, holy; through Jesus Christ our Lord

and Savior, who with thee and the Holy Spirit lives and reigns, ever one God, world without end. Amen. *The Gallican Sacramentary*

OLD TESTAMENT READING: *Isaiah 62:1-5*

REFLECTIONS FROM THE CHURCH FATHERS

Betrothal and Marriage. CYRIL OF ALEXANDRIA: "You will be a crown of beauty in the hand of the Lord and a royal diadem in the hand of your God." Now this compares both each holy soul and the collective church, that is, the company of the saints, to a garland tied together from many flowers or to a royal diadem, shining with Indian jewels and with a variety of beautiful forms. For many are the noble characteristics of the saints, and there is not one type of distinction but many and various . . . and Christ himself said about his own sheep or the flock of those believing in him, "No one shall snatch them from the hand of the Father." . . . "As a young man marries a virgin." This is said to the church about the time in the beginning when it was constituted from the Jewish tribes. For the godly disciples were Jewish according to their human origin, but they stood out from the others and took the lead since they had apostolic status. Yet they retained a great love and respect for their religion, so that there seemed to be great affection toward it as a man ought to feel toward a young virgin bride when he lies with her. *Commentary on Isaiah 5.5.62.3-5.*

Sharing His Name. THEODORET OF CYR: Those who believe in the Lord received a new title; they are not called after Abraham or Israel or Judah but are named after the master, Christ. For they are called Christians by everyone, since they have put on Christ through the most holy baptism. *Commentary on Isaiah 19.62.2.*

The Sons Are the Apostles, the Priests and the Righteous Ones. EPHREM THE SYRIAN: "For as a young man marries a virgin, so shall your sons marry you." He calls sons the apostles, the priests and the

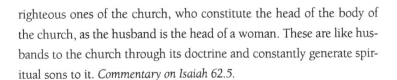

righteous ones of the church, who constitute the head of the body of the church, as the husband is the head of a woman. These are like husbands to the church through its doctrine and constantly generate spiritual sons to it. *Commentary on Isaiah 62.5.*

PSALM OF RESPONSE: *Psalm 36:5-10*

NEW TESTAMENT READING: *1 Corinthians 12:1-11*

REFLECTIONS FROM THE CHURCH FATHERS

The Work of the Spirit Alone. CHRYSOSTOM: Paul calls the gifts spiritual because they are the work of the Spirit alone, owing nothing to human initiative. *Homilies on the Epistles of Paul to the Corinthians 29.2.*

Visible Signs of Grace. THEODORET OF CYR: In former times those who accepted the divine preaching and who were baptized for their salvation were given visible signs of the grace of the Holy Spirit at work in them. Some spoke in tongues which they did not know and which nobody had taught them, while others performed miracles or prophesied. The Corinthians also did these things, but they did not use the gifts as they should have done. They were more interested in showing off than in using them for the edification of the church. *Commentary on the First Epistle to the Corinthians 240.*

Varieties of Service. CHRYSOSTOM: One who hears about gifts might be upset if someone else has a greater one. But when it comes to service, things are the other way around. In this case, labor and sweat are implied. Why do you complain if they have been given more to do so as to spare you? *Homilies on the Epistles of Paul to the Corinthians 29.4.*

Manifestation of the Spirit. AMBROSIASTER: Each person receives a gift so that, governing his life by divine constraints, he may be useful both to himself and to others while presenting an example of good behavior. *Commentary on Paul's Epistles.*

Not Many Spirits. AUGUSTINE: Without the spirit of faith no one will rightly believe. Without the spirit of prayer no one will profitably pray. It is not that there are so many spirits, "but in all things one and the same Spirit works, who apportions to each one individually as he wills." *Letter to Sixtus 191.*

GOSPEL READING: *John 2:1-11*

REFLECTIONS FROM THE CHURCH FATHERS

Jesus Honors His Mother in Doing What She Asks. CHRYSOSTOM: Why, after he had said, "My hour has not yet come," and denied his mother's initial request, did he do what his mother told him to do? The main reason was so that those who opposed him and thought that he was under subjection to the "hour" might have sufficient proof that he was subject to no hour. For if he was, how could he have done this miracle before the hour appointed for it? He also wished to show honor to his mother and let it eventually become evident, in the company of so many, that he had not contradicted the woman who had borne him. *Homilies on the Gospel of John 22.1.*

The King Pours His Wine for the Guests. EPHREM THE SYRIAN:
Let Cana thank you for gladdening her banquet!
The bridegroom's crown exalted you for exalting it,
And the bride's crown belonged to your victory.
In her mirror allegories are expounded and traced,
For you portrayed your church in the bride,
And in her guests, yours are traced,
And in her magnificence she portrays your advent.
Let the feast thank him, for in multiplying his wine
Six miracles were beheld there:

The six wine jugs set aside for water
Into which they invited the King to pour his wine.
Hymns on Virginity 33.1-2.

The Miracle Manifests the King of Glory. BEDE: By this sign he made manifest that he was the King of glory, and so the church's bridegroom. He came to the marriage as a common human being, but as Lord of heaven and earth he could convert the elements as he wished. How beautifully appropriate it is that when he began the signs that he would show to mortals while he was still mortal he turned water into wine. But when he had become immortal through his resurrection, he began the signs that he would show only to those who were pursuing the goal of immortal life. . . . Therefore, let us love with our whole mind, dearly beloved, the marriage of Christ and the church, which was prefigured then in one city and is now celebrated over the whole earth. *Homilies on the Gospels 1.14.*

CLOSING PRAYER

Lord, inspire us to read your Scriptures and meditate on them day and night. We beg you to give us real understanding of what we need, that we in turn may put its precepts into practice. Yet we know that understanding and good intentions are worthless, unless rooted in your graceful love. So we ask that the words of Scriptures may also be not just signs on a page but channels of grace into our hearts. *Origen*

Bear Good Fruit

◄ THEME

The joy of the Lord is our strength (Neh 8:1-3, 5-6, 8-10). We desire to follow the Lord in everything we do (Ps 19), proclaiming freedom (Lk 4:14-21) with the knowledge that we are a small but important part of something greater than ourselves (1 Cor 12:12-31a).

◄ OPENING PRAYER: *Third Sunday After Epiphany*

May God the Father and the eternal high priest Jesus Christ build us up in faith and truth and love and grant us our portion among the saints with all those who believe on our Lord Jesus Christ. We pray for all saints, for kings and rulers, for the enemies of the cross of Christ, and for ourselves we pray that our fruit may abound and we may be made perfect in Christ Jesus our Lord. *Polycarp*

◄ OLD TESTAMENT READING: *Nehemiah 8:1-3, 5-6, 8-10*

REFLECTIONS FROM THE CHURCH FATHERS

Instruction Through Divine Discourses. **BEDE:** As Nehemiah was seeking to make plans and decide who should reside in the city that they had built, the seventh month arrived, for it was not far off. For since the wall had been completed on the twenty-fifth day of the sixth month, not more than five days remained until the beginning of the seventh month. The whole of this seventh month, from its first day until the twenty-second, was consecrated with ceremonies prescribed by the Law; when these had been duly celebrated, only then did he return with the leaders and common people to decide who should be residents of the rebuilt city. The point to note here is the devotion and also the like-mindedness of the people who as one person (that is, with one and the same faith and love) came together at the Lord's temple, and they themselves asked their *pontifex* to bring the book and recount for them the commandments of the Law that they must observe, so that along with the rebuilt city, a structure of good works pleasing to God might spring up in case, just as before, neglect of religion should lead to the ruination of the city as well. *On Ezra and Nehemiah 3.26.*

BEDE: And it is appropriate that the city was completed in the sixth month and that the people gathered in it to hear the Law in the seventh; for in the Law there are six days for working and a seventh for resting. And this, after we have done good work, is the form of our rest that is most beloved and most acceptable to the Lord: to abstain from servile work (that is, from sin) and devote ourselves to hearing and fulfilling his commandments with due diligence This is why the Feast of Trumpets, by whose blast the people, amid their prayers and offerings, were more fervently moved to remembrance of the divine law, was placed in the beginning of this seventh month also. *On Ezra and Nehemiah 3.26.*

⌁ **PSALM OF RESPONSE:** *Psalm 19*

⌁ **NEW TESTAMENT READING:** *1 Corinthians 12:12-31a*

REFLECTIONS FROM THE CHURCH FATHERS

Every Member Necessary. **THEODORET OF CYR:** Paul is pointing out that just as the body has many members, some of which are more important than others, so it is with the church also. But every member is necessary and useful. *Commentary on the First Epistle to the Corinthians 246.*

Many Members Supply What Other Parts Lack. AMBROSIASTER: The unity of the body consists in the fact that its many members supply the things which the other parts lack. *Commentary on Paul's Epistles.*

The Analogy of the Bad Haircut. AUGUSTINE: Aren't the hairs of your head certainly of less value than your other members? What is cheaper, more despicable, more lowly in your body than the hairs of your head? Yet if the barber trims your hair unskillfully, you become angry at him because he does not cut your hair evenly. Yet you do not maintain that same concern for unity of the members in the church. *The Usefulness of Fasting 6.*

Greater Attention to Inferior Parts. CHRYSOSTOM: Paul points out that if division in the body is to be avoided, greater attention must be given to the lesser parts, so that they will not be harmed or feel excluded. If they were badly treated they would be destroyed, and their destruction would be the ruin of the body. *Homilies on the Epistles of Paul to the Corinthians 32.3.*

All Suffer Together. AUGUSTINE: Far be it from us to refuse to hear what is bitter and sad to those whom we love. It is not possible for one member to suffer without the other members suffering with it. *Letters 99.*

Not Individuals Voluntarily Joined. SEVERIAN OF GABALA: We are not individual members who elect to join together to form a whole but rather organic members of a wider whole, which is the whole body. *Pauline Commentary from the Greek Church.*

Not by Merit. AMBROSIASTER: The graces of the Lord which are seen in person do not relate to the merit of the individual but to the honoring of God. *Commentary on Paul's Epistles.*

GOSPEL READING: *Luke 4:14-21*

REFLECTIONS FROM THE CHURCH FATHERS

The Choice of Isaiah. ORIGEN: It was no accident that he opens the scroll and finds the chapter of the reading that prophesies about him. This too was an act of God's providence. . . . Precisely the book of Isaiah was found, and the reading was no other but this one, which spoke about the mystery of Christ. *Homilies on the Gospel of Luke 32.4.*

Jesus Begins His Ministry with a Reference to the Trinity. AMBROSE: Scripture speaks of Jesus himself as God and man, perfect in both natures. It speaks of the Father and the Holy Spirit. For the Holy Spirit is shown as Christ's partner when he descends in bodily shape as a dove on Christ, when the Son of God was baptized in the river and when the Father spoke from heaven. So what greater testimony to us who are weak than that Christ signified with his own voice that he himself spoke by the prophets? *Exposition on the Gospel of Luke 4.44-45.*

Good News to the Poor. EUSEBIUS: Our Savior, after reading this prophecy through in the synagogue one day to a multitude of Jews, shut the book and said, "This day is this Scripture fulfilled in your ears." He began his own teaching from that point. He began to preach the gospel to the poor, putting in the forefront of his blessings "Blessed are the poor in spirit, for theirs is the kingdom of heaven." Yes, he proclaimed forgiveness to those who were hampered by evil spirits and bound for a long time like slaves by demons. He invited all to be free and to escape from the bonds of sin when he said, "Come to me, all you that labor and are heavy laden, and I will refresh you." *Proof of the Gospel 3.1.88C-89A.*

Acceptable Year of the Lord Embraces Jesus' Miracles and Death. CYRIL OF ALEXANDRIA: What does preaching the acceptable year of the Lord mean? It signifies the joyful tidings of his own advent, that the time of the Lord—yes, the Son—had arrived. For that was the acceptable year in which Christ was crucified on our behalf, because we then were made acceptable to God the Father as the fruit borne by him. That is why the Lord said, "When I am lifted up from the earth, I will draw all men to myself." Truly he returned to life the third day, having trampled on the power of death. After that resurrection he said to his disciples, "All power has been given to me." That too is in every respect an acceptable year. In it we were received into his family and were admitted to him, having washed away sin by holy baptism and been made partakers of his divine nature by the communion of the Holy Spirit. That too is an acceptable year, in which he manifested his glory by inexpressible miracles. *Commentary on Luke, Homily 12.*

CLOSING PRAYER

Almighty and everlasting God, by whose Spirit the whole body of the church is governed and sanctified: Receive our supplications and prayers which we offer before thee for all estates of people in thy holy church, that every member of the same in his vocation and ministry may truly and godly serve thee, through our Lord and Savior Jesus Christ. Amen. *The Gelasian Sacramentary*

Love

THEME

God is with us; he is our fortress and rock of refuge (Ps 71:1-6). He knew us before we were born (Jer 1:4-10). Because of his love for us, we are to love others with a patient, kind and enduring love (1 Cor 13:1-13). This love was shown to us by Christ, who came to earth as a man and endured threats and abuse and finally, death, so that we might live with him eternally (Lk 4:21-30).

OPENING PRAYER: *Fourth Sunday After Epiphany*

O God, our refuge and strength, who are the author of all godliness, be ready, we beseech thee, to hear the devout prayers of thy church; and grant that those things which we ask faithfully, we may obtain effectually, through Jesus Christ our Lord. Amen. *The Gregorian Sacramentary*

OLD TESTAMENT READING: *Jeremiah 1:4-10*

REFLECTIONS FROM THE CHURCH FATHERS

God Cares for the Weak and Frail. ORIGEN: We forget that the words "Let us make man according to our image and according to our likeness" apply to each person. When we fail to remember the one who formed a person in the womb and formed all people's hearts individually and understands all their works, we do not perceive that God is a helper of those who are lowly and inferior, a protector of the weak, a provider of shelter of those who have been given up in despair and Savior of those who have been given up as hopeless. *Commentary on the Gospel of John 13.167-68.*

Jeremiah, Like Moses, Resisted the Call. GREGORY OF NAZIAN-ZUS: I resort once again to history. When I consider the men of best repute in ancient days, who were ever preferred by grace to the office of ruler or prophet, I discover that some readily complied with the call while others deprecated the gift. I also learn that those who drew back were not blamed for their timidity, nor were those who came forward accused of being too eager. The former stood in awe of the greatness of the ministry; the latter trustfully obeyed him who called them. Aaron was eager, but Moses resisted; Isaiah readily submitted, but Jeremiah was afraid of his youth and did not venture to prophesy until he had received from God a promise and a power beyond his years. *In Defense of His Flight to Pontus, Oration 2.114.*

The Privilege and Freedom of Our Calling. CHRYSOSTOM: Prophets had power either to speak or to refrain from speaking. They were not bound by necessity but were honored with a privilege. For this reason Jonah fled, for this reason Ezekiel delayed, and for this reason Jeremiah excused himself. And God drives them not only by compulsion but also by advising, exhorting, threatening. He does not darken their mind, because to cause distraction, madness and great darkness is the proper work of a demon. It is God's work to illuminate and with consideration to teach what is necessary. *Homilies on First Corinthians 29.2-3.*

Freed to Overcome Tribulations. JEROME: You should not consider the matter of age, he said, for you have learned through another prophet's words that "a man's gray hair is his wisdom." May you only be willing to continue, for you will have me as a companion by whose assistance you will accomplish everything: "Open your mouth, and I will fill it." Neither should you consider the number of those against whom you are about to speak, but consider me only, who is with you to deliver you, says the Lord. The Lord delivers, however, not so that the prophet will be free of persecutions and difficulties, for we read that he was severely afflicted. Instead, the Lord liberates one who suffers everything to overcome these tribulations rather than yielding to them. *Six Books on Jeremiah 1.4.1-2.*

The Lord Provides the Words. ORIGEN: We pray that words may be given us, as it is written in the book of Jeremiah that the Lord said to the prophet: "Behold, I have put my words in your mouth as fire. See, I have set you this day over the nations and over the kingdoms, to root out and to pull down, and to destroy, and to throw down, and to build and to plant." *Against Celsus 4.1.*

PSALM OF RESPONSE: *Psalm 71:1-6*

NEW TESTAMENT READING: *1 Corinthians 13:1-13*

REFLECTIONS FROM THE CHURCH FATHERS

A Nuisance Without Love. CHRYSOSTOM: In other words, says Paul, if I have no love I am not just useless but a positive nuisance. *Homilies on the Epistles of Paul to the Corinthians 32.6.*

Tongues of Angels Not Perceived by the Ear. THEODORET OF CYR: Paul chooses speaking in tongues as his example because the Corinthians thought that it was the greatest of the gifts. This was because it had been given to the apostles on the day of Pentecost, before any of the others. The tongues of angels are those which are perceived by the mind, not by the ear. *Commentary on the First Epistle to the Corinthians 251.*

Giving One's Body to Be Burned. AUGUSTINE: Giving one's body to be burned is not a license to commit suicide but a command not to resist suffering if the alternative is being forced to do wrong. *Letter 173, to Donatus.*

What Is Good. THEODORET OF CYR: Love hates what is unjust and rejoices in what is good and honorable. *Commentary on the First Epistle to the Corinthians 253.*

When I Was a Child. CLEMENT OF ALEXANDRIA: This is a figure of speech for the way Paul lived under the law, when he persecuted the Word and was still senseless and childish, blaspheming God. *Christ the Educator 1.6.3.*

GOSPEL READING: *Luke 4:21-30*

REFLECTIONS FROM THE CHURCH FATHERS

Nazareth Rejects Jesus Out of Envy. AMBROSE: The Savior deliberately explains why he performed no miracles of virtue in his own country, to prevent someone from thinking that we should value affection for our country very little. He who loved all could not but love his fellow citizens. But those who envy his country deprive themselves of love, for "love does not envy, it is not puffed up." Yet his country does not lack divine blessings. Isn't it a greater miracle that Christ was born there? So, you see what measure of evil envy, the country in which he toiled as a citizen, which was worthy that the Son of God be born there. *Exposition of the Gospel of Luke 4.47.*

An Attempt to Kill Jesus. CYRIL OF ALEXANDRIA: So they threw him out of their city, pronouncing by their action their own condemnation. So they confirmed what the Savior had said. They themselves were banished from the city that is above, for not having received Christ. That he might not convict them only of impiety in words, he permitted their disrespect of him to proceed to deeds. Their violence was irrational and their envy untamed. Leading him to the brow of the hill, they sought to throw him from the cliff. But he went through the midst of them without taking any notice, so to say, of their attempt. He did not refuse to suffer—he had come to do that very thing—but to wait for a suitable time. Now, at the beginning of his preaching, it would have been the wrong time to have suffered before he had proclaimed the word of truth. *Commentary on Luke, Homily 12.*

The Time of Jesus' Passion Had Not Yet Come. AMBROSE: At the same time, understand that he was not forced to suffer the passion of his body. It was voluntary. He was not taken by the Jews but given by himself. Indeed, he is taken when he wants to be. He glides away when he wants to. He is hung when he wants to be. He is not held when he does not wish it. Here he goes up to the summit of the hill to be thrown down. But, behold, the minds of the furious men were suddenly changed or confused. He descended through their midst, for the hour of his passion had not yet come. Indeed, he still preferred to heal the Jews, rather than destroy them, so that through the unsuccessful outcome of their frenzy, they would cease to want what they could not attain. *Exposition of the Gospel of Luke 4.55-56.*

CLOSING PRAYER

Almighty and everlasting God, give to us the increase of faith, hope and charity; and that we may obtain that which thou promise, make us to love that which thou command, through Jesus Christ our Lord. Amen. *The Leonine Sacramentary*

God's Steadfast Love

THEME

The holiness of God reminds us of our own sin and need for salvation (Is 6:1-13). Even in the middle of trouble, God's steadfast love and watchful care protect us (Ps 138), and his grace toward us through the death and resurrection of Jesus Christ offers us eternal life (1 Cor 15:1-11). Just as Christ urged Simon Peter to do, we must share this good news with others (Lk 5:1-11).

OPENING PRAYER: *Fifth Sunday After Epiphany*

We beseech thee, O Lord, in thy loving-kindness, to pour thy holy light into our souls, that we may ever be devoted to thee, by whose wisdom we were created and by whose providence we are governed; through Jesus Christ our Lord. Amen. *The Gelasian Sacramentary*

OLD TESTAMENT READING: *Isaiah 6:1-13*

REFLECTIONS FROM THE CHURCH FATHERS

God As King. JEROME: We have talked about standing; we have talked about walking; let us talk about sitting. Whenever God is represented as seated, the portrayal takes one of two forms: either he appears as the ruler or as the judge. If he is like a king, one sees him as Isaiah does: "I saw the Lord seated on a high and lofty throne." There he is presented as the sovereign king. *Homilies on the Psalms 14 (Psalm 81).*

Understand the Distinctions. AMBROSE: Cherubim and seraphim with unwearied voices praise him and say, "Holy, holy, holy is the Lord God of hosts." They say it not once, lest you should believe that there is but one; not twice, lest you should exclude the Spirit; they say not holies (in the plural), lest you should imagine that there is plurality, but they repeat three times and say the same word, that even in a hymn you may understand the distinction of persons in the Trinity and the oneness of the Godhead, and while they say this they proclaim God. *On the Holy Spirit 3.16.110.*

Heaven. AUGUSTINE: What are we going to do there? Tell me. Sleep? Yes, here people who have nothing to do just sleep. But there is no sleep there, because there is no weariness. So we aren't going to perform works of necessity, aren't going to sleep—what are we going to do? None of us must be afraid of boredom; none of us must imagine it's going to be so boring there. Do you find it boring now to be well? You can get tired of anything and everything in this age; can you get tired of being well? If you don't get tired of good health, will you get tired of immortality? *Sermon 211A.2.*

Remorse for Sin. PETER CHRYSOLOGUS: But let us at this time feel remorse with all the affection of our hearts. Let us admit that we are wretched in this misery of the flesh. Let us weep with holy groans because we, too, have unclean lips. Let us do all this to make that one of the seraphim bring down to us, by means of the tongs of the law of grace, a flaming sacrament of faith taken for us from the heavenly altar. Let us do this to make him touch the tip of our lips with such delicate touch as to take away our iniquities, purge away our sins and so enkindle our mouths to the full flame of complete praise that the burning will be one that results in salvation, not pain. Let us beg, too, that the heat of that coal may penetrate all the way to our hearts. Thus we may draw not only relish for our lips from the great sweetness of this mystery but also complete satisfaction for our sense and minds. *Sermon 57.*

⊰ PSALM OF RESPONSE: *Psalm 138*

⊰ NEW TESTAMENT READING: *1 Corinthians 15:1-11*

REFLECTIONS FROM THE CHURCH FATHERS

The Gospel Received. AMBROSIASTER: Paul is showing the Corinthians that if they have been led away from his teaching, especially from belief in the resurrection of the dead on which it is based, they will lose everything they have believed. *Commentary on Paul's Epistles.*

He Was Buried. CHRYSOSTOM: This serves to confirm that Christ died a genuine human death and points us once more to the Scriptures for proof. Nowhere does Scripture mean the death of sin, when it makes mention of our Lord's death, but only the death of the body, and a burial and resurrection of that same body. *Homilies on the Epistles of Paul to the Corinthians 38.4.11.*

Matthias Included? OECUMENIUS: Note that he does not say "to the eleven," and neither does John (Jn 20:24), who writes that Thomas was "one of the twelve." We should probably say that either he has included Matthias with the other apostles by anticipation or else that he is still thinking of Judas, even after his betrayal and hanging. *Pauline Commentary from the Greek Church.*

Last in Time. AMBROSIASTER: Paul is least because he was the last in time, not because he was inferior in any way to the others. *Commentary on Paul's Epistles 4.*

Unfit. CHRYSOSTOM: Paul says this because he was a humble man and also because it is what he really thought about himself. He was forgiven for having persecuted the church, but it was a shame he never forgot. It taught him the greatness of God's grace toward him. *Homilies on the Epistles of Paul to the Corinthians 38.6.5.*

I Worked Harder Than Any. CHRYSOSTOM: If Paul was so humble, why did he call attention to his labors? He had to do this in order to justify his right to be a trustworthy witness and a teacher. *Homilies on the Epistles of Paul to the Corinthians* 38.7.14.

God Grants Efficacy to Our Labors. BASIL THE GREAT: This is the perfect and consummate glory in God: not to exult in one's own righteousness, but recognizing oneself as lacking true righteousness, to be justified by faith in Christ alone. Paul gloried in despising his own righteousness. In seeking after the righteousness by faith which is of God through Christ, he sought only to know him and the power of his resurrection and the fellowship of his sufferings, being made conformable to his death, so as to attain to the resurrection from the dead. . . . It is God who grants efficacy to our labors. *On Humility* 20.17.

GOSPEL READING: *Luke 5:1-11*

REFLECTIONS FROM THE CHURCH FATHERS

First Catch of Fish the Church in the Present Time. AUGUSTINE: So let me recall with you those two catches of fish made by the disciples at the command of the Lord Jesus Christ: one before his passion, the other after his resurrection. These two catches of fish stand for the whole church, both as it is now and as it will be at the resurrection of the dead. Now, as you can see, it contains countless numbers, both good and bad. After the resurrection it will contain only the good, and a definite number of them. So call to mind that first catch, where we may see the church as it is in this present time. . . . The nets were cast. They caught so many fish that two boats were filled, and the very nets were torn by that vast quantity of fish. Then he said to them, "Follow me, and I will make you fishers of men." They received from him the nets of the Word of God, they cast them into the world as into a deep sea, and they caught the vast multitude of Christians that we can see and marvel at. Those two boats, though, stood for the two peoples,

Jews and Gentiles, synagogue and church, those circumcised and those uncircumcised. *Sermon 248.2.2.*

Christ Continues to Catch People in the Nets of Preaching. CYRIL OF ALEXANDRIA: But note that neither Simon nor his companions could draw the net to land. Speechless from fright and astonishment—for their wonder had made them mute—they beckoned to their partners, to those who shared their labors in fishing, to come and help them in securing their prey. For many have taken part with the holy apostles in their labors, and still do so, especially those who inquire into the meaning of what is written in the holy Gospels. Yet besides them there are also others: the pastors and teachers and rulers of the people, who are skilled in the doctrines of truth. For the net is still being drawn, while Christ fills it and calls to conversion those who, according to the Scripture phrase, are in the depths of the sea, that is to say, those who live in the surge and waves of worldly things. *Commentary on Luke, Homily 12.10.*

CLOSING PRAYER

Lord, you are our teacher, and we would ask you to be kind to us, your little children. . . . May we all live in your peace; and as we journey toward your dwelling place, may we sail through the waters of sin in such a way that we remain untouched by the waves but carried calmly along by the Holy Spirit. *Clement of Alexandria*

Trust

⊰ THEME

The Lord is worthy of our trust; he alone knows our minds and hearts (Jer 17:5-10). When we meditate on Scripture and delight in the words of the Lord, we are like a fruitful tree, flourishing by a stream (Ps 1). Because of Christ's death and resurrection (1 Cor 15:12-20), if we choose to follow him, we will have a great reward in heaven (Lk 6:17-26).

⊰ OPENING PRAYER: *Sixth Sunday After Epiphany*

O God, the strength of all them that put their trust in thee, mercifully accept our prayers, and because through the weakness of our mortal nature we can do no good thing without thee, grant us the help of thy grace, that in keeping of thy commandments we may please thee, both in will and deed, through Jesus Christ our Lord. Amen. *The Gelasian Sacramentary*

⊰ OLD TESTAMENT READING: *Jeremiah 17:5-10*

REFLECTIONS FROM THE CHURCH FATHERS

Trust in the Lord. AUGUSTINE: Blessed are all who trust in God. If the blessed are those who trust in him, then the wretched are those who trust in themselves. Cursed, you see, is everyone who puts his hopes in humankind, so do not put them even in yourself, because you too are human. If you put your hopes in another person, that is the wrong kind of humility. But if you put your hopes in yourself, that is dangerous pride. What is the difference, anyway? Each is pernicious, neither is to be chosen. Humble in the wrong way, you cannot lift yourself up; dangerously proud, you are heading for a fall. *Sermon 13.2.*

There Is One Refuge: God. BASIL THE GREAT: One thing you must flee, sin. One refuge from evil must be sought, God. Do not trust in princes. Do not be exalted in the uncertainty of wealth. Do not be proud of bodily strength. Do not pursue the splendor of human glory. None of these things save you. All are transient. All are deceptive. There is one refuge: God. "Cursed is the one who trusts in humankind" or in any human thing. *Homilies on the Psalms 18.1 (Psalm 45).*

PSALM OF RESPONSE: *Psalm 1*

NEW TESTAMENT READING: *1 Corinthians 15:12-20*

REFLECTIONS FROM THE CHURCH FATHERS

The Pivot of Christian Testimony. AMBROSE: How grave an offense it is not to believe in the resurrection of the dead. If we do not rise again, Christ died in vain and did not rise again. For if he did not rise for us, he did not rise at all, because there is no reason why he should rise for himself. *On His Brother Satyrus 2.103.*

The General Resurrection and Christ's Being Raised. PELAGIUS: The one depends on the other. Either you believe both, or you believe neither. *Commentary on the First Epistle to the Corinthians 15.*

Not a Resurrection of the Soul Only. PELAGIUS: Some heretics claim that there is a resurrection of the soul but not of the body, though this makes no sense. How can there be a resurrection of something which has not fallen into the ground and died? *Commentary on the First Epistle to the Corinthians 15.*

Forgiveness of Sins. PELAGIUS: If Christ lied about his resurrection, then he lied about his claim to forgive our sins also. *Commentary on the First Epistle to the Corinthians 15.*

If Christ Has Not Been Raised. CHRYSOSTOM: If Christ did not rise again, neither was he slain, and if he was not slain, our sins have not been taken away. If our sins have not been taken away, we are still in them, and our entire faith is meaningless. *Homilies on the Epistles of Paul to the Corinthians 39.4.*

Hope in Christ. AMBROSIASTER: It is clear that we hope in Christ both for this life and for the next one. Christ does not abandon his servants but gives them grace, and in the future they will dwell in eternal glory. *Commentary on Paul's Epistles.*

If the Body Does Not Rise. CHRYSOSTOM: Even if the soul remains, being infinitely immortal without the flesh it will not receive those hidden blessings. If the body does not rise again, the soul remains uncrowned with the blessings stored up for it in heaven. In that case, we have nothing to hope for, and our rewards are limited to this life. What could be more wretched than that? *Homilies on the Epistles of Paul to the Corinthians 39.4.*

GOSPEL READING: *Luke 6:17-26*

REFLECTIONS FROM THE CHURCH FATHERS

Jesus Descended to Heal the Lowly. AMBROSE: Note all things carefully. He ascends with the apostles and descends to the crowds. How would a crowd see Christ, except at a low level? It does not follow him to the heights; it does not climb to majestic places. So when he descends, he finds the weak, for the weak cannot be high up. Thus also Matthew teaches that the weak were healed down below. First each was healed, so that little by little, with increasing virtue, he could ascend to the mountain. On the plain he heals each, that is, he calls them back from recklessness. He turns away the harm of blindness. He descends to heal our wounds, so that in an effective and abundant manner he makes us partakers in his heavenly nature. *Exposition of the Gospel of Luke 5.46.*

To Lift the Eyes. ORIGEN: The phrase "lift up your eyes" occurs in many places in Scripture. By this expression, the divine Word admonishes us to exalt and lift up our thoughts. It invites us to elevate the insight that lies below in a rather sickly condition and is stooped and completely incapable of looking up. *Commentary on the Gospel of John 1.274-77.*

Four Beatitudes; Four Cardinal Virtues. AMBROSE: Let us see how St. Luke encompassed the eight blessings in the four. We know that there are four cardinal virtues: temperance, justice, prudence and fortitude. One who is poor in spirit is not greedy. One who weeps is not proud but is submissive and tranquil. One who mourns is humble. One who is just does not deny what he knows is given jointly to all for us. One who is merciful gives away his own goods. One who bestows his own goods does not seek another's, nor does he contrive a trap for his neighbor. Those virtues are interwoven and interlinked, so that one who has one may be seen to have several, and a single virtue befits the saints. Where virtue abounds, the reward too abounds. . . . Thus temperance has purity of heart and spirit, justice has compassion, patience has peace, and endurance has gentleness. *Exposition of the Gospel of Luke 5.62-63, 68.*

Woe to Those Who Misuse Their Possessions. AMBROSE: Although there are many charms of delights in riches, yet there are more incentives to practice virtues. Although virtue does not require assistance and the contribution of the poor person is more commended than the generosity of the rich, yet with the authority of the heavenly saying, he condemns not those who have riches but those who do not know how to use them. The pauper is more praiseworthy who gives with eager compassion and is not restrained by the bolts of looming scarcity. He thinks that he who has enough for nature does not lack. So the rich person is the more guilty who does not give thanks to God for what he has received but vainly hides wealth given for the common use and conceals it in buried treasures. Then the offense consists not in the wealth but in the attitude. *Exposition of the Gospel of Luke 5.69.*

Weeping Is a Requirement, Laughter a Reward of Wisdom. AUGUSTINE: If you propose a choice between these two things, which is better, to laugh or to cry? Is there anybody who wouldn't prefer to laugh? Because repentance involves a beneficial sorrow, the Lord presented tears as a requirement and laughter as the resulting benefit. How? When he says in the Gospel, "Blessed are those who cry, because they shall laugh." So crying is a requirement, laughter the reward, of wisdom. He wrote laughter to mean joy. *Sermon 175.2.*

CLOSING PRAYER

I know, O Lord, and do with all humility acknowledge myself an object altogether unworthy of your love; but sure I am, you are an object altogether worthy of mine. I am not good enough to serve you, but you have a right to the best service I can pay. Do you then impart to me some of that excellence, and that shall supply my own want of worth. Help me to cease from sin according to your will, that I may be capable of doing you service according to my duty. Enable me so to guard and govern myself, so to begin and finish my course that, when the race of life is run, I may sleep in peace and rest in you. Be with me to the end, that my sleep may be rest indeed, my rest perfect security and that security a blessed eternity. *Augustine*

Repentance

⁙ THEME

God is merciful, slow to anger and full of love toward his children. He calls us to repentance (Joel 2:1-2, 12-17). We look to God as our refuge, our protector and our guardian from all trouble (Ps 91:1-2, 9-16). God gave his only son, Jesus, to become fully human, with all the same temptations we experience (Lk 4:1-13), then to die for our sins and be resurrected (Rom 10:8b-13) so that we might spend eternity with him.

⁙ OPENING PRAYER: *First Sunday in Lent*

Father of mercies, hear our prayers, we beseech thee; spare them who repent, that they whose consciences by sin are accused, by thy merciful pardon may be absolved; through Jesus Christ our Lord. Amen. *The Gelasian Sacramentary*

⁙ OLD TESTAMENT READING: *Joel 2:1-2, 12-17*

REFLECTIONS FROM THE CHURCH FATHERS

Confess and Repent. CYPRIAN: Let each one confess his sin, I beseech you, brethren, while he who has sinned is still in this world, while his confession can be admitted, while the satisfaction and remission effected through the priest is pleasing with the Lord. Let us turn to the Lord with our whole mind, and, expressing repentance for our sin with true grief, let us implore God's mercy. Let the soul prostrate itself before him; let sorrow give satisfaction to him; let our every hope rest on him. He himself tells how we ought to ask. He says, "Return to me with all your hearts, in fasting and in weeping, and in mourning, and rend your hearts, not your garments." Let us return to the Lord with a whole heart; let us placate his wrath and displeasure by fastings, weepings and mournings, as he himself admonishes. *The Lapsed 29.5.*

Mercy Flows from God's Being. THEODORET OF CYR: "Rend your hearts, not your garments," that is, have recourse to thoughts of compunction, soften the obduracy of your thinking, accept beneficial advice, abandon the way of vice and travel by that way which leads directly to God. After all, many are the founts of compassion and mercy that flow from him, and in his exercise of longsuffering he is not in the custom of putting his threats into effect. In fact, he indicated as much by saying "repenting of the troubles," that is, by instilling dread by the threats of punishment, and by the changes in human beings for the better transforming the threats into something pleasant. The God of all, you see, does not intend one thing at one time and another thing at another, or like us repent of what he does. Rather, while making threats he has mercy within himself, and he offers it to those who are sorry for their sins, and while making promises of good things he knows those who are good and those who are unworthy of his gifts, extending them to the former and giving to the latter the opposite of what he promises. *Commentary on Joel 2.13.*

Rend Hearts in Repentance. FULGENTIUS OF RUSPE: How well does the holy prophet teach that the seeds of good works must be watered by a river of tears! No seeds germinate unless they are watered; nor does fruit come forth from the seed if deprived of the aid of water. Accordingly, we too, if we wish to keep the fruits of our seeds, let us not stop watering our seeds with tears that must be poured out more from the heart than from the body. Therefore it is said to us through the prophet that we rend "our hearts and not our garments," something we can do when we recall that we ourselves, even if not in deed, frequently sin at least in thought. Because the "earthly tent burdens the thoughtful mind" and our land does not cease to produce thorns and thistles for us. We are unable to get to eating our bread, unless we will have been worn out by weariness and the sweat of our brow. *Letter 9.*

PSALM OF RESPONSE: *Psalm 91:1-2, 9-16*

NEW TESTAMENT READING: *Romans 10:8b-13*

REFLECTIONS FROM THE CHURCH FATHERS

The Word Is Near You. ORIGEN: By this Paul indicates that Christ is in the heart of all men by virtue of his being the Word or reason (logos) embedded in all things by sharing in which all people are rational. *On First Principles 1.3.6.*

Faith Not Foreign to Our Nature. AMBROSIASTER: This is said in Deuteronomy (30:14) in order to show that belief in Christ is not all that foreign to our mind or to our nature. Even though we cannot see him with our eyes, what we believe is not out of harmony with the nature of our minds and our way of speaking. *Commentary on Paul's Epistles.*

The Simplicity of Confession. AUGUSTINE: The innumerable and multiple rites by which the Jewish people had been oppressed have been taken away, so that in the mercy of God we might attain salvation by the simplicity of a confession of faith. *Augustine on Romans 67.*

Believers Not Put to Shame. CYRIL OF ALEXANDRIA: Israel ought not to suppose that salvation by faith is a blessing peculiar to it. For Scripture says that everyone who calls on the name of the Lord will be saved, whether Jew or Gentile, whether slave or free. The universal God saves everyone without distinction, because all things belong to him.

Thus we say that all things are recapitulated in Christ. *Explanation of the Letter to the Romans.*

Lord of All. PELAGIUS: There is one Lord of all, who abounds in mercy and possesses salvation, with which he is generous to all. *Pelagius's Commentary on Romans.*

GOSPEL READING: *Luke 4:1-13*

REFLECTIONS FROM THE CHURCH FATHERS

Jesus Says Neither "I Can" Nor "I Cannot." CYRIL OF ALEXANDRIA: Therefore it was that Christ, knowing the monster's plan, neither made the change nor said that he was either unable or unwilling to make it. Rather, the Lord shakes him off as annoying and meddlesome, saying, "Man shall not live by bread alone." He means this: If God grants a man the ability, he can survive without eating and live as Moses and Elijah, who by the Word of the Lord passed forty days without taking food. If, therefore, it is possible to live without bread, why should I make the stone bread? He purposely does not say, "I cannot," that he may not deny his own power. Nor does he say, "I can," lest the devil, knowing that he is God, for whom alone such things are possible, should depart from him. Observe, I beg you, how the nature of man in Christ casts off the faults of Adam's gluttony. By eating we were conquered in Adam, by abstinence we conquered in Christ. *Commentary on Luke, Homily 12.*

Jesus Restores Kingdoms Seized by Fraud. CYRIL OF ALEXANDRIA: It is written, "You shall worship the Lord your God, and him only shall you serve." It is fitting that he made mention of this commandment, striking as it were at his very heart. Before his advent, Satan had deceived all under heaven and was himself worshiped everywhere. But the law of God, ejecting him from the dominion he had usurped by fraud, has commanded people to worship him only who by nature and in truth is God and to offer service to him alone. *Commentary on Luke, Homily 12.*

Satan Uses Scripture Selectively by Convenience. EPHREM THE SYRIAN: Satan studied only those passages from Scriptures that were convenient to him and omitted those which were harmful to him. The heretics are like this too. They appropriate from Scripture those passages that suit their erroneous teaching and omit those that refute their errors, thereby demonstrating that they are disciples of this master. *Commentary on Tatian's Diatessaron 4.8B-C.*

The Pinnacle of the Temple Is Christ. PRUDENTIUS:
Still the pinnacle stands, outlasting the temple's destruction,
For the corner raised up from that stone which the builders rejected
Will remain throughout all ages forever and ever.
Now it is head of the temple and holds the new stones together.
Scenes from Sacred History 31.

CLOSING PRAYER

We give thee thanks—yes, more than thanks, O Lord our God, for all thy goodness at all times and in all places, because thou has shielded, rescued, helped and guided us all the days of our lives and brought us to this hour. We pray and beseech thee, merciful God, to grant in thy goodness that we may spend this day, and all the time of our lives, without sin, in fullness of joy, holiness and reverence of thee. But drive away from us, O Lord, all envy, all fear and all temptations. Bestow on us what is good and meet. Whatever sin we commit in thought, word or deed, do thou in thy goodness and mercy be pleased to pardon. And lead us not into temptation but deliver us from evil; through the grace, mercy and love of thine only-begotten Son. Amen. *Liturgy of St. Mark*

Following Christ

⌁ THEME

God keeps his promises (Gen 15:1-12, 17-18); he is our light and our salvation. Because of his care, we need not be afraid (Ps 27) and can rejoice in knowing Jesus Christ, no matter what the cost (Phil 3:17–4:1). Blessed is he who comes in the name of the Lord (Lk 13:31-35)!

⌁ OPENING PRAYER: *Second Sunday in Lent*

I beseech you, merciful God, to allow me to drink from the stream that flows from your fountain of life. May I taste the sweet beauty of its waters, which sprang from the very depths of your truth. O Lord, you are that fountain from which I desire with all my heart to drink. Give me, Lord Jesus, this water, that it may quench the burning spiritual thirst within my soul, and purify me from all sin. I know, King of glory, that I am asking from you a great gift. But you give to your faithful people without counting the cost, and you promise even greater things in the future. Indeed, nothing is greater than yourself, and you have given yourself to humankind on the cross. Therefore, in praying for the waters of life, I am praying that you, the source of those waters, will give yourself to me. You are my light, my salvation, my food, my drink, my God. *Columbanus*

⌁ OLD TESTAMENT READING: *Genesis 15:1-12, 17-18*

REFLECTIONS FROM THE CHURCH FATHERS

A Reward Bestowed. AMBROSE: What is the meaning then of the expression "he brought him outside"? The prophet is as it were led out, so that he goes outside of the body and sees the limitations imposed by the flesh that is his garment and the infusion of the Holy Spirit who makes a kind of visible descent. We too must exit from the confinement of this our temporary dwelling. We must purify the place where our soul dwells from all uncleanness, throw out every stain of wickedness, if we wish to receive the spirit of wisdom, because "wisdom will not enter a wicked soul." Abraham believed, not because he was drawn by a promise of gold or silver but because he believed from the heart. "It was reckoned to him as righteousness." A reward was bestowed that corresponded to the rest of his merit. *On Abraham 2.8.48.*

A Symbol Was Given. AUGUSTINE: Here also, in fine, a symbol was given, consisting of these animals: a heifer, a she-goat, a ram and two birds, a turtledove and pigeon, that he might know that the things which he had not doubted should come to pass were to happen in accordance with this symbol. The heifer may be a sign that the people should be put under the law, the she-goat that the same people were to become sinful, the ram that they should reign. Perhaps these animals are said to be of three years old for this reason: that there are three remarkable divisions of time, from Adam to Noah, and from him to Abraham, and from him to David. David, on the rejection of Saul, was first established by the will of the Lord in the kingdom of the Israelite nation. In this third division, which extends from Abraham to David, people grew up as if passing through the third age of life. Or perhaps it may be that they had some other more suitable meaning. Still I have no doubt whatever that spiritual things were prefigured by them as well as by the turtledove and pigeon. *City of God 16.24.*

No Discrepancy Between Genesis and Exodus. DIDYMUS THE BLIND:
This word anticipates the sojourn of the people in Egypt, for they were
to sojourn as it were in a land not their own. They would be reduced to
slavery by the Pharaoh and mistreated in many ways by him and by the
Egyptians. There is no discrepancy between what is said here and what
is written in Exodus. There it is said, "After 430 years, the army of the
Lord left the land of Egypt." Here: "After four hundred years." It should
be noted that it is not said that they left when four hundred years were
completed but rather after four hundred years, which leaves room for
the thirty years. And the promise "I will judge the nation to which you
will be enslaved" was realized in the very way described in Exodus: God
afflicted the Egyptians with ten plagues, and in the end "they sank as
lead in the mighty waters." Finally, they were to leave "with much bag-
gage," as history would show. From this we learn that if God maltreats
someone for a time, he does this not as a matter of indifference but only
for some good purpose. Consider too whether this passage might also
allude to the sojourn of the saints. *On Genesis 231.*

⊲ **PSALM OF RESPONSE:** *Psalm 27*

⊲ **NEW TESTAMENT READING:** *Philippians 3:17–4:1*

REFLECTIONS FROM THE CHURCH FATHERS

Now with Tears. AMBROSIASTER: Those who bring him to tears are
the very ones who had already overthrown the Galatians. By treacher-
ous proceedings they were destroying the churches in the name of
Christ. . . . He speaks of these people with grief and tears. They were
impeding the salvation of the faithful by raising questions about the
eating of or abstinence from food. It is as though salvation were in food
or as if God *were a belly*, one whom they believed to take delight in
worldly foods according to the law while they gloried in the circumcision of their private parts. This is what it is to "think earthly thoughts."

One who "thinks spiritual thoughts" glories in faith, hope and charity. *Epistle to the Philippians 3.19.*

Living As Expatriates. CLEMENT OF ALEXANDRIA: We know that this is well said, for we ought to live as strangers and expatriates in the world . . . not using the creation to satisfy our passions but high-mindedly and with thanksgiving. *Stromata 3.95.*

The Beloved Stand Together As One in Christ. MARIUS VICTORI-NUS: Love, the sum of every virtue for the Christian, does not fittingly come to pass if the faithful do not stand united as one, thinking in harmony. This is what Paul means here by "Stand firm in the Lord, my beloved." We may understand that he wants them to be united in understanding from the fact that he calls them (literally) "most beloved brethren." Mutual love is the result of thinking in unison and standing together in Christ. When all have equal faith in Christ all of us stand together in him. *Epistle to the Philippians 4.1.*

GOSPEL READING: *Luke 13:31-35*

REFLECTIONS FROM THE CHURCH FATHERS

The Miracles of Jesus Point to His Passion. CYRIL OF ALEXANDRIA: But what did he tell them to say? "Behold, I cast out demons and perform cures today and tomorrow, and the third day I finish my course." You see that he declares his intention of performing what he knew would grieve the troop of Pharisees. So they drive him from Jerusalem, fearing that by the display of miracles he will win many to faith in himself. But inasmuch as their purpose there did not escape him since he was God, he declares his intention of performing what they hated and says that he shall also rebuke unclean spirits and deliver the sick from their sufferings and be perfected. This means that of his own will he will endure the passion on the cross for the salvation of the world. He knew, therefore, as it appears, both how and when he would endure death in the flesh. *Commentary on Luke, Homily 100.*

Jesus Must Die in Jerusalem. EPHREM THE SYRIAN: It was prophetic that Moses had given the Israelites the order to offer the lamb in
sacrifice and there to accomplish an image of the redemption. Herod
did not kill the Lord with the infants of Bethlehem, nor did the Naza-
renes when they hurled him down from the mountain, since it was not
possible for him to die outside of Jerusalem. For it cannot be that a
prophet should perish outside of Jerusalem. Take note that although it
was Jerusalem that killed him, nevertheless Herod and Nazareth were
united with regard to his death, and vengeance will be required of both
for his death. Learn also from this that not only will vengeance for his
blood be required of the inhabitants of Jerusalem, but also everyone
who saw and denied him will be convicted for having killed him. In
saying "between the sanctuary and the altar," he has indeed shown their
perversity, in that they did not respect even the place of atonement.
Commentary on Tatian's Diatessaron 18.10.

CLOSING PRAYER

O Lord Jesus Christ, give us a measure of your spirit that we may be
enabled to obey your teaching to pacify anger, to take part in pity, to
moderate desire, to increase love, to put away sorrow, to cast away
vainglory, not to be vindictive, not to fear death, ever entrusting our
spirit to immortal God, who with you and the Holy Spirit lives and
reigns world without end. *Apollonius*

Help with Temptation

THEME

God is powerful—he can work through our weaknesses to accomplish his purposes (Ex 3:1-15). We seek the Lord and his steadfast love; we praise him and marvel at his power and glory (Ps 63:1-8). We ask him for help to stand against temptation and to find ways to escape it (1 Cor 10:1-13). When we fall into sin, we are called to repentance (Lk 13:1-9).

OPENING PRAYER: *Third Sunday in Lent*

May the strength of God pilot us. May the power of God preserve us. May the wisdom of God instruct us. May the hand of God protect us. May the way of God direct us. May the shield of God defend us. May the host of God guard us against the snares of evil and the temptations of the world. May Christ be with us. Christ before us, Christ in us, Christ over us. May your salvation, O Lord, be always ours this day and for evermore. *Patrick*

OLD TESTAMENT READING: *Exodus 3:1-15*

REFLECTIONS FROM THE CHURCH FATHERS

The Angel Was God. HILARY OF POITIERS: The vision and the voice are in the one place, nor is anyone else heard except the one who is seen. He who is an angel of God when he is seen is the same one who is the Lord when he is heard, but he himself who is the Lord when he is heard is recognized as the God of Abraham, Isaac and Jacob. When he is called the angel of God, it is revealed that this is not his true nature and that he is not alone, for he is the angel of God. When he is called the Lord and God, he is proclaimed as possessing the glory and the name of his own nature. Accordingly you have in an angel who appeared in the bush him who is also the Lord and God. *On the Trinity 4.32.*

The Power of God's Word Shown in the Burning Bush. PRUDENTIUS:
It was the Word, breathed from the Father's mouth,
Who of the Virgin took a mortal frame.
The human form that not yet in the flesh
Appeared to Moses wore a brow like ours,
Since God, who would by power of the Word
Assume a body, made the face the same.
Flames rose and seemed to burn the thorny bush.
God moved amid the branches set with spines,
And tresses of the flames swayed harmlessly,
That he might shadow forth his Son's descent
Into our thorny members sin infests
With teeming briers and fills with bitter woes.
For tainted at its root that noxious shrub
Had sprouted from its baneful sap a crop
Of evil shoots beset with many thorns.
The sterile branches suddenly grew bright
As God enkindled with his mighty power
The leafy boughs, not harmed the tangled briers.
He touched the scarlet berries, blood-red fruits,
And grazed the twigs that grew from deadly wood,
Shed by the tortured bush with cruel pangs.
The Divinity of Christ 49-70.

Beautiful for Preaching the Gospel. AMBROSE: Pass by like Moses, that you may see the God of Abraham and of Isaac and of Jacob and that you may see a great vision. This is a great vision, but if you wish to see it, remove the sandals from your feet, remove every bond of iniquity, remove the bonds of the world, leave behind the sandals which are earthly. Likewise, Jesus sent the apostles without sandals, without money, gold and silver, so that they would not carry earthly things with them. For the man who seeks the good is praised not for his sandals but for the swiftness and grace of his feet, as Scripture says, "How beautiful are the feet of those who preach the gospel of peace, of those who bring glad tidings of good things!" Therefore remove the sandals from your feet, that they may be beautiful for preaching the gospel. *Flight from the World 5.25.*

Dead Works. AUGUSTINE: What are the shoes? Well, what *are* the shoes we wear? Leather from dead animals. The hides of dead animals are what we protect our feet with. So what are we being ordered to do? To give up dead works. This is symbolically what he instructs Moses to do in his honor, when the Lord says to him, "Take off your shoes. For the place you are standing in is holy ground." There's no holier ground than the church of God, is there? So as we stand in it let us take off our shoes, let us give up dead works. *Sermon 101.7.*

PSALM OF RESPONSE: *Psalm 63:1-8*

NEW TESTAMENT READING: *1 Corinthians 10:1-13*

REFLECTIONS FROM THE CHURCH FATHERS

Grace and Baptism. THEODORET OF CYR: The cloud is the grace of the Holy Spirit, while the sea represents baptism. *Commentary on the First Epistle to the Corinthians 226.*

Food for the Soul. GREGORY OF NYSSA: The divine apostle also, in calling the Lord "spiritual food and drink," suggests that he knows that human nature is not simple, but that there is an intelligible part mixed with a sensual part and that a particular type of nurture is needed for each of the elements in us—sensible food to strengthen our bodies and spiritual food for the well-being of our souls. *On Perfection.*

Manifest a Life Worthy of Grace. CHRYSOSTOM: Why does Paul say these things? He was pointing out that just as the Israelites got no benefit from the great gift which they enjoyed, so the Corinthian Christians would get nothing out of baptism or holy communion unless they went on and manifested a life worthy of that grace. *Homilies on the Epistles of Paul to the Corinthians 23.3.*

Warnings for Us. ORIGEN: These things were written as examples for us, so that when we read about their sins we shall know to avoid them. *Commentary on 1 Corinthians 4.46.*

The Purpose of Temptation. SEVERIAN OF GABALA: Paul did not pray that we should not be tempted, for a man who has not been tempted is untried, but that we should be able to bear our temptations as we ought. *Pauline Commentary from the Greek Church.*

Ability to Bear Temptation Comes from Grace. CHRYSOSTOM: Paul implies that there must be temptations which we cannot bear. What are these? Well, all of them in effect. For the ability to bear them comes from God's grace, which we obtain by asking for it. God gives us patience and brings us speedy deliverance. In this way the temptation becomes bearable. *Homilies on the Epistles of Paul to the Corinthians 24.1.*

⌁ GOSPEL READING: *Luke 13:1-9*

REFLECTIONS FROM THE CHURCH FATHERS

The Lord's Three Visits Through the Patriarchs, the Prophets and the Gospel. AUGUSTINE: The Lord also has something very fitting to say about a fruitless tree, "Look, it is now three years that I have been coming to it. Finding no fruit on it, I will cut it down, to stop it blocking up my field." The gardener intercedes. . . . This tree is the human race. The Lord visited this tree in the time of the patriarchs, as if for the first year. He visited it in the time of the law and the prophets, as if for the second year. Here we are now; with the gospel the third year has dawned. Now it is as though it should have been cut down, but the merciful one intercedes with the merciful one. He wanted to show how merciful he was and so he stood up to himself with a plea for mercy. "Let us leave it," he says, "this year too. Let us dig a ditch around it." Manure is a sign of humility. "Let us apply a load of manure; perhaps it may bear fruit." Since it does bear fruit in one part, and in another part does not bear fruit, its Lord will come and divide it. What does that mean, "divide it"? There are good people and bad people now in one company, as though constituting one body. *Sermon 254.3.*

Whether the Vinedresser Is the Door or the Father. CYRIL OF AL-EXANDRIA: If any one should say that the vinedresser is the Son, this view also has a suitable reason on its side. He is our advocate with the Father, our propitiation and the gardener of our souls. He constantly prunes away whatever is harmful and fills us with rational and holy seeds so we may produce fruits for him. He spoke of himself, "A sower went out to sow his seed." It does not influence the glory of the Son to assume the character of the vinedresser. The Father assumes it himself, without being exposed to any blame for so doing. The Son said to the holy apostles, "I am the vine, you are the branches; my Father is the vinedresser." *Commentary on Luke, Homily 96.*

CLOSING PRAYER

Stir up, we beseech thee, O Lord, the wills of thy faithful people; that they, plenteously bringing forth the fruit of good works, may by thee be plenteously rewarded; through Jesus Christ our Lord. *The Gregorian Sacramentary*

Caring for the Lost

THEME

God cares for his people (Josh 5:9-12) and forgives our sins. We can trust him and his steadfast love—he is our refuge in times of distress (Ps 32). Through Christ, we become a new creation (2 Cor 5:16-21) and are heirs to the kingdom of God (Lk 15:1-3, 11-32).

OPENING PRAYER: *Fourth Sunday in Lent*

Show me, O Lord, your mercy, and delight my heart with it. Let me find you whom I so longingly seek. See, here is the man whom the robbers seized, mishandled and left half dead on the road to Jericho. O kind-hearted Samaritan, come to my aid! I am the sheep who wandered into the wilderness—seek after me, and bring me home again to your fold. Do with me what you will, that I may stay by you all the days of my life and praise you with all those who are with you in heaven for all eternity. *Jerome*

OLD TESTAMENT READING: *Joshua 5:9-12*

REFLECTIONS FROM THE CHURCH FATHERS

The Reproach of Sins. ORIGEN: All persons, even if they come from the law, even if they have learned through Moses, still have the reproach of Egypt in them, the reproach of sins. Who will be like Paul even according to the observance of the law? Just hear him saying, "According to the righteousness based on the law, I lived without blame."

Nevertheless, he himself publicly announces and says, "For we were even ourselves at some time foolish, unbelieving, wandering, enslaved to desires and various forms of pleasure, in malice and envy, hateful, hating one another." Do those things not seem to you to be reproaches, even the reproaches of Egypt? But since Christ came and gave to us the second circumcision through "the baptism of regeneration" and purified our souls, we have cast away all these things, and in exchange for them we have received the affirming of a good conscience toward God. At that time, through the second circumcision, the reproaches of Egypt were taken away from us and the blemishes of sins were purified. No one, therefore, fears the reproaches of past transgressions, if he has been wholly converted and has repented from the heart, and, by faith, has parted the waters of the Jordan and been purified through the second circumcision of the gospel. You hear that "today, I have taken the reproach of Egypt away from you." *Homilies on Joshua* 5.6.

Joshua's Manna Fulfilled by the Sacrament of Christ's Body and Blood. BEDE: And Jesus said to them, "I have eagerly desired to eat this Passover with you before I suffer." He desired first of all to eat the typical Passover with his disciples and thus to reveal the mystery of his passion to the world, so that the judge of the ancient and lawful Passover would emerge and forbid this to be displayed to have pertained to the type of its dispensation by further carnal teaching but would demonstrate instead through the passing shadow that the light of the true Passover has now come. . . . And for three and one half years (after his baptism), although provoking gradual movement toward the promised heaven, Christ does not cease to observe the sacraments of the law, as though to be nourished with the customary manna, until, while eating the desired Passover with his disciples at a foreordained time, as morning was breaking, he finally offers the most pure sacrament of his body and blood, consecrated on the altar of the cross for imbuing the faithful, as though it were the unleavened bread of the promised land. *Exposition of the Gospel of Luke* 6.22.

❧ **PSALM OF RESPONSE:** *Psalm 32*

❧ **NEW TESTAMENT READING:** *2 Corinthians 5:16-21*

REFLECTIONS FROM THE CHURCH FATHERS

Ordered Freedom. AUGUSTINE: We are then truly free when God orders our lives, that is, forms and creates us not as human beings—this he has already done—but as good people, which he is now doing by his grace, that we may indeed be new creatures in Christ Jesus. Accordingly the prayer: "Create in me a clean heart, O God." *Enchiridion 9:31.*

An Offering for Our Sins. AMBROSIASTER: Christ did not have to be born as a man, but he became man because of sin. It was only because all flesh was subject to sin that he was made sin for us. In view of the fact that he was made an offering for sins, it is not wrong for him to be said to have been made "sin," because in the law the sacrifice which was offered for sins used to be called a "sin." After his death on the cross Christ descended to hell, because it was death, working through sin, which gave hell its power. Christ defeated death by this death and brought such benefit to sinners that now death cannot hold those who are marked with the sign of the cross. *Commentary on Paul's Epistles.*

He Suffered As If a Condemned Sinner. CHRYSOSTOM: God allowed his Son to suffer as if a condemned sinner, so that we might be delivered from the penalty of our sins. This is God's righteousness, that we are not justified by works (for then they would have to be perfect, which is impossible), but by grace, in which case all our sin is removed. *Homilies on the Epistles of Paul to the Corinthians 11.5.*

Called to Be What We Are. THEODORET OF CYR: Christ was called what we are in order to call us to be what he is. *Commentary on the Second Epistle to the Corinthians 318.*

❧ **GOSPEL READING:** *Luke 15:1-3, 11-32*

REFLECTIONS FROM THE CHURCH FATHERS

The Parable Calls the Pharisees to Rejoice Over the Repentance of Sinners. CYRIL OF ALEXANDRIA: What is the object of the parable? Let us examine the occasion that led to it so we will learn the truth. The blessed Luke had said a little before of Christ the Savior of us all. . . . The Pharisees and scribes made this outcry at his gentleness and love to people. They wickedly and impiously blamed him for receiving and teaching people whose lives were impure. Christ very necessarily set before them the present parable. He clearly shows them that the God of all requires even him who is thoroughly steadfast, firm, holy and has attained to the highest praise for sobriety of conduct to be earnest in following his will. When any are called to repentance, even if they have a bad reputation, he must rejoice rather and not give way to an unloving irritation because of them. *Commentary on Luke, Homily 107.*

To Return to the Father's House. EPHREM THE SYRIAN:
Jacob led out his sheep
And brought them to his father's home;
A symbol for those with discernment,
A parable for those with perception
Is to be found in this homecoming:
Let us too return to our Father's house,
My brothers, and do not become
Captivated with desire
For this transient earth
—for your true city is in Eden.
Blessed indeed is that person
Who has seen his dear ones in its midst.
Hymns on Paradise 14.7.

The First Confession Seeks Reconciliation. AMBROSE: "Father," it says, "I have sinned against heaven and before you." This is the first confession before the Creator of nature, the Patron of mercy and the Judge of guilt. Although God knows all things, he awaits the words of your confession. . . . Confess, so that Christ may rather intercede for you, he whom we have as an advocate with the Father. Confess, so that the church may pray for you and that the people may weep for you. Do not fear that perhaps you might not receive. The advocate promises pardon. The patron offers grace. The defender promises the reconciliation with the Father's good will to you. Believe because it is the truth. Consent because it is a virtue. He has a reason to intercede for you, unless he died for you in vain. The Father also has a reason for forgiveness, because the Father wants what the Son wants. *Exposition of the Gospel of Luke 7.224-25.*

Restoring Him to Sonship. PETER CHRYSOLOGUS: "Give him a ring for his finger." The father's devotion is not content to restore only his innocence. It also brings back his former honor. "And give him sandals for his feet." He was rich when he departed, but how poor he has returned! Of all his substance, he does not even bring back shoes on his feet! "Give him sandals for his feet" that nakedness may not disgrace even a foot and that he may have shoes when he returns to his former course of life. *Sermon 3.*

⫸ CLOSING PRAYER

Keep, I pray, my faith unsullied, and till my spirit departs, grant that I may speak what I believe: so that I may always hold fast to what I professed in the creed, when I was baptized in the Father, and the Son, and the Holy Spirit. . . . Amen. *Hilary of Poitiers*

God Makes a Way

THEME

The Lord is doing something new! He makes a way for us in the wilderness and causes rivers to flow in the desert (Is 43:16-21). Because of the great things he has done for us, we are filled with joy (Ps 126). Christ's love, mercy (Jn 12:1-8) and sacrifice mean we make him our highest priority (Phil 3:4b-14).

OPENING PRAYER: *Fifth Sunday in Lent*

Loving Savior, be pleased to show yourself to us who knock, so that in knowing you we may love only you, love you alone, desire you alone, contemplate only you day and night and always think of you. Inspire in us the depth of love that is fitting for you to receive as God. So may your love pervade our whole being, possess us completely and fill all our senses, that we may know no other love but love for you who are everlasting. May our love be so great that the many waters of sky, land and sea cannot extinguish it in us: "many waters could not extinguish love." *Columbanus*

OLD TESTAMENT READING: *Isaiah 43:16-21*

REFLECTIONS FROM THE CHURCH FATHERS

God Makes a Path. PROCOPIUS OF GAZA: How has he led chariots and horses? It is clear that Pharaoh pursued Israel by his own decision, for God had already spoken in this way to him: "I have raised you up as to show my power in you and so that my name might be made known throughout the earth." Thus in a marvelous way God saves those who are fleeing from the desire for earthly things as they are pursued by the devil. God shows them that the wild waves of the present life are passable and that they will not be overwhelmed by trials but will arrive securely in the desert with a stilled and purified mind. They will eat the heavenly bread and drink the water from the rock. This is to share in Christ and to go through the Jordan and gain the Promised Land. *Commentary on Isaiah 43.14-28.*

The New Creation Requires Unexpected Means. AMBROSE: Although he took a body, although he became man to redeem humanity and recall it from death, still, being God, he came to earth in an unusual way so that, as he had said, "Behold, I make all things new," he might thus be born from the womb of an immaculate virgin and be believed to be, as it is written, "God with us." *Letter 44.*

A New Eye Is Required. CLEMENT OF ALEXANDRIA: The Word says, "Look, I am doing something new, which no eye has seen, no ear heard, no human heart felt." These are to be seen, heard and grasped by a new eye, a new hearing and a new heart when the Lord's disciples speak, listen and act in the Spirit. *Stromata 2.4.15.3.*

⫗ PSALM OF RESPONSE: *Psalm 126*

⫗ NEW TESTAMENT READING: *Philippians 3:4b-14*

REFLECTIONS FROM THE CHURCH FATHERS

The Ladder of the Law No Longer Needed. CHRYSOSTOM: So the law served as a ladder. Note that when a person has gone up a ladder, he no longer needs it. Yet he does not despise it but gives it thanks, because it is due to the ladder that he is in the state of no longer needing it. . . . It is not the law that is a privation but apostasy from Christ through adherence to the law. So when it leads us away from Christ it is a loss. When it leads us to him, no longer so. *Homily on Philippians 12.3.7-9.*

Not That I Have Already Obtained. AMBROSIASTER: Throughout the letter Paul bears witness to his joy in them and praises their obedience and faith. He is, however, concerned that they, like all who are subject to human conceits, might become elated as though they were already worthy. So he tells them openly, speaking of his own person, that something is still wanting for perfect righteousness. He urges them to good works. If he who is adorned with such dignity confesses that he is still wanting in perfection, they would understand how much more they must work to acquire the blessings of righteousness. *Epistle to the Philippians 3.12.1.*

Making My Own the One Who Made Me His Own. MARIUS VICTORINUS: Christ by his sufferings has set free all who follow him. He embraces everyone, but especially those who follow. The one who wants to follow and embrace Christ is bound to follow Christ in all his sufferings. Only in this way may he embrace Christ as Christ embraces him. For if Christ set everyone free by his sufferings, he embraces everyone in his sufferings. *Epistle to the Philippians 3.12.*

Though We Know Not the Future We Know the One Who Knows It. THEODORET OF CYR: This is how we should think about the crowns laid up for us. For even if we do not perceive exactly what these are like, we ought at least to know that God, as Master of the contest, will reveal this to us. *Epistle to the Philippians 3.15.*

GOSPEL READING: *John 12:1-8*

REFLECTIONS FROM THE CHURCH FATHERS

Imprinting the Memory of Lazarus's Resurrection. BEDE: Being sure of the glory of his resurrection, Jesus first came to Bethany, a town near Jerusalem, where Lazarus was, whom he had raised from the dead. Then he went to Jerusalem, where he himself was to suffer and rise from the dead. He went to Jerusalem so that he might die there, but to Bethany so that the raising up of Lazarus might be imprinted more deeply on the memory of all. *Homilies on the Gospels 2.4.*

Give Your Excess to the Poor. AUGUSTINE: Let us look into the mystery this incident imported. Whatever soul among you wishes to be truly faithful, anoint the feet of the Lord with precious ointment like Mary did. That ointment was righteousness, and therefore it was exactly a pound weight: but it was ointment of pure nard, very precious. From his calling it "pistics" we ought to infer that there was some locality from which it derived its preciousness, but this does not exhaust its meaning, and it harmonizes well with a sacramental symbol. The root of the word in the Greek (*pistis*) is by us called "faith." You were seeking to work righteousness. "The just shall live by faith." Anoint the feet of Jesus: follow the Lord's footsteps by living a good life. Wipe them with your hair: what you have in excess, give to the poor, and then you have wiped the feet of the Lord. For the hair seems to be the superfluous to you but necessary for the feet of the Lord. Perhaps on this earth the Lord's feet are still in need. For of whom but of his members is he yet to say in the end, "Inasmuch as you did it to one of the least of mine, you did it to me"? You spent what was superfluous for yourselves, but you have done what was grateful to my feet. *Tractates on the Gospel of John 50.6.*

Under the Guise of Religion. GAUDENTIUS OF BRESCIA: Judas valued cheating above everything else—except his hatred of the Savior. Nevertheless, under the pretext of piety, he rings out these deceitful words. . . . Impious beyond measure and filled with a savage disposition, influenced by his fraudulent greed, it is evident that he expresses this particular charge, attempting to hide it under the guise of religion. *Sermon 13.*

Care, Reproof and Vindication. **THEODORE OF MOPSUESTIA:** If, he says, you are really sincere in your mercy for the poor, there is much time left for you to benefit them. There will never be a shortage of them in this world. But it will not be easy for you to perform a service for me: I am staying with you for a short time, and then I will leave. First he purified the woman from the blame with these words by modestly saying that a greater honor had to be attributed to him than to the poor because he was staying with them for a short time. Then he reproved the intention of Judas because Judas did not care about the poor at all, nor should the woman be reproached because of the perfume she had poured. *Commentary on John 5.12.8.*

CLOSING PRAYER

Let us take refuge like deer beside the fountain of waters. Let our soul thirst, as David thirsted, for the fountain. What is the fountain? Listen to David: "With you is the fountain of life." Let my soul say to this fountain: "When shall I come and see you face to face?" For the fountain is God himself. *Ambrose*

A Teachable Heart

☙ THEME

The Lord gives us a teachable heart so that we might encourage others
(Is 50:4-9a). When we are grieved and discouraged, we turn to God in
trust for help (Ps 31:9-16) knowing that he gave his only son Jesus, who
came to earth (Lk 19:28-40) to die for us on the cross (Phil 2:5-11).

☙ OPENING PRAYER: *Palm Sunday*

O you from whom to be turned is to fall, to whom to be turned is to
rise and in whom to stand is to abide forever, grant us in all our duties
your help, in all our perplexities your guidance, in all our dangers your
protection and in all our sorrows your peace; through Jesus Christ our
Lord. *Augustine*

☙ OLD TESTAMENT READING: *Isaiah 50:4-9a*

REFLECTIONS FROM THE CHURCH FATHERS

The Tongue That Knows When to Speak. JUSTIN MARTYR: The
power of his mighty word with which he always refuted the Pharisees
and scribes, and indeed all the teachers of your race who disputed with
him, was stopped like a full and mighty fountain whose waters have
been suddenly shut off when he remained silent and would no longer
answer his accusers before Pilate, as was recorded in the writings of the
apostles, in order that those words of Isaiah might bear fruit in action:

"The Lord gives me a tongue, that I may know when I ought to speak." And his words, "You are my God, depart not from me," teach us to put all our trust in God, the Creator of all things, and to seek aid and salvation from him alone; and not to imagine, as other people do, that we can attain salvation by means of birth, or wealth, or power or wisdom. *Dialogue with Trypho 102.*

In Silence We Learn How to Speak. AMBROSE: Now what ought we to learn before everything else, but to be silent that we may be able to speak? Lest my voice should condemn me before that of another acquits me, for it is written: "By your words you shall be condemned." What need is there, then, that you should hasten to undergo the danger of condemnation by speaking when you can be more safe by keeping silent? How many have I seen to fall into sin by speaking, but scarcely one by keeping silent; and so it is more difficult to know how to keep silent than how to speak. . . . A person is wise, then, who knows how to keep silent. Lastly, the Wisdom of God said, "The Lord has given to me the tongue of learning, that I should know when it is good to speak." Justly, then, is one wise who has received of the Lord to know when he ought to speak. Wherefore the Scripture says well: "A wise person will keep silence until there is opportunity." *Duties of the Clergy 1.2.5.*

A Call to Self-Control. BASIL THE GREAT: If you remain unruffled, you silence your insolent assailant by giving him a practical illustration of self-control. Were you struck? So also was the Lord. Were you spat on? The Lord also suffered this, for "he did not turn his face from the shame of the spittle." . . . You have not been condemned to death or crucified. *Homily Against Those Who Are Prone to Anger.*

Our Pride in Contrast to God's Humility. MACARIUS OF EGYPT: Now if God willed to accept and to lower himself to such sufferings, dishonors and humiliations, then no matter how much you humble yourself, you whose nature is mud and subject to death, you will never resemble your Lord in this. God for your sake humbled himself, but you, for your own sake, do not humble yourself. You are proud and puffed up. God came and took up your burden to give you his rest, but you do not wish to endure labors and suffering. By your labors your wounds are healed. *First Syriac Epistles 7.*

PSALM OF RESPONSE: *Psalm 31:9-16*

NEW TESTAMENT READING: *Philippians 2:5-11*

REFLECTIONS FROM THE CHURCH FATHERS

Proof of His Full Divinity As the Form of God. NOVATIAN: If Christ were only a man, he would have been said to have been "in the image of God," not "in the form of God." We know that humanity was made in the image, not the form, of God. *On the Trinity 22.2.*

The Emptying As an Assumption of the Body. ORIGEN: In "emptying himself" he became a man and was incarnate while remaining truly God. Having become a man, he remained the God that he was. He assumed a body like our own, differing only in that it was born from the Virgin by the Holy Spirit. *On First Principles 1, Preface 4.*

His Participation in Slavery Is an Expression of His Divine Compassion. EUSEBIUS: Read the record of his compassion. It pleased him, being the Word of God, to "take the form of a slave." So he willed to be joined to our common human condition. He took to himself the toils of the members who suffer. He made our human maladies his own. He suffered and toiled on our behalf. This is in accord with his great love of humankind. *Demonstration of the Gospel 10.1.22.*

His Humiliation Demonstrates His Voluntarily Divested Majesty. HILARY OF POITIERS: Humility is hard, since the one who humbles himself has something magnificent in his nature that works against his lowering. The one who becomes obedient, however, undertakes the act of obedience voluntarily. It is precisely through the act of humbling that he becomes obedient. *On the Trinity 11.30.*

Humanity Re-Created. ATHANASIUS: The glory of the Father is that the human race not only was created but was re-created when lost. It was given life once again when dead, so as to become a renewed temple of God. For the powers in heaven also, the angels and the archangels, worship him and now worship the Lord "in the name of Jesus." This joy and exaltation belongs to human beings, because the Son of God, having himself become a human being, is now worshiped. The heavenly powers are not offended when they behold all of us being led into our heavenly abode as we share in his body. This could not have happened in any other way. It happened only because, "being in the form of God and taking the form of a slave, he humbled himself," agreeing to assume our bodily condition "even to death." *Against the Arians 1.42.*

GOSPEL READING: *Luke 19:28-40*

REFLECTIONS FROM THE CHURCH FATHERS

Jesus Turns from Teaching to His Passion in Jerusalem. CYRIL OF ALEXANDRIA: As long as it was fitting that he should travel the country of the Jews trying to win by lessons and admonitions superior to the law many to the grace that is by faith, he did not cease to do so. The time was now calling Christ to the passion for the salvation of the whole world. He therefore goes up to Jerusalem to free the inhabitants of the earth from the tyranny of the enemy, to abolish death and to destroy the sin of the world. First, he points out to the Israelites by a plain fact, that a new people from among the heathen shall be subject to him, while they themselves are rejected as the murderers of the Lord. *Commentary on Luke, Homily 129.*

A Manger and a Donkey. EPHREM THE SYRIAN: "Untie the donkey and bring it to me." He began with a manger and finished with a donkey, in Bethlehem with a manger, in Jerusalem with a donkey. *Commentary on Tatian's Diatessaron 18.1.*

Jacob's Blessing on Judah. JUSTIN MARTYR: People from every nation look for him who was crucified in Judea, after whose coming the country of the Jews was immediately given over to you as the loot of war. The words "tying his foal to the vine and washing his robe in the blood of the grape" allegorically signified the things that would happen to Christ and the deeds he would perform. *First Apology 32.*

Peace of Heaven and Earth. CYRIL OF ALEXANDRIA: The disciples praise Christ the Savior of all, calling him King and Lord, and the peace of heaven and earth. Let us also praise him, taking the psalmist's harp and saying, "How great are your works, O Lord! In wisdom you have made them." Only wisdom is in his works because he guides all useful things in their proper manner and assigns to his acts the season that suits them. *Commentary on Luke, Homily 130.*

CLOSING PRAYER

O Lord our God, refresh us with quiet sleep when we are wearied with the day's labor, that, being assisted with the help which our weakness needs, we may be devoted to thee both in body and mind; through Jesus Christ our Lord. Amen. *The Leonine Sacramentary*

The Resurrection

THEME

He is risen (Jn 20:1-18)! In Christ's resurrection is peace for the world and the promise of a new creation (Is 65:17-25). The Lord is our strength and our salvation. This is the day the Lord has made—let us rejoice and be glad in it (Ps 118:1-2, 14-24). Death is destroyed. Christ is risen—he is risen indeed (1 Cor 15:19-26).

OPENING PRAYER: *Easter*

O God, who by thine only-begotten Son have overcome death and opened to us the gate of everlasting life, grant us, we beseech thee, that we who celebrate the solemnities of our Lord's resurrection may by the renewing of thy Spirit arise from the death of the soul, through the same Jesus Christ our Lord. *The Gelasian Sacramentary*

OLD TESTAMENT READING: *Isaiah 65:17-25*

REFLECTIONS FROM THE CHURCH FATHERS

Newness Means a Change into Something Better. JEROME: Those who interpret the new heaven and earth to be a change for the better, rather than the destruction of the elements, cite this passage: "You founded the earth in the beginning, Lord, and the heavens are the work of your hands. They will perish, but you will endure; they will grow old like a garment, and you will roll them up like cloth, and they will be changed." In this psalm is demonstrated clearly a perdition and destruction that is not an annihilation but a transformation for the better. Neither does what is written elsewhere indicate that there will be a complete destruction of what was there at the beginning, but rather a transformation: "The moon will shine like the sun, and the sun's light will be strengthened sevenfold." And that this may be better understood, let us use an example from our own human condition: when an infant grows into a boy, and a boy into an adolescent, and an adolescent into a man and a man into an old man, the same person continues to exist throughout his succession of ages. For he remains the same man as he was, even though it can be said that he has changed a little and that the previous ages have passed away. Understanding this truth, the apostle Paul said, "For the form of this world is perishing." Notice that he said "form," not "substance." *Commentary on Isaiah 18.13.*

The Cross and Its Life-Giving Fruit. **THEODORET OF CYR:** For us the saving cross is the tree of life. For it received like fruit the life-giving body by which those who stretch out their hands and pick the fruit will live life eternally. *Commentary on Isaiah 20.65.22.*

The World to Come Is Paradise Regained. **GREGORY OF ELVIRA:** The earth will freely give its produce, and all evil will be removed, just as Isaiah said . . . for God has refashioned such a world in his kingdom just as it had been made in the beginning before the first-made human being ruined it, who after he had disobeyed the word of God all things were spoiled and ruined and cursed by God's word: "The earth will be cursed in your works." The former shape of this world will become the kingdom of the saints and the liberation of the creatures. *Origen's Tractates on the Books of Holy Scripture 5.36.*

⊴ PSALM OF RESPONSE: *Psalm 118:1-2, 14-24*

⊴ NEW TESTAMENT READING: *1 Corinthians 15:19-26*

REFLECTIONS FROM THE CHURCH FATHERS

By a Man. ATHANASIUS: For by the sacrifice of his own body he both put an end to the law which was against us and made a new beginning of life for us, by the hope of resurrection which he has given us. For since from man it was that death prevailed over men, for this cause conversely, by the Word of God being made man has come about the destruction of death and the resurrection of life. *On the Incarnation 10.*

Suppose the Word Did Not Become Flesh. BASIL THE GREAT: If the sojourn of the Lord in the flesh did not take place, the Redeemer did not pay to death the price for us. He did not by his own power destroy the dominion of death. If that which is subject to death were one thing and that which was assumed by the Lord another, then death would not have ceased performing its own works, nor would the sufferings of the God-bearing flesh have been our gain. He would not have destroyed sin in the flesh. We who had died in Adam would not have been made alive in Christ. *Letter 261, to the Citizens of Sozopolis.*

None Except Through That Door. AUGUSTINE: We commonly say that all enter a certain house through one door, not because all humanity enters that house but because no one enters except through that door. It is in this sense that as all die in Adam so do all those who live in Christ. . . . Aside from the one Mediator of God and humankind, the man Christ Jesus, there is no other name under heaven whereby we must be saved. *Against Julian 24.*

Beggaring Description. CYRIL OF JERUSALEM: This body shall be raised but not in its present weakness. It shall be raised the very same body, but by putting aside corruption it shall be transformed, just as iron becomes fire when combined with fire, as the Lord who raises us knows. This body therefore shall rise, but it will not abide in its present condition, but as an eternal body. No longer will it, as now, need nourishment for life or stairs for its ascent. It will become spiritual, a marvelous thing, beggaring description. *Catechetical Lecture 18.*

Christ's Reign Fulfilled. THEODORET OF CYR: The final victory will be the fulfillment, not the end of Christ's reign. *Commentary on the First Epistle to the Corinthians 270.*

GOSPEL READING: *John 20:1-18*

REFLECTIONS FROM THE CHURCH FATHERS

The Womb of the Earth Gives Birth. HESYCHIUS OF JERUSALEM: Hidden first in a womb of flesh, he sanctified human birth by his own birth. Hidden afterward in the womb of the earth, he gave life to the dead by his resurrection. Suffering, pain and sighs have now fled away. For who has known the mind of God, or who has been his counselor, if not the Word made flesh who was nailed to the cross, who rose from the dead and who was taken up into heaven? This day brings a message of joy: it is the day of the Lord's resurrection when, with himself, he raised up the race of Adam. Born for the sake of human beings, he rose from the dead with them. On this day paradise is opened up by the risen one, Adam is restored to life and Eve is consoled. On this day the divine call is heard, the kingdom is prepared, we are saved and Christ is adored. On this day, when he had trampled death underfoot, made the tyrant a prisoner and despoiled the underworld, Christ ascended into heaven as a king in victory, as a ruler in glory, as an invincible char- ioteer. He said to the Father, "Here am I, O God, with the children you have given me." And he heard the Father's reply, "Sit at my right hand until I make your enemies your footstool." To him be glory, now and forever, through endless ages, Amen. *Easter Homily 5-6.*

Mary Goes to the Tomb on Behalf of the Women. ROMANUS THE MELODIST: It was dark, but love lighted the way for her. *Kontakion on the Resurrection 29.1-3.*

Mary's Secret and the Disciples' Examination. EUSEBIUS: The Scripture shows much examination and carefulness on the part of the disciples, not readily assenting to their words but at first suspending judgment until they recognized the truth fully and clearly. *To Marinus, Supplement 3.*

Neatness of Linens Proves No Theft. CHRYSOSTOM: When Mary came and said these things, the apostles heard them and drew near to the sepulcher with great eagerness. They see the linen clothes lying there, which was a sign of the resurrection. For if they had removed the body, they would not have stripped it first, nor, if any had stolen it, would they have taken the trouble to remove the napkin and roll it up and lay it in a place by itself apart from the linens. They would have taken the body as it was. Therefore, John tells us by anticipation that it was buried with much myrrh, which glues linen to the body no less firmly than lead. He tells us this so that when you hear that the napkin lay apart from the linens, you may not endure those who say that he was stolen. For a thief would not have been so foolish as to expend so much effort on a trifling detail. *Homilies on the Gospel of John 85.4.*

CLOSING PRAYER

Accept, we beseech thee, our evening thanksgiving, O thou fountain of all good, who has led us in safety through the length of the day, who daily blesses us with so many temporal mercies and has given us the hope of resurrection to eternal life; through Jesus Christ our Lord. Amen. *From an Ancient Collect*

Lay Aside Doubt

🔹 THEME

We bear witness to Jesus' death and resurrection and tell everyone the good news (Acts 5:27-32). Like Thomas, we lay aside our doubts (Jn 20:19-31) and now anticipate his second coming (Rev 1:4-8). Let everything that has breath praise the Lord (Ps 150)!

🔹 OPENING PRAYER: *Second Sunday of Easter*

O God, our true life, to know you is life, to serve you is freedom, to enjoy you is a kingdom, to praise you is the joy and happiness of the soul. I praise and bless and adore you, I worship you, I glorify you. I give thanks to you for your glory. I humbly beg you to live with me, to reign in me, to make this heart of mine a holy temple, a fit habitation for your divine majesty. *Augustine*

🔹 READING FROM ACTS: *Acts 5:27-32*

REFLECTIONS FROM THE CHURCH FATHERS

Bringing This Man's Blood on Us. BEDE: The high priest had forgotten the doom that he had called down on himself and his own when he said, "His blood be on us and on our children." *Commentary on the Acts of the Apostles 5.28.*

Not Defiance but Compassion. CHRYSOSTOM: It was not with defiance that the apostles answered them, for they were teachers. And yet who, backed by an entire city and enjoying such grace, would not have spoken and uttered something big? But not these men. For they were not angered, but they pitied and wept over them and looked for a way to free them from their error and anger. No longer did they say to them, "You must judge," but they declared, "He whom God raised, this man we proclaim." It is by the will of God that these things are done, he says. They did not say, "Did we not say to you even then, that 'we cannot but speak the things which we have seen and heard'?" For they do not lust after honor. *Homilies on the Acts of the Apostles 13.*

PSALM OF RESPONSE: *Psalm 150*

NEW TESTAMENT READING: *Revelation 1:4-8*

REFLECTIONS FROM THE CHURCH FATHERS

Pertaining to All the Churches. APRINGIUS OF BEJA: What is the importance of the people of Asia that they alone deserve to receive the apostolic revelation? However, there is a mystery in the number and a sacrament in the name of the province. . . . The number seven, therefore, signifies the period of the present life, so that the apostle is not merely writing to seven churches and to that world in which he was then present, but it is understood that he is giving these writings to all future ages, even to the consummation of the world. Therefore, he mentions the number in a most holy manner, and he names "Asia," which means "elevated" or "walking," indicating that celestial fatherland which we call the "catholic church." For exalted by the Lord and always moving toward the things which are above, it is the church which advances by spiritual exercises and is always desirous of the things of heaven. *Tractate on the Apocalypse 1.4.*

As Firstborn of the Dead, Christ Is the Source of Life. **IRENAEUS:** Great, then, was the mercy of God the Father. He sent the creative Word, who, when he came to save us, put himself in our position, and in the same situation in which we lost life. He loosed the prison bonds, and his light appeared and dispelled the darkness in the prison, and he sanctified our birth and abolished death, loosing those same bonds by which we were held. He showed forth the resurrection, becoming himself the firstborn from the dead, and raised in himself prostrate humankind, being lifted up to the heights of heaven, at the right hand of the glory of the Father. Just as God had promised through the prophet, saying, "I will raise up the tabernacle of David." This means that which is fallen, the body sprung from David. This was in truth accomplished by our Lord Jesus Christ, in the triumph of our redemption, that he raises us in truth, setting us free to the Father . . . as the firstborn of the dead, head and source also of the life unto God. *Proof of the Apostolic Preaching 38-39.*

Christ Is Alpha and Omega, Creator and Redeemer. **AUGUSTINE:** Do you want to gaze on him as the first? "All things were made through him." Do you seek him as the last? "For Christ is the end of the law, that everyone who has faith may be justified." In order for you to live at some time or other, you had him as your creator. In order for you to live always, you have him as your redeemer. *Sermon 299B.1, On the Birthday of the Holy Apostles Peter and Paul.*

GOSPEL READING: *John 20:19-31*

REFLECTIONS FROM THE CHURCH FATHERS

An Evening More by Grief Than by Time. **PETER CHRYSOLOGUS:** It was evening more by grief than by time. It was evening for minds darkened by the somber cloud of grief and sadness because although the report of the resurrection had given the slight glimmer of twilight, nevertheless the Lord had not yet shone through with his light in all its brilliance. *Sermon 84.2.*

Admit the Limits of Your Sense to Understand. HILARY OF POIT-IERS: The Lord stoops to the level even of our feeble understanding. He works a miracle of his invisible power in order to satisfy the doubts of unbelieving minds. Explain, my critic, the ways of heaven—explain his action if you can. The disciples were in a closed room. They had met and held their assembly in secret since the passion of the Lord. The Lord presents himself to strengthen the faith of Thomas by meeting his challenge. He gives him his body to feel, his wounds to handle. . . . Yet where does the one who is standing in their midst come from? Your senses and your words are powerless to account for it. The fact is certain, but it lies beyond the region of human explanation. If, as you say, our account of the divine birth is a lie, then prove that this account of the Lord's entrance is a fiction. If we assume that an event did not happen because we cannot discover how it was done, we make the limits of our understanding into the limits of reality. But the certainty of the evidence proves the falsehood of our contradiction. The Lord did stand in a closed house in the midst of the disciples; the Son was born of the Father. Deny not that he stood, because your puny wits cannot ascertain how he came there; renounce instead a disbelief in God the only-begotten and perfect Son of God the unbegotten and perfect Father that is based only on the incapacity of sense and speech to comprehend. *On the Trinity 3.20.*

Blessings Hidden in Suffering. AMBROSE: There are some . . . who think a blessed life is impossible in this body, weak and fragile as it is. For we have to suffer pain and grief, weeping, illness—all in this body. . . . It is not a blessing to be in the midst of suffering. But it is a blessing to be victorious over it and not to be bullied by the power of temporal pain. Suppose that things come that are considered terrible because of the grief they cause, such as blindness, exile, hunger, violation of a daughter, loss of children? . . . It is true that in these sufferings there is something bitter and that we cannot use mind over matter to hide this pain. I should not deny that the sea is deep because in shore it is shallow, or that the sky is clear because sometimes it is covered with clouds, or that the earth is fruitful because in some places there is only barren ground or that the crops are rich and full because they sometimes have wild oats mingled with them. So, too, count it as true that the harvest of a happy conscience may be mingled with some bitter feelings of grief. In the sheaves of the whole of a blessed life, if by chance any misfortune or bitterness has crept in, is it not as though the wild oats were hidden or as though the bitterness of the tares was concealed by the sweet scent of the corn? *Duties of the Clergy 2.5.19-21.*

CLOSING PRAYER

Receive, O Lord, in heaven above
Our prayers and supplications pure;
Give us a heart all full of love
And steady courage to endure.
Thy holy name our mouths confess,
Our tongues are harps to praise thy grace;
Forgive our sins and wickedness,
Who in this vigil seek thy face.
Let not our song become a sigh,
A wail of anguish and despair;
In loving-kindness, Lord most high,
Receive tonight our evening prayer.
O raise us in that day, that we
May sing, where all thy saints adore,
Praise to thy Father, and to thee,
And to thy Spirit, evermore. Amen.
Ephrem the Syrian

Out of the Dark

THEME

Just as Saul heard the voice of the Lord on the road to Damascus, was blinded and then regained his sight (Acts 9:1-6), so we who turn from our sins and follow the Lord find joy and healing (Ps 30). Because we love and trust in God's Son, who became a man and dwelled among us (Jn 21:1-19), we offer him all praises and glory (Rev 5:11-14).

OPENING PRAYER: *Third Sunday of Easter*

Almighty and everlasting God . . . , hear our prayers which we offer to thee for that blinded people, that by acknowledging the light of thy truth, which is Christ, they may be rescued from their own darkness; through the same Jesus Christ our Lord. Amen. *The Gelasian Sacramentary*

READING FROM ACTS: *Acts 9:1-6*

REFLECTIONS FROM THE CHURCH FATHERS

The Lord Shared Our Human State. BASIL THE GREAT: For it is written, "And when all things are made subject to him, then the Son himself will also be made subject to him who subjected all things to him." Do you not fear, O man, the God who is called unsubjected? For he makes your subjection his own, and because of your struggle against virtue, he calls himself unsubjected. Thus, he even said at one time that he himself was the one persecuted; for he says, "Saul, Saul, why do you persecute me?" when Saul was hastening to Damascus, desiring to put in bonds the disciples of Christ. Again, he calls himself naked, if anyone of his brothers is naked. "I was naked," he says," and you covered me." And still again, when another was in prison, he said that he himself was the one imprisoned. For he himself took up our infirmities and bore the burden of our ills. And one of our infirmities is insubordination, and this he bore. Therefore, even the adversities that happen to us the Lord makes his own, taking on himself our sufferings because of his fellowship with us. *Letter 8.*

Paul Drawn by Christ Himself. CHRYSOSTOM: The eunuch was on the road and Paul was on the road, but the latter was drawn by no other than Christ himself, for this was too great a work for the apostles. It was great indeed that with the apostles at Jerusalem and no one of authority at Damascus, he returned from there converted. And those at Damascus knew that he had not come from Jerusalem converted, for he brought letters that he might place the believers in chains. Like a consummate physician, Christ brought help to him, once the fever reached its height. It was necessary that he should be quelled in the midst of his frenzy, for then especially he would fall and condemn himself as one guilty of dreadful audacity. *Homilies on the Acts of the Apostles 19.*

Blindness Leads to Sight. BEDE: By no means would he have been able to see well again unless he had first been fully blinded. Also, when he had rejected his own wisdom, which was confusing him, he could commit himself totally to faith. *Commentary on the Acts of the Apostles 9.8.*

PSALM OF RESPONSE: *Psalm 30*

NEW TESTAMENT READING: *Revelation 5:11-14*

REFLECTIONS FROM THE CHURCH FATHERS

The Lamb Slain Is Christ's Humanity. CAESARIUS OF ARLES: This is not said of his Godhead, in which are all the treasures of wisdom, so that he should receive wisdom. Rather, this is said of his assumed manhood, that is, concerning his body, which is the church. Or, it might be said of his martyrs who were slain for his name. For the church receives all things in its Head, as the Scriptures say, "He has given us all things with him." The Lamb himself receives, as he said in the Gospel, "All authority in heaven and on earth has been given to me." However, he receives this authority according to his humanity, not according to his divinity. *Exposition on the Apocalypse 5.12, Homily 4.*

God Receives Praise from Every Existing Thing. ANDREW OF CAESAREA: From all beings, whether intelligent or sensible, whether living or simply existing in some way, God, as the Creator of all things, is glorified by words proper to their natures. Also praised is his only begotten and consubstantial Son who graciously renewed humankind and the creation that was made through him. And it is written that, as man, he received authority over all things in heaven and upon the earth. *Commentary on the Apocalypse 5.11-13.*

Angels and Men Form One Church. ANDREW OF CAESAREA: Through these, one flock and one church from angels and from men is indicated which has been formed through Christ, the God who united that which was separate and has destroyed the partition wall of separation. And so, as we have heard, with the four living creatures who surpass the other angelic ranks, also the elders, who represent the fullness of those who are being saved, are worthy of the hymn and worship of God. Of which may also we be found worthy in Christ himself, the Giver of peace and our God, with whom together with the Father and the Holy Spirit be glory and might forever and ever. Amen. *Commentary on the Apocalypse 5.14.*

GOSPEL READING: *John 21:1-19*

REFLECTIONS FROM THE CHURCH FATHERS

Jesus Eats to Prove the Resurrection. JEROME: Our Lord ate to prove the resurrection, not to give his palate the pleasure of tasting of honey. He asked for a fish broiled on the coals that he might confirm the doubting apostles who did not dare approach him because they thought they saw not a body but a spirit. *Against John of Jerusalem 34.*

Looking Forward to Our Resurrection. CHRYSOSTOM: Perhaps when you heard these things, you glowed and called those happy who were then with him along with those who shall be with him at the day of the general resurrection. Let us then make every effort so that we may see that admirable face. For if when now we hear, we are so enflamed, and desire to have been in those days that he spent on earth, and to have heard his voice and seen his face and to have approached and touched and ministered to him—consider how great a thing it will be to see him no longer in a mortal body or doing human actions but with a bodyguard of angels, being ourselves also in a form of unmixed purity, and beholding him and enjoying the rest of that bliss which surpasses all language. Therefore I beseech you, let us use every means so as not to miss such glory. For nothing is difficult if we are willing, nothing burdensome if we apply ourselves. "If we endure, we shall also reign with him." *Homilies on the Gospel of John 87.3.*

Threefold Confession of Peter's Love. AMBROSE: It is Peter, chosen by the Lord himself to feed his flock, who merits three times to hear the words "Feed my little lambs; feed my lambs; feed my sheep." And so, by feeding well the flock of Christ with the food of faith, he effaced the sin of his former fall. For this reason he is admonished three times to feed the flock. He is asked three times whether he loves the Lord in order that he may confess him three times whom he had denied three times before his crucifixion. *On the Christian Faith 5, Prologue 2.*

Shepherds in the Line of Christ and Peter. APHRAHAT: O pastors! Imitate that diligent pastor, the chief of the whole flock, who cared so greatly for his flock. He brought near those who were far away. He brought back the wanderers. He visited the sick. He strengthened the weak. He bound up the broken. He guarded those who were well fed. He gave himself up for the sake of the sheep. He chose and instructed excellent leaders, and committed the sheep into their hands and gave them authority over all his flock. For he said to Simon Cephas, "Feed my sheep and my lambs and my ewes." So Simon fed his sheep and fulfilled his calling and handed over the flock to you and departed. And so you also must feed and guide them well. For the pastor who cares for his sheep engages in no other pursuit along with that. He does not make a vineyard, or plant gardens or fall into the troubles of this world. Never have we seen a pastor who left his sheep in the wilderness and became a merchant, or one who left his flock to wander and became a husbandman. But if he deserts his flock and does these things, he thereby hands over his flock to the wolves. *Demonstration 10.4.*

Service to Christ. THEODORE OF MOPSUESTIA: The Savior does not say to him, fast, or keep watch for me. But, since the pastoral care of souls is more worthy and more useful to the community, he entrusts him with this. I, he says, need nothing: feed my sheep, and return to me the love with which I loved you, because I will take your care for them as care devoted to me. *Commentary on John 7.21.17.*

CLOSING PRAYER

We beg you, Lord, to help and defend us. Deliver the oppressed, pity the insignificant, raise the fallen, show yourself to the needy, heal the sick, bring back those of your people who have gone astray, feed the hungry, lift up the weak, take off the prisoners' chains. May every nation come to know that you alone are God, that Jesus Christ is your child, that we are your people, the sheep of your pasture. *Clement of Rome*

Our Shepherd

🔹 THEME

Through Christ, we are able to do more than we could in our own strength, just as Peter worked a miracle at Joppa (Acts 9:36-43). The Lord is our shepherd (Rev 7:9-17); he takes care of all of our needs (Ps 23) and offers us eternal life, if we listen to his voice and follow him (Jn 10:22-30).

🔹 OPENING PRAYER: *Fourth Sunday of Easter*

O sovereign and almighty Lord, bless all thy people and all thy flock. Give peace, thy help, thy love to us, thy servants the sheep of thy fold, that we may be united in the bond of peace and love, one body and one spirit, in one hope of our calling, in thy divine and boundless love; for the sake of Jesus Christ, the great Shepherd of the sheep. Amen. *Liturgy of St. Mark*

🔹 READING FROM ACTS: *Acts 9:36-43*

REFLECTIONS FROM THE CHURCH FATHERS

True Fame. CHRYSOSTOM: If you want to be remembered and are anxious for true repute, imitate her, and build edifices like that, not going to expense on lifeless matter but displaying great generosity in regard to your fellow human beings. This is the remembrance that is worth admiring and brings great benefit. *Homilies on Genesis 30.8.*

An Allegory of Law and Gospel. ARATOR: If we are rightly inspired, the renewed day of her soul is clearly suitable for allegory, a soul, turned back to the voice of Peter, which the darkness of exceedingly ancient peril had pressed down: the life burdened previously in the bosom of the dark law, rising just like a second soul, stands up in the church's presence, and the light of works, the companion of faith, drives away the shadows, a salvation that had not been promised by the voice of the law, because grace undertakes to give gifts of eternal life to those reborn in the font. *On the Acts of the Apostles 1.*

The Merits of Mercy. CYPRIAN: So powerful were the merits of mercy, so much did just works avail! She who had conferred on suffering widows the assistance for living deserved to be recalled to life by the petition of widows. *Works and Almsgiving 6.*

He Raised Her Up. BEDE: When she was touched by Peter's hand, Tabitha rose again, since there is no better way for the soul that has become weak because of its sins to regain its strength than the example of the saints. *Commentary on the Acts of the Apostles 9.41.*

PSALM OF RESPONSE: *Psalm 23*

NEW TESTAMENT READING: *Revelation 7:9-17*

REFLECTIONS FROM THE CHURCH FATHERS

Bodies Glorified Through Resurrection. BEDE: Let us think attentively about the eternal feast of the martyrs, which is in heaven, and by following in their footsteps insofar as we can, let us also take care to become ourselves participants in this heavenly feast, for as the apostle bears witness, if we have been companions of his passion, we will at the same time be companions of his consolation. Nor should we mourn their death as much as we should rejoice about their attaining the palm of righteousness. . . . Hence, says John, they were standing before the throne "in the sight of the Lamb, dressed in white robes, and palms were in their hands." For they now stand before God's throne, crowned, who once lay, worn down by pain, before the thrones of earthly judges. They stand in the sight of the Lamb, and for no cause can they be separated from contemplating his glory there, since here they could not be separated from his love through punishments. They shine in white robes and have palms in their hands, who possess the rewards for their works; while they get back their bodies, glorified through resurrection, which for the Lord's sake they suffered to be scorched by flames, torn to pieces by beasts, worn out by scourges, broken by falls from high places, scraped by hoofs and completely destroyed by every kind of punishment. *Homilies on the Gospels 1.10.*

Baptism and the Eucharist Make White. OECUMENIUS: And, it says, "They have washed their robes and made them white in the blood of the Lamb." To be sure, one might think that robes dipped in blood would be red, not white. And so, how is it that they have become white? Because, according to the opinion of all-wise Paul, baptism is completed in the death of the Lord and wipes clean from every filth of sin, so that those baptized in him are made white and clean. *Commentary on the Apocalypse 7.9-17.*

Spiritual Joy and Gladness. TYCONIUS: All of these things will happen to us spiritually when sins have been forgiven and we rise to life, that is, when the "old man has been stripped off and we have put on Christ" and are filled "with the joy of the Holy Spirit." For this is the life that the Lord promised to his church when he said, "Behold, I create Jerusalem a rejoicing, and my people a joy. I will rejoice over Jerusalem, and be glad in my people; no more will be heard in it the sound of weeping or the cry of distress." *Commentary on the Apocalypse 7.17.*

✦ **GOSPEL READING:** *John 10:22-30*

REFLECTIONS FROM THE CHURCH FATHERS

Jesus Preferred Acts over Words. ORIGEN: And since he avoided unnecessary talk about himself and preferred to show by acts rather than words that he was the Christ, the Jews for that reason said to him, "If you are the Christ, tell us plainly." *Against Celsus 1.48.*

The Voice of the Shepherd. AUGUSTINE: What is the voice of the shepherd? "And that repentance and forgiveness of sins should be preached in his name throughout all the nations, beginning from Jerusalem." There is the voice of the shepherd. Recognize it and follow if you are a sheep. *Sermon 46.32.*

Christ, Who Is Life, Gives Life. CYRIL OF ALEXANDRIA: Christ promises his followers eternal life as a compensation and reward. They receive exemption from death and corruption and from the torments the judge inflicts on transgressors. By giving life, Christ shows that by nature he *is* life. He does not receive it from another but supplies it from his own resources. And by eternal life we understand not only length of days which all, both good and bad, shall possess after the resurrection but also the passing of those days in bliss. It is also possible to understand by "life" a reference to the mystical blessing of the Eucharist by which Christ implants in us his own life through the participation of his own flesh by the faithful, according to the text, "He who eats my flesh and drinks my blood has eternal life." *Commentary on the Gospel of John 7.1.*

One with the Father. NOVATIAN: This word can be true of no human being, "I and the Father are one." Christ alone declared this word out of the consciousness of his divinity. *On the Trinity 13.*

Unity Is the Ground of Unanimity. HILARY OF POITIERS: Now seeing that the heretics cannot get around these words because they are so clearly stated and understood, they nevertheless try to explain them away. They maintain that the words "I and the Father are one" refer to a mere union of unanimity only; a unity of will, not of nature, that is, that the two are one not by essence of being but by identity of will. . . . They make use of the example of our own union with God, as though we were united to the Son and through the Son to the Father by mere obedience and a devout will and not through the true communion of our nature with his that is promised to us through the sacrament of the body and blood. . . . Thus we do not deny the unanimity between the Father and the Son—for heretics falsely say that since we do not accept the concord by itself as the bond of unity we declare the Father and the Son to be in disagreement. We do not deny such a unanimity (but the unanimity results from the unity). The Father and the Son are one in nature, honor, power and the same nature cannot will contrary things. *On the Trinity 8.5, 17-19.*

✠ CLOSING PRAYER

O good Shepherd, seek me out, and bring me home to your fold again. Deal favorably with me according to your grace, till I may dwell in your house all the days of my life and praise you forever and ever with those who are there. Amen. *Jerome*

Love One Another

THEME

The good news is this: Jesus Christ died for our sins and was resurrected so that no one should perish, but all should have eternal life (Acts 11:1-18). We should then love one another, as Christ loved us (Jn 13:31-35), even as we look forward to an eternity with him (Rev 21:1-6). Let all the earth and heavens praise the Lord (Ps 148)!

OPENING PRAYER: *Fifth Sunday of Easter*

You wake us to delight in your praises; for you made us for yourself, and our heart is restless until it reposes in you. *Augustine*

READING FROM ACTS: *Acts 11:1-18*

REFLECTIONS FROM THE CHURCH FATHERS

Peter Was a Humble Shepherd. GREGORY THE GREAT: For if, when he was blamed by the believers, he had paid regard to the authority that he had received in holy church, he might have replied that the sheep should not dare to find fault with the shepherd to whom they had been committed. But, had he said anything of his own power in answer to the complaint of the believers, he would not have been truly a teacher of gentleness. He pacified them, therefore, by giving a reason humbly, and he even produced witnesses to defend him from blame, saying, "Moreover these six brothers accompanied me." If, then, the pastor of the church, the prince of the apostles, who singularly did signs and miracles, did not disdain humbly to give a reason in defending himself from blame, how much more ought we sinners, when we are blamed for anything, to pacify those who blame us by giving a reason humbly! *Letter 45.*

All Are Called to the Gospel of Christ. BEDE: I am amazed at how some people interpret this as having to do with certain foods that were prohibited by the old law but that are now to be consumed, since neither serpents nor reptiles can be eaten. Nor did Peter himself understand it in this way. Rather he understood it as meaning that all people are equally called to the gospel of Christ and nothing is naturally defiled. For when he was reproached, he explained the symbolism of this vision, not as giving the reason why he ate beasts but why he associated with Gentiles. *Commentary on the Acts of the Apostles 11.6.*

Dismantling a Holiness Based on Exclusion. CHRYSOSTOM: Peter shows that he did nothing himself. "For it was the very thing that we obtained," he says, "that those men received." "If then God gave the same gift to them as he gave to us when we believed in the Lord Jesus, who was I that I could withstand God?" To silence them more effectively, he added, "the same gift." Do you see how he does not allow them to have less? "When they believed," he says, "God gave the same gift to them as he gave to us when we believed in the Lord Jesus." He makes them clean, and he does not say "to you" but "to us." That is, why do you feel aggrieved when we call them partners? "When they heard this they were silenced. And they glorified God, saying, 'Then to the Gentiles also God has granted repentance to life.'" Do you see how it all came about through the oratory of Peter, who did well to report the events? They glorified God because he had given them repentance. They were humbled by these words. From this point on the door of faith was open to the Gentiles. *Homilies on the Acts of the Apostles 24.*

⁂ PSALM OF RESPONSE: *Psalm 148*

⁂ NEW TESTAMENT READING: *Revelation 21:1-6*

REFLECTIONS FROM THE CHURCH FATHERS

The Renewal of the Old. ANDREW OF CAESAREA: This passage does not speak of the obliteration of creation but of its renewal into something better. For as the apostle says, "This creation will be freed from the bondage of corruption into the freedom of the glory of the children of God." Also the holy psalmist says, "You change them like a raiment, and they pass away." The renewal of that which has grown old does not involve the annihilation of its substance but rather indicates the smoothing out of its agedness and its wrinkles. It is a custom among us to say concerning persons who have in some way become better or have become worse, "someone has become someone else." And so it is indicated concerning the heaven and the earth that they have "passed away" instead of have "changed." And this is also the same with us who have received death; we will change from a former condition to a better lot. *Commentary on the Apocalypse 21.1.*

In This Life, Holiness Results in More Abundant Weeping. PRIMASIUS: It is certain that all these benefits belong to the future life and not to this life. Indeed, in this life the more one is holy and the more full a person is of holy desires, the more abundant will be his weeping in prayer. For this reason we read, "My tears have been my food day and night," and again, "Every night I flood my bed with tears." *Commentary on the Apocalypse 21.4.*

Christ Created the World and Consummates It. BEDE: Just as he testified at the beginning of the book that he was the Alpha and the Omega, so now this is repeated for the third time, so that no one might believe that there is any other god before him or any other god after him, as Isaiah says. Indeed, since he is speaking of the end of the world,

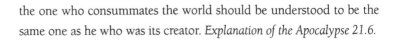

the one who consummates the world should be understood to be the same one as he who was its creator. *Explanation of the Apocalypse 21.6.*

GOSPEL READING: *John 13:31-35*

REFLECTIONS FROM THE CHURCH FATHERS

Jesus Speaks As If the Resurrection Had Taken Place. AUGUSTINE: He predicts his own resurrection, which was to follow immediately, not at the end of the world like ours. . . . And so he says, "Now is the Son of Man glorified." The now refers not to his approaching passion but to the resurrection that was immediately to follow it, as if that which was so very soon to be had already taken place. *Tractates on the Gospel of John 63.3.*

Seeking Jesus as the Word. ORIGEN: For in that "little while" in which they would not see him, they would seek Jesus, and for this reason they would weep and lament, although their grief would change to joy when the saying was fulfilled. "And again a little while and you will see me." But to seek Jesus is to seek the Word, and wisdom, and justice, and truth and the power of God, all of which Christ is. *Commentary on the Gospel of John 32.385, 387.*

Love Fulfills the Law. APOSTOLIC CONSTITUTIONS: He who then had forbidden murder now forbids anger without cause. He who had forbidden adultery now forbids all unlawful lust. He who had forbidden stealing now pronounces him most happy who supplies those that are in want out of his own labors. He who had forbidden hatred now pronounces him blessed who loves his enemies. *Constitutions of the Holy Apostles 6.23.*

Love Is a Greater Sign Than Miracles. CHRYSOSTOM: Passing over the miracles that they were to perform, he makes love the distinguishing mark of his followers. . . . Miracles do not attract unbelievers as much as the way you live your life. And nothing brings about a proper life as much as love. *Homilies on the Gospel of John 72.5.*

CLOSING PRAYER

I bind to myself today
The strong name of the Trinity,
By invocation of the same,
The Three in One, and One in Three.
I bind this day to me forever,
By power of faith, Christ's incarnation,
His baptism in the Jordan River,
His death on cross for my salvation,
His bursting from the spiced tomb,
His riding up the heavenly way,
His coming at the day of doom,
I bind to myself today.
I bind to myself today
The virtues of the starlit heaven,
The glorious sun's life-giving ray,
The whiteness of the moon at even,
The flashing of the lightning free,
The whirling wind's tempestuous shocks,
The stable earth, the deep salt sea,
Around the old eternal rocks.
I bind to myself today
Your power, O God, to hold and lead,
Your eye to watch, your might to stay,
Your ear to hearken to my need,
Your wisdom, O my God, to teach,
Your hand to guide, your shield to ward,
Your living Word to give me speech,
Your heavenly host to be my guard.

I bind to myself the name,
The strong name of the Trinity,
By invocation of the same,
The Three in One, and One in Three.
Patrick

Healing

THEME

As we follow the early Christians' example, such as that of Lydia (Acts 16:9-15), we praise God and ask for his blessings (Ps 67) and his healing from our sickness of sin (Jn 5:1-9). We anticipate living in the light of his presence forever (Rev 21:10, 22–22:5).

OPENING PRAYER: *Sixth Sunday of Easter*

O God, who purifies the hearts of those who confess their sins to thee and absolves the conscience of all bonds of iniquity: give pardon to the guilty and vouchsafe healing to the wounded, that they may receive remission of all their sins, persevere henceforward in sincere devotion and attain everlasting redemption, through our only Savior Jesus Christ. Amen. *The Gelasian Sacramentary*

READING FROM ACTS: *Acts 16:9-15*

REFLECTIONS FROM THE CHURCH FATHERS

God's Shepherds. ORIGEN: Listen, shepherds of the churches! Listen, God's shepherds! His angel always comes down from heaven and proclaims to you, "Today a Savior is born for you, who is Christ the Lord." For, unless that Shepherd comes, the shepherd of the churches will be unable to guard the flock well. Their custody is weak, unless Christ pastures and guards it along with them. We just read in the apostle, "We are coworkers with God." A good shepherd, who imitates the good Shepherd, is a coworker with God and Christ. He is a good shepherd precisely because he has the best Shepherd with him, pasturing his sheep along with him. For, "God established in his church apostles, prophets, evangelists, shepherds and teachers. He established everything for the perfection of the saints." Let this suffice for a simpler explanation. But we should ascend to a more hidden understanding. Some shepherds were angels that governed human affairs. Each of these kept his watch. They were vigilant day and night. But, at some point, they were unable to bear the labor of governing the peoples who had been entrusted to them and accomplish it diligently. When the Lord was born, an angel came and announced to the shepherds that the true Shepherd had appeared. *Homilies on the Gospel of Luke 12.2-3.*

God Wants the Willing. **CHRYSOSTOM:** Notice again the absence of pride. She was a woman, and she was lowly and a manual laborer. Note, however, that the woman was a lover of wisdom. The first evidence of this is her testimony that God called her. See how the writer of the story was not ashamed to report the habits of life. . . . And as for us, let us not be ashamed of these students or of any student of these things. Peter stays with the tanner, and Paul with the dealer in purple and a foreign one for that matter. Where is their pride? Therefore let us pray to God that he may open our heart. In fact God opens those hearts that want to be opened, as he can see those that are hardened. The opening is God's part, being attentive hers: this is something that is, in fact, both human and divine. *Catena on the Acts of the Apostles 16.13.*

⸙ **PSALM OF RESPONSE:** *Psalm 67*

⸙ **NEW TESTAMENT READING:** *Revelation 21:10, 22–22:5*

REFLECTIONS FROM THE CHURCH FATHERS

The Seer Contemplates the Sublime Life of the Saints. ANDREW OF CAESAREA: That he was "carried away in the Spirit" indicates that through the Spirit he was elevated in his mind from earthly things to the contemplation of heavenly realities. The image of the "great mountain" indicates the sublime and transcendent life of the saints, in which the wife of the Lamb, the Jerusalem above, will be made beautiful and glorified by God. *Commentary on the Apocalypse 21.10-11.*

The Church Is Led by the Eternal Sun. BEDE: The city has no need of sun or moon because the church is not governed by the light or the elements of the world. Rather, it is led through the darkness of the world by Christ, the eternal Sun. *Explanation of the Apocalypse 21.23.*

The Church of the Future. PRIMASIUS: He is here describing the church of the future when, unlike at the present time, the evil will not be mixed in along with the good and allowed to live with them. For the good alone will reign with Christ with whom and in whom they will live happily forever, namely, in that heavenly Jerusalem that is the mother of all. Indeed, it says that they are written in the book of the Lamb, to whom he said, "Rejoice that your names are written in heaven." *Commentary on the Apocalypse 21.127.*

Understanding and Wisdom. APRINGIUS OF BEJA: Neither the night of sin nor the darkness of unrighteousness will ever appear again. Nor in that bliss will they [the saints] live by the words of any teacher; nor established in such a fullness will they require the light of another's understanding. The Lord himself will give them great understanding and wisdom, for all knowledge that is desired is revealed in the brightness of his countenance. And they shall reign in all wisdom and truth. *Tractate on the Apocalypse 22.5.*

GOSPEL READING: *John 5:1-9*

REFLECTIONS FROM THE CHURCH FATHERS

Opportunities for Revelation. THEODORE OF MOPSUESTIA: He chose the time when everybody gathered to offer his help to everyone. Therefore he went to Jerusalem at that time. He did not think it was necessary to travel around and go to every place where people were ill, so that it might not appear that he was looking for fame. Instead he healed one only and through him he revealed himself to many. *Commentary on John 2.5.1.*

The Cure of Baptism Foreshadowed. CHRYSOSTOM: What kind of a cure is this? What mystery does it signify to us? . . . What is it that is shown in outline? A baptism was about to be given that possessed much power. It was the greatest of gifts, a baptism purging all sins and making people alive instead of dead. These things then are foreshown as in a picture by the pool. . . . And this miracle was done so that those at the pool who had learned over and over for such a long time how it is possible to heal the diseases of the body by water might more easily believe that water can also heal the diseases of the soul. *Homilies on the Gospel of John 36.1.*

The Angel Declared the Descent of the Holy Spirit. AMBROSE: What did the angel declare in this type but the descent of the Holy Spirit, which was to come to pass in our day and should consecrate the waters when invoked by the prayers of the priest? That angel, then, was a herald of the Holy Spirit, inasmuch as by means of the grace of the Spirit medicine was to be applied to our infirmities of soul and mind. The Spirit, then, has the same ministers as God the Father and Christ. He fills all things, possesses all things, works all and in all in the same manner as God the Father and the Son work. *On the Holy Spirit 1.7.88.*

Itinerary of Love. AUGUSTINE: What significance is there, then, in the bed, I ask you? What, except that that sick man was carried on the bed, but when healed, he carries the bed? What was said by the apostle? "Bear your burdens, each for the other, and so you will fulfill the law of Christ." Now the law of Christ is love, and love is not fulfilled unless we bear our burdens, each for the other. "Bearing with one another," he says, "in love, eager to preserve the unity of the Spirit in the bond of peace." When you were sick, your neighbor was carrying you. You have been healed; carry your neighbor. So you will fulfill, O man, what was lacking to you. "Take up," therefore, "your bed." But when you have taken it up, do not stay; "walk." In loving your neighbor, in being concerned about your neighbor, you are taking a trip. Where are you taking a trip to except to the Lord God? For we have not yet reached the Lord, but we have our neighbor with us. Therefore carry him with whom you are walking that you may reach him with whom you long to stay. Therefore "take up your bed, and walk." *Tractates on the Gospel of John 17.9, 2-3.*

CLOSING PRAYER

Watch, dear Lord, with those who wake, or watch or weep tonight, and give your angels charge over those who sleep; tend your sick ones, O Lord Christ, rest your weary ones, bless your dying ones, soothe your suffering ones, pity your afflicted ones, shield your joyous ones, and all for your love's sake. Amen. *Augustine*

Power and Glory

◁ THEME

Jesus calls us to love one another (Jn 17:20-26). Just as he cared for Paul and Silas in jail (Acts 16:16-34), so he will release us from our imprisonment of sin. Even the heavens proclaim his power and glory (Ps 97). Come, Lord Jesus (Rev 22:12-14, 16-17, 20-21)!

◁ OPENING PRAYER: *Seventh Sunday of Easter*

Almighty God, give us wisdom to perceive you, intellect to understand you, diligence to seek you, patience to wait for you, eyes to behold you, a heart to meditate on you and life to proclaim you, through the power of the Spirit of our Lord Jesus Christ. *Attributed to Benedict of Nursia*

◁ READING FROM ACTS: *Acts 16:16-34*

REFLECTIONS FROM THE CHURCH FATHERS

How Powerful the Words of Christ's Servants. AMMONIUS: After the demon had repeatedly testified that the message of the apostles was saving, Paul ordered him to come out in order to demonstrate to those who believed him that every believer was stronger than the demon and to show that each had power both to allow the demon to stay as one subject to the believer and to release him. See how powerful the words of the servants of Christ were: as soon as they gave a command, the demons came out. *Catena on the Acts of the Apostles 16.17.*

Paul's Power Shown in Weakness. **CHRYSOSTOM:** Do you see how his power was perfected in weakness? If Paul had been freed and had shaken that building, the event would not have been so wonderful. "Therefore," he says, "remain in chains! Let the walls be shaken from every side, and let the prisoners be freed—so that my power may appear all the greater, when through you, the one confined and in fetters, all who are in chains are freed." This is what amazed the jailer, that Paul, held in such constraints, was able, through prayer alone, to shake the foundations, open the doors of the prison and free all who were in chains. *Homilies Concerning the Statues 1.16.*

The Refusal to Believe. **AMMONIUS:** From this event it can be established that the faith of people is something in their power. See how, after such a fright, only the jailer believed. And yet, most of all, those imprisoned should have been moved to believe, since they had experienced a greater wonder when they saw their iron chains suddenly broken. Being foolish, they were frightened at the moment when the foundations of the prison were shaken and the doors were opened. But being despisers of God, after such a sign, they forgot what had happened, so that they did not speak to the jailer or to anyone about the terror that had happened. For, no doubt, had they heard from the jailer or from the followers of Paul the reason for such a wonder, they would perhaps have been converted. *Catena on the Acts of the Apostles 16.29-30.*

His Sins Were Washed Away. **BEDE:** A beautiful exchange—for them he washed the wounds from their flows, and through them he was relieved of the wounds of his own guilty acts. *Commentary on the Acts of the Apostles 16.33.*

PSALM OF RESPONSE: *Psalm 97*

NEW TESTAMENT READING: *Revelation 22:12-14, 16-17, 20-21*

REFLECTIONS FROM THE CHURCH FATHERS

We Must Be Eager to Do Good and Not Be Lazy. CLEMENT OF ROME: What, then, brothers, ought we to do? Should we grow slack in doing good and give up love? May the Lord never permit this to happen at any rate to us! Rather, we should be energetic in doing "every good deed" with earnestness and eagerness. The good laborer accepts the bread he has earned with his head held high; the lazy and negligent workman cannot look his employer in the face. We must, then, be eager to do good; for everything comes from him. *1 Clement 33-34.*

So That No One Will Be Ignorant. OECUMENIUS: "To testify" means to bear witness, not in private or in secret but so that the churches everywhere will hear and no one, feigning ignorance, will with evil intent do evil. *Commentary on the Apocalypse 22.15-19.*

Christ Will Shine. ANDREW OF CAESAREA: He is the "morning star," since he rose for us early in the morning after the three days. Moreover, after the night of the present life he will manifest himself to the saints in the early morning of the common resurrection and bring to pass the unending day. *Commentary on the Apocalypse 22.16.*

Baptism and Absolution Are Freely Given. APRINGIUS OF BEJA: Salvation is given without any price and without any barter. Rather, he who desires to be saved, he will enter and will either receive free of charge the regeneration of baptism, or he will receive the remedy of repentance without cost or charge. The prophet spoke in a similar manner: "All who thirst, come to the waters; and you who have no money, hasten, come, buy and eat." *Tractate on the Apocalypse 22.17.*

◌ GOSPEL READING: *John 17:20-26*

REFLECTIONS FROM THE CHURCH FATHERS

Call for Unity. CYPRIAN: The Lord's loving-kindness, no less than his mercy, is great in respect of our salvation in that, not content to redeem us with his blood, he in addition prayed for us. See now what the desire of his petition was, that just as the Father and Son are one, so it may be evident how greatly someone sins who divides unity and peace, since even the Lord himself petitioned for this same thing. He no doubt desired that his people should in this way be saved and live in peace since he knew that discord cannot come into the kingdom of God. *The Lord's Prayer 30.*

Unity from Diversity in God. CYRIL OF ALEXANDRIA: Our Lord Jesus Christ did not pray for the twelve apostles alone. He prayed for all who were destined in every age to yield to and obey the words that call them to be holy by believing and to be purified through participation in the Holy Spirit. . . . "May they all be one," he prayed. "As you, Father, are in me and I am in you, may they also be one in us." . . . By his own wisdom and the Father's counsel he devised a way of bringing us all together and blending us into a unity with God and one another, even though the differences between us give us each in both body and soul a separate identity. For in Holy Communion he blesses with one body, which is his own, those who believe in him, and he makes them one body with himself and one another. Who could separate those who are united to Christ through that one sacred body or destroy their true union with one another? If "we all share one loaf" we all become one body, for Christ cannot be divided. So it is that the church is the body of Christ, and we are its members. For since we are all united to Christ through his sacred body, having received that one indivisible body into our own, our members are not our own but his. *Commentary on the Gospel of John 11.11.*

Peace in Unity Is a Witness. CHRYSOSTOM: This is similar to what he said earlier, "By this shall all know that you are my disciples, if you love one another." And how will they believe this? "Because," he says, "you are a God of peace." And if therefore the disciples keep that same peace that they have learned from me, their hearers will know the teacher by the disciples. But if they quarrel, people will deny that they are the disciples of a God of peace and will not allow that I, not being peaceable, have been sent from you. Do you see how he proves his unanimity with the Father to the very end? *Homilies on the Gospel of John 82.2.*

CLOSING PRAYER

O God of unchangeable power and eternal light, look favorably on thy whole church, that wonderful and sacred mystery; and by the tranquil operation of thy perpetual providence, carry out the work of human salvation; let the whole world feel and see that things which were cast down are being raised up, that those which had grown old are being made new and that all things are returning to perfection; through him from whom they took their origin, even Jesus Christ thy Son our Lord. Amen. *The Gelasian Sacramentary*

God's Peace

THEME

It is not our achievements that matter (Gen 11:1-9) but the breath-taking works of the Lord (Ps 104:24-34, 35b). Because we are his children and fellow heirs with Christ (Rom 8:14-17), empowered by God, we are able to achieve more than we could ever accomplish by ourselves. Christ has left his peace with us, so we need not be troubled or afraid (John 14:8-17, 25-27).

OPENING PRAYER: *Day of Pentecost*

We beseech thee, O Lord, let the power of the Holy Spirit be present with us, that he may both mercifully cleanse our hearts and protect us from all adversities, through Jesus Christ our Lord. Amen. *The Leonine Sacramentary*

OLD TESTAMENT READING: *Genesis 11:1-9*

REFLECTIONS FROM THE CHURCH FATHERS

After God Confuses the Language, a War Breaks Out. EPHREM THE SYRIAN: It is likely that they lost their common language when they received these new languages. For if their original language had not perished their first deed would not have come to nothing. It was when they lost their original language, which was lost by all the nations, with one exception, that their first building came to naught. In addition, because of their new languages, which made them foreigners to each other and incapable of understanding one another, war broke out among them on account of the divisions that the languages brought among them. Thus war broke out among those who had been building that fortified city out of fear of others. And all those who had been keeping themselves away from the city were scattered throughout the entire earth. *Commentary on Genesis 8.3.2-8.4.2.*

The Doom of the Tower Must Be Regarded As a Warning. CHRYSOS-TOM: There are many people even today who in imitation of them want to be remembered for such achievements, by building splendid homes, baths, porches and avenues. I mean, if you were to ask each of them why they toil and labor and lay out such great expense to no good purpose, you would hear nothing but these very words. They would be seeking to ensure that their memory survives in perpetuity and to have it said that "this is the house belonging to so-and-so," "this is the property of so-and-so." This, on the contrary, is worthy not of commemoration but of condemnation. For hard on those words come other remarks equivalent to countless accusations—"belonging to so-and-so the grasping miser, despoiler of widows and orphans." So such behavior is calculated not to earn remembrance but to encounter unremitting accusations, achieve notoriety after death and incite the tongues of onlookers to calumny and condemnation of the person who acquired these goods. But if you are anxious for undying reputation, I will show you the way to succeed in being remembered for every achievement and also, along with an excellent name, to provide yourself with great confidence in the age to come. How then will you manage both to be remembered day after day and also become the recipient of tributes even after passing from one life to the next? If you give away these goods of yours into the hands of the poor, letting go of precious stones, magnificent homes, properties and baths. *Homilies on Genesis 30.7.*

PSALM OF RESPONSE: *Psalm 104:24-34, 35b*

NEW TESTAMENT READING: *Romans 8:14-17*

REFLECTIONS FROM THE CHURCH FATHERS

Led by the Spirit. CHRYSOSTOM: Note the great honor here. For as believers we do not merely live in the Spirit; we are led by him as well. The Spirit is meant to have the same power over us as a pilot has over his ship or a charioteer over his horses. And it is not only the body but the soul also which is meant to be controlled in this way. If you put your confidence in baptism to the point that you neglect your behavior after it, Paul says that even if you are baptized, if you are not led by the Spirit afterward you will lose the dignity bestowed on you and the honor of your adoption. This is why he does not talk about those who received the Spirit in the past but rather about those who are being led by the Spirit now. *Homilies on Romans 14.*

The Assurance That Dares to Say "Abba, Father." AMBROSIASTER: Paul says this because once we have received the Holy Spirit we are delivered from all fear of evil deeds, so that we might no longer act in such a way as to be afraid once more. Beforehand we were under fear, because once the law was given everyone was considered guilty. Paul called the law "the spirit of fear" because it made people afraid on account of their sins. But the law of faith, which is what is meant by "the Spirit of sonship," is a law of assurance, because it has delivered us from fear by pardoning our sins and thus giving us assurance. Set free by the grace of God from fear, we have received the Spirit of sonship so that, considering what we were and what we have become by the gift of God, we might govern our life with great care lest the name of God the Father be disgraced by us and we incur all the things we have escaped from. . . . We have received such grace that we can dare to say to God: "Abba! Father!" For this reason, Paul warns us not to let our trust

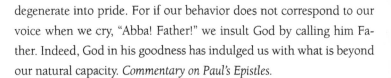

degenerate into pride. For if our behavior does not correspond to our voice when we cry, "Abba! Father!" we insult God by calling him Father. Indeed, God in his goodness has indulged us with what is beyond our natural capacity. *Commentary on Paul's Epistles.*

Slaves Fear; Sons Love. **PELAGIUS:** The Jews received a spirit which constrained them into service by means of fear. For it is the nature of slaves to fear and of sons to love, as it is written: "The slave shall fear his master, and the son shall love his father." Those who were not willing to work out of the desire of love are compelled by the constraint of fear, but let us perform all things willingly so that we may show that we are sons. He who calls to his father declares himself a son. He ought therefore to resemble his father in character, lest he incur a greater penalty for having assumed the name of his father in vain. *Pelagius's Commentary on Romans.*

Ready If Necessary to Suffer. **CYRIL OF ALEXANDRIA:** Good works can hardly be done without suffering, yet the suffering of the saints is nourished by a great hope. For nothing earthly is promised but rather eternal glory. *Explanation of the Letter to the Romans.*

GOSPEL READING: *John 14:8-17, 25-27*

REFLECTIONS FROM THE CHURCH FATHERS

The Father's Portrait in the Son. **AMBROSE:** By means of this image the Lord showed Philip the Father. Yes, he who looks on the Son sees, in portrait, the Father. Notice what kind of portrait is spoken of. It is truth, righteousness, the power of God. It is not silent, for it is the word. It is not insensible, for it is Wisdom. It is not vain and foolish, for it is power. It is not soulless, for it is the life. It is not dead, for it is the resurrection. *On the Christian Faith 1.7.50.*

To Love Is to Submit to Christ. **CHRYSOSTOM:** At all times it is works and actions that we need, not a mere show of words. It is easy for anyone to say or promise something, but it is not so easy to act on that word or promise. . . . "If you love me," Christ said, "keep my commandments." . . . I have commanded you to love one another and to do to one another as I have done to you. To love me is to obey these commands and to submit to me, your beloved. *Homilies on the Gospel of John 75.1.*

Peace Defines a Christian. CAESARIUS OF ARLES: Peace, indeed, is serenity of mind, tranquility of soul, simplicity of heart, the bond of love, the fellowship of charity. It removes hatred, settles wars, restrains wrath, tramples on pride, loves the humble, pacifies the discordant and makes enemies agree. For it is pleasing to everyone. It does not seek what belongs to another or consider anything as its own. It teaches people to love because it does not know how to get angry, or to extol itself or become inflated with pride. It is meek and humble to everyone, possessing rest and tranquility within itself. When the peace of Christ is exercised by a Christian, it is brought to perfection by Christ. . . . Anyone who has received this peace should keep it, and one who has destroyed it should look for it, while anyone who has lost it should seek it. *Sermon 174.1.*

CLOSING PRAYER

O God of peace, good beyond all that is good, in whom is calmness and concord: do thou make up the dissensions which divide us from one another and bring us into unity of love in thee, through Jesus Christ our Lord. *Dionysius of Alexandria*

Father, Son and Spirit

◁ THEME

Wisdom, in the form of Jesus, has always been with the Father (Prov 8:1-4, 22-31). When we see the beauty of creation, we are amazed that God has given us the chance to be his children (Ps 8). We are grateful that we may be at peace with God through Jesus Christ (Rom 5:1-5) and that we are given the gift of the Holy Spirit (Jn 16:12-15).

◁ OPENING PRAYER: *Trinity Sunday*

Almighty and everlasting God, who has given to thy servants grace, by the confession of a true faith, to acknowledge the glory of the eternal Trinity, and in the power of the divine majesty to worship the unity; we beseech thee, that thou would keep us steadfast in this faith and evermore defend us from all adversities, who lives and reigns one God, world without end. Amen. *The Gregorian Sacramentary*

◁ OLD TESTAMENT READING: *Proverbs 8:1-4, 22-31*

REFLECTIONS FROM THE CHURCH FATHERS

The Son, the First Offspring from the Father, Was Not Created.
ATHENAGORAS: The Son is the first offspring of the Father. I do not mean that he was created, for, since God is eternal mind, he had his word within himself from the beginning, being eternally wise. . . . Indeed we say that the Holy Spirit himself, who inspires those who utter prophe-

cies, is an effluence from God, flowing from him and returning like a ray of the sun. Who, then, would not be astonished to hear those called atheists who admit God the Father, God the Son and the Holy Spirit, and who teach their unity in power and their distinction in rank? . . . We affirm too, a crowd of angels and ministers, whom God, the maker and creator of the world, appointed to their several tasks through his Word. He gave them charge over the good order of the universe, over the elements, the heavens, the world, and all it contains. *A Plea Regarding Christians 10.*

"Creation" Indicates Relationship. DIDYMUS THE BLIND: Since wisdom is already eternal, it is not subjected to time. The "beginning," then, is yoked together with created things. But having existed before creation as wisdom, the Son of God—even though he says, "The Lord created me"—this assertion ("The Lord created me") must be understood as referring not to substance but to his relationship toward creatures. For wisdom says that its works were at the beginning of the creative and providential ways of God, that is, a "Cause," introducing still another way of speaking. The Son of God was made man when he assumed the form of a servant. He is eternal before the ages, as he is God the Word. It says he was "created" because he was born of Mary and was made flesh. For those desiring to walk like God and with God, consult this teacher, an example of perfect life, who gives his teaching to those who follow him. The fact that the word "to create" does not mean everywhere "to make substance" is confirmed by David, who says, "Create in me a pure heart, O God." He asks for such a creation not as if he does not have a heart; but since he had polluted it, he desires to have it back pure. . . . And so the interpreters proclaimed, "He created me." *Commentary on the Proverbs of Solomon, Fragment 8.22.*

There Was Never a "When" When He Did Not Exist. ATHANASIUS: The Lord is God's true and natural Son, and he is known to be not just eternal but one who exists concurrently with the eternity of the Father.

. . . Being Son, he is inseparable from the Father, and there was never a "when" when he did not exist. He always existed. Moreover, since he is the image and radiance of the Father, he also possesses the Father's eternity. *Four Discourses Against the Arians 3.28-29.*

PSALM OF RESPONSE: *Psalm 8*

NEW TESTAMENT READING: *Romans 5:1-5*

REFLECTIONS FROM THE CHURCH FATHERS

The Guarantee of Peace. ORIGEN: It is obvious from this that the apostle is inviting everyone who has understood that he is justified by faith and not by works to that "peace which passes all understanding," in which the height of perfection consists. But let us investigate further in order to see what the apostle means when he talks about peace, and especially about that peace which is through our Lord Jesus Christ. Peace reigns when nobody complains, nobody disagrees, nobody is hostile and nobody misbehaves. Therefore, we who once were enemies of God, following the devil, that great enemy and tyrant, now, if we have thrown down his weapons and in their place taken up the sign of Christ and the standard of his cross, have peace with God. But this is through our Lord Jesus Christ, who has reconciled us to God through the offering of his blood. Let us therefore have peace, so that the flesh will no longer war with the spirit, nor will the law of God be opposed by the law of our member. *Commentary on the Epistle to the Romans.*

God Reconciled Us to Himself. CHRYSOSTOM: What does it mean to have peace? Some say that it means that we should not fall out with one another because of disagreements over the law. But it seems to me that he is speaking much more about our current behavior. . . . Paul means here that we should stop sinning and not go back to the way we used to live, for that is to make war with God. How is this possible? Paul says that not only is it possible, it is also reasonable. For if God reconciled us to himself when we were in open warfare with him, it is surely reasonable that we should be able to remain in a state of reconciliation. *Homilies on Romans 9.*

Suffering Prepares Us for Endurance. CHRYSOSTOM: Consider how great the things to come are, when we can rejoice even at things which appear to be distressful. . . . Sufferings are in themselves a good thing, insofar as they prepare us for endurance. *Homilies on Romans 9.*

GOSPEL READING: *John 16:12-15*

REFLECTIONS FROM THE CHURCH FATHERS

The Mystery of the Spirit. HILARY OF POITIERS: According to the apostle, Lord, your Holy Spirit fully understands and penetrates your inmost depths. He also intercedes on my behalf, saying to you things for which I cannot find the words. Nothing can penetrate your being but what is divine already. Nor can the depths of your immense majesty be measured by any power that itself is alien or extrinsic to you. So, whatever enters into you is yours already, nor can anything that has the power to search your very depths ever have been other than your own. . . . Your Holy Spirit proceeds through your Son from you. Though I may fail to grasp the full meaning of that statement, I give it nonetheless the firm assent of my mind and heart. *On the Trinity 12.55-57.*

Taught by God the Spirit. AUGUSTINE: Beloved, you should not expect to hear from us what the Lord refrained from telling his disciples because they were still unable to bear them. Rather, seek to grow in the love that is shed abroad in your hearts by the Holy Spirit who is given to you so that, fervent in spirit and loving spiritual things, you may be able—not by any sign apparent to your bodily eyes or any sound striking on your bodily ears but by the inward eyesight and hearing—to become acquainted with that spiritual light and that spiritual word that carnal people are unable to bear. For that cannot be loved that is altogether unknown. But when what is known, in however small a measure, is also loved, by the same love, one is led on to a better and fuller knowledge. If, then, you grow in the love that the Holy Spirit spreads abroad in your heart, "He will teach you all truth," or, as the other codices have it, "He will guide you in all truth"; as it is said, "Lead me in your way, O Lord, and I will walk in your truth." So shall the result be, that not from outward teachers will you learn those things that the Lord at that time declined to utter, but you will all be taught by God, so that the very things that you have learned and believed by means of lessons and sermons supplied from without . . . your minds themselves may have the power to perceive. *Tractates on the Gospel of John 96.4.*

Reciprocal Sharing. GREGORY OF NAZIANZUS: All things that the Father has are the Son's. And . . . all that belongs to the Son is the Father's. Nothing then is peculiar to any person because all things are in common. For their being itself is common and equal, even though the Son receives it from the Father. *On the Son, Theological Oration 4.30.11.*

CLOSING PRAYER

Breathe in me, Holy Spirit, that I may think what is holy. Move me, Holy Spirit, that I may do what is holy. Attract me, Holy Spirit, that I may love what is holy. Strengthen me, Holy Spirit, that I may guard what is holy. Guard me, Holy Spirit, that I may keep what is holy. *Augustine*

Confessing Our Sins

THEME

We, like David, are capable of great sin (2 Sam 11:26–12:10, 13-15), yet when we confess our sins, God forgives us (Ps 32). This forgiveness and healing from sins does not come about by our own power but by the grace of God through Jesus Christ (Gal 2:15-21), the greatest healer (Lk 7:36–8:3).

OPENING PRAYER: *Proper 6*

Like the thief I cry to thee, "Remember me." Like Peter I weep bitterly. Like the publican I call out, "Forgive me, Savior." Like the harlot I shed tears. Accept my lamentation, as once thou accepted the entreaties of the woman of Canaan. Have mercy on me, O God, have mercy on me.
Andrew of Crete

OLD TESTAMENT READING: *2 Samuel 11:26–12:10, 13-15*

REFLECTIONS FROM THE CHURCH FATHERS

Diseased Tissue in David's Heart. AUGUSTINE: For I admit my wrongdoing, and my offense confronts me all the time. "I have not thrust my deed behind my back; I do not look askance at others while forgetting myself; I do not presume to extract a speck of straw from my brother's eye while there is a timber in my own; my sin is in front of me, not behind my back. It was behind me until the prophet was sent to me and put to me the parable of the poor man's sheep." . . . Obviously the king was unaware of the trap into which he had fallen, and he decreed that the rich man deserved to die and must make fourfold restitution for the sheep. It was a very severe view, and entirely just. But his own sin was not yet before his eyes; what he had done was still behind his back. He did not yet admit his own iniquity and hence would not remit another's. But the prophet had been sent to him for this purpose. He brought the sin out from behind David's back and held it before his eyes, so that he might see that the severe sentence had been passed on himself. To cut away diseased tissue in David's heart and heal the wound there, Nathan used David's tongue as a knife. *Explanations of the Psalms 50.*

Temporal Punishment Remained. ISAAC OF NINEVEH: And David, who was a man after God's own heart, who because of his virtues was found worthy to generate from his seed the promise of the fathers and to have Christ shine forth from himself for the salvation of all the world, was he not punished because of adultery with a woman, when he held her beauty with his eyes and was pierced in his soul by that arrow? For it was because of this that God raised up a war against him from within his own household, and he who came forth from his loins pursued him. These things befell him even after he had repented with many tears, such that he moistened his couch with his weeping, and after God had said to him through the prophet, "The Lord has forgiven your sin." *Ascetical Homilies 10.*

No Shame in Repentance. PACIAN OF BARCELONA: May we by all means be filled with revulsion for sin but not for repentance. May we be ashamed to put ourselves at risk but not to be delivered. Who will snatch away the wooden plank from the shipwrecked so that he may not escape? Who will begrudge the curing of wounds? Does David not say, "Every single night I will bathe my bed, I will drench my couch in my tears." And again, "I acknowledge my sin, and my iniquity I have not concealed." And further, "I said, 'I will reveal against myself my sin to my God,' and you forgave the wickedness of my heart." Did not the prophet answer David as follows when, after the guilt of murder and adultery for the sake of Bathsheba, he was penitent? "The Lord has taken away from you your sin." *Letter 1.5.3.*

PSALM OF RESPONSE: *Psalm 32*

NEW TESTAMENT READING: *Galatians 2:15-21*

REFLECTIONS FROM THE CHURCH FATHERS

No One Can Fulfill the Law in Every Respect by Moral Effort Alone.
JEROME: In this place we must consider how many are the precepts of the law which no one can fulfill. And it must also be said that some works of the law are done even by those who do not know it. But those who perform it are not justified, because this happens without faith in Christ. *Epistle to the Galatians 1.2.16.*

One Who Reestablishes the Law Is a Transgressor Against Not Faith but the Law Itself. CHRYSOSTOM: Note the shrewdness of Paul. For they wanted to show that the one who does not keep the law is a transgressor; but he turns the argument upside down, showing that the one who observes the law is a transgressor not against faith but against the law itself. What he says is as follows: "The law has ceased, as we ourselves agree, in so far as we have left it and taken refuge in the salvation of faith. If we now strive to establish it, we become transgressors by this very fact, as we strive to observe the precept dissolved by God." *Homily on Galatians 2.18.*

Snatched from Death. AMBROSIASTER: There is no doubt that Christ lives in the one who is delivered from death by faith. When Christ forgives the sins of one who is worthy of death, he himself lives in that person, since by his protection the person is snatched from death. *Epistle to the Galatians 2.20.*

On Not Nullifying Grace. **AMBROSIASTER:** Since a future life is promised to Christians, the one who now lives with God's assistance lives in the faith of the promised life. For this one contemplates his image, having the pledge of the future life, which was procured for us by Christ's love in accordance with God's will. The one who is grateful to Christ is therefore the one who endures in faith toward him. He knows that he has no benefit from anyone but Christ and treats Christ with dishonor if he compares any other to him. *Epistle to the Galatians 2.21.*

⌐ GOSPEL READING: *Luke 7:36–8:3*

REFLECTIONS FROM THE CHURCH FATHERS

Jesus Tells the Parable to Bring About Reconciliation with Simon. **EPHREM THE SYRIAN:** Our Lord devised a statement that was like an arrow. He put conciliation at its tip and anointed it with love to soothe the parts of the body. He no sooner shot it at the one who was filled with conflict, than conflict turned to harmony. Directly following the humble statement of our Lord, who said, "Simon, I have something to say to you," he who had secretly withdrawn responded, "Speak, my Lord." A sweet saying penetrated a bitter mind and brought out fragrant fruit. He who was a secret detractor before the saying gave public praise after the saying. Humility with a sweet tongue subdues even its enemies to do it honor. Humility does not put its power to the test among its friends but among those who hate its display of its trophies. *Homily on Our Lord 24.2.*

Christ Is Our Love Who Forgives Sins. **AMBROSE:** Christ is love. Love is good, since it offered itself to death for transgressions. Love is good, which forgave sins. Let our soul clothe itself with love of a kind that is "strong as death." Just as death is the end of sins, so also is love, because the one who loves the Lord ceases to commit sin. For "charity thinks no evil and does not rejoice over wickedness, but endures all things." If someone does not seek his own goods, how will he seek the goods of another? That death through the bath of baptism, through which every sin is buried, is strong and forgives every fault. The woman in the Gospel brought this kind of love. The Lord says, "Her many sins have been forgiven her, because she has loved much." *Isaac, or the Soul 8.75-76.*

The Apostles Follow Jesus' Example. AUGUSTINE: If anyone does not believe that wherever they preached the gospel the apostles brought women of holy life with them, so that these women might minister the necessities of life to them from their abundance, let him hear the Gospel and realize that the apostles did this by the example of our Lord himself. *The Work of Monks 5.6.*

CLOSING PRAYER

O Word of our God, I betrayed you, the Truth, with my falsehood, when I promised to hallow the hours that vanish away. In overtaking me, night does not find me undarkened by sin. I did indeed pray, and I thought to stand blameless at eve. But some way and somewhere my feet have stumbled and fallen; for a storm cloud swooped on me, envious lest I be saved. Kindle for me your light, O Christ, restore me by your presence. *Gregory of Nazianzus*

The Love of God

THEME

Isaiah's prophetic verses foretell the love and compassion of God in sending his only Son to an unwelcoming world (Is 65:1-9); just as this psalm foretells Christ's death (Ps 22:19-28). Christ's sacrifice allows us to be made children of God through faith (Gal 3:23-29). Like the man Jesus healed of evil spirits, we should declare how much God has done for us (Lk 8:26-39).

OPENING PRAYER: *Proper 7*

You only I love; you only I follow; you only I seek; you only am I ready to serve. Because you alone are justly Lord, I desire to be under your rule. Command, I ask you, as you will, but heal and open my ears that I may hear your voice. Heal and open my eyes that I may see your beckoning. Tell me where I must go that I may see you; and I hope to do all that you command. Receive, I pray you, your fugitive, most clement Father and Lord. Enough have I served your enemies whom you have put under your feet. Enough have I been the plaything of deceits. Receive me, your servant, now fleeing from these things. *Augustine*

OLD TESTAMENT READING: *Isaiah 65:1-9*

REFLECTIONS FROM THE CHURCH FATHERS

The Unsought Messiah. THEODORE OF HERACLEA: "I was ready to be sought by those who did not seek me." These words should be understood as about the Savior, who, sent by the Father's love and coming with his own compassionate love, was revealed to all people. He became savior of those who had not made him welcome nor had invited him. *Fragments on Isaiah.*

Ingratitude for Divine Care and Concern. THEODORET OF CYR: It is the nations who did not have a prophet sent to them who recognize their maker and benefactor, whereas those who received all sorts of care gained no profit but continued in their sinful habits. The phrase "all day long I have held out my hands" refers to the care for them that he gave for all that time, but the saving suffering of the cross in which he stretched out his hands is also alluded to here. *Commentary on Isaiah 20.65.2.*

God Came to Seek and Restore His Image. LEO THE GREAT: If, dearly beloved, we comprehend faithfully and wisely the beginning of our creation, we shall find that humankind was made in God's image, to the end that he might imitate the Creator and that our race attains its highest natural dignity, by the form of the divine goodness being reflected in us, as in a mirror. And assuredly to this form the Savior's grace is daily restoring us, so long as that which in the first Adam fell is raised up again in the second. And the cause of our restoration is nothing else but the mercy of God, whom we would not have loved unless he had first loved us and dispelled the darkness of our ignorance by the light of his truth. *Sermon 12.1.*

Christ Is the Haven for the Spiritual. THEODORET OF CYR: Those who have attained the summit of perfection have as their harbor not life, or the resurrection or any of these admirable things but the desired One himself, for whose sake they counted misfortune a delight, and weary toil the sweetest repose, and time spent in the desert more desirable than city life, and poverty fairer than wealth and irksome slavery sweeter than any position of authority. This is the reward awaited by the doers of virtue. "It is an inheritance for those who serve God," as the prophet Isaiah exclaims. *On Divine Providence 9.11.*

◁ PSALM OF RESPONSE: *Psalm 22:19-28*

◁ NEW TESTAMENT READING: *Galatians 3:23-29*

REFLECTIONS FROM THE CHURCH FATHERS

Why the Law Was Given. THEODORET OF CYR: Now it was necessary that the law be given, as it fulfilled our need of a custodian. And it freed us from our previous impiety, taught us knowledge of God and then brought us to Christ the Lord as though to some wise teacher, so that we might be instructed by him in perfect learning and acquire the righteousness that is through faith. *Epistle to the Galatians 3.24.*

How One Is Made a Son in Baptism. CHRYSOSTOM: Since he has said something great and remarkable, he also explains how one is made a son. "For as many of you as were baptized into Christ have put on Christ." Why didn't he say, "All you who were baptized into Christ have been born of God," since that is the inference from showing that they were sons? Because what he says is more awe-inspiring. For if Christ is the Son of God and you put him on, having the Son inside yourself and being made like him, you have been made one in kind and form. *Homily on Galatians 3.27.*

The Analogy of Glowing with the Spirit, Where All Distinctions Disappear. JEROME: When one has once put on Christ and, having been sent into the flame, glows with the ardor of the Holy Spirit, it is not apparent whether he is of gold or silver. As long as the heat takes over the mass in this way there is one fiery color, and all diversity of race, condition and body is taken away by such a garment. *Epistle to the Galatians 2.3.27-28.*

⊰ GOSPEL READING: *Luke 8:26-39*

REFLECTIONS FROM THE CHURCH FATHERS

The Demons' Response Fearful yet Prideful. CYRIL OF ALEXAN-
DRIA: I beseech you to again observe the incomparable majesty of
Christ who transcends all. With irresistible might and unequalled authority he crushes Satan by simply willing that it should be. *Commentary on Luke, Homily 44.*

Demons Know Better Than Heretics Who Jesus Is. HILARY OF
POITIERS: Did not the devils know the real nature of this name? It is
fitting that the heretics should be found guilty, not by the teachings of
the apostles but by the mouth of demons. The latter often exclaim,
"What have I to do with you, Jesus, Son of the Most High God?" The
truth drew out this reluctant confession, and being forced to obey, their
grief testifies to the strength of this nature. This power overcomes
them, since they abandon bodies that they have possessed for a long
time. They pay their tribute of honor when they acknowledge the nature of Christ. In the meantime, Christ testifies that he is the Son by his
miracles as well as by his name. O heretic, where do you find the name
of a creature or the favor of an adoption among those words by which
the demons admit who he is? *On the Trinity 6.49.*

Freed from His Sepulchral Prison. PRUDENTIUS:
In his sepulchral prison the savage demon had broken
Fetters of iron that bound him; he darts forth and kneels before Jesus.
But the Lord sets the man free and orders the devil to madden
Herds of the swine and to plunge with them into the depths of
    the vast sea.
Scenes from Sacred History 36.

The Demoniac Goes from Synagogue to Church. AMBROSE: It says,
"The herdsmen saw this and fled." Neither professors of philosophy

nor leaders of the synagogue can offer any cure when people perish. Christ alone takes away the sins of the people, provided they do not refuse to submit to healing. He does not want to cure the unwilling and soon abandon the weak for whom it seems that his presence is a burden, like the peoples of the Gerasenes. They went out from that country, which appears to be an image of the synagogue, and begged him to depart from them, because they were very afraid. . . . Why does Christ not accept the healed man but advise him to return home? Perhaps this occurs to avoid a cause of boasting and give an example to unbelievers, although that home may be an inn by nature. Since he received the healing of his mind, Christ commanded him to depart from the tombs and the graves and to return to that spiritual home. He who had in him the grave of the mind became a temple of God. *Exposition of the Gospel of Luke 6.50, 53.*

⌐ CLOSING PRAYER

O Lord, you have mercy on all; take away from me my sins, and mercifully set me ablaze with the fire of your Holy Spirit. Take away from me the heart of stone, and give me a human heart, a heart to love and adore you, a heart to delight in you, to follow and enjoy you, for Christ's sake. Amen. *Jerome*

Fruit of the Spirit

THEME

Just as Elisha was obedient and learned from Elijah (1 Kings 19:15-16, 19-21), so we choose to follow God and bless him for his counsel (Ps 16). We seek to live and walk by the Spirit and not by the flesh, cultivating the fruit of the Spirit (Gal 5:1, 13-25) and putting Christ above all else (Lk 9:51-62).

OPENING PRAYER: *Proper 8*

May the very God of all, who spoke by the Holy Spirit through the prophets, who sent the Holy Spirit on the apostles on the day of Pentecost in this place, send the Spirit at this time also on you; and by him keep us also, imparting his benefit in common to us all, that we may ever render up the fruits of the Holy Spirit, in Christ Jesus our Lord; by whom and with whom, together with the Holy Spirit, be glory to the Father, both now and ever, and forever and ever. Amen. *Cyril of Jerusalem*

OLD TESTAMENT READING: *1 Kings 19:15-16, 19-21*

REFLECTIONS FROM THE CHURCH FATHERS

Elisha Is the Type of the Apostles. EPHREM THE SYRIAN: "So he set out from there and found Elisha son of Shaphat. He passed by him and threw his mantle over him." With his mantle Elijah took Elisha from

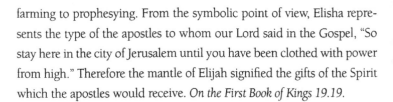

farming to prophesying. From the symbolic point of view, Elisha represents the type of the apostles to whom our Lord said in the Gospel, "So stay here in the city of Jerusalem until you have been clothed with power from high." Therefore the mantle of Elijah signified the gifts of the Spirit which the apostles would receive. *On the First Book of Kings 19.19.*

The Call of Elisha Came from Christ. JOHN THE MONK:
After receiving the garment from the prophetical hand,
At the same time you have received the privilege,
When you were transformed from worker into a prophet
Through the radiance of the Spirit that was glorified.
Since you foreknew, O Christ, the inclination to goodness
Of the heart of Elisha, he has understood with no doubt
The glorious call that you had established and followed it.
Canon 6, On Elisha the Prophet, Ode 1.

Elisha Leaves Behind All Worldly Goods. ISHO'DAD OF MERV: "He slaughtered the oxen." He did that not as a sacrifice to God, because Elisha was not a priest, but he killed them for a banquet which he offered to his people. From now on, he was lifted above earthly things and did not make use of anything that belonged to this world. *Books of Sessions 1 Kings 19.21.*

PSALM OF RESPONSE: *Psalm 16*

NEW TESTAMENT READING: *Galatians 5:1, 13-25*

REFLECTIONS FROM THE CHURCH FATHERS

Why Be Yoked Again? JEROME: He adds "again," not because the Galatians had previously kept the law . . . but in their readiness to observe the lunar seasons, to be circumcised in the flesh and to offer sacrifices, they were in a sense returning to the cults that they had previously served in a state of idolatry. *Epistle to the Galatians 2.5.1.*

Called to Freedom but Not As an Occasion for Sin. AUGUSTINE: From this point Paul begins to discuss those works of the law which . . . no one denies also pertain to the new covenant, but with another aim, appropriate to those who perform good works "in freedom." These acts aim for the rewards of a love that hopes for eternal things and looks forward in faith. This is quite unlike the Jews, who were forced to fulfill these commandments from fear, and not that righteous fear which endures to eternity but one that made them fear for the present life. The result is that they fulfill certain works of the law which consist in ceremonies but are completely unable to fulfill those that consist in good conduct. For nothing fulfills these except love. . . . And so the apostle now says, "You are called into freedom, brethren, but on condition that you do not let your freedom be an opportunity for the sin nature. Do not suppose, on hearing the word *freedom,* that you can sin with impunity." *Epistle to the Galatians 43 (1B.5.13).*

Both Covenants from the One Lord. EPIPHANIUS: What need is there for the holy apostle to make use of the law, if the new covenant is foreign to the old legislation? He wants to show both covenants are from the one Lord. They are best perceived as sharing the same intent. The fulfillment of the law is through the love of one's neighbor, because love is that which effects the perfect good. He therefore says that love is the fulfilling of the law. *Panarion 42.12.3, Fifth Refutation of Marcion.*

The Whole Law Fulfilled by Love. MARIUS VICTORINUS: The whole work of the law is fulfilled by this one command: love. For one who loves another neither murders nor commits adultery nor steals. . . . Now Paul himself adds a text: "You shall love your neighbor as yourself." But we ought to understand by "neighbor" every human being and then constantly view Christ as our neighbor. "And you too must love one another but in the spirit." Here he now seems, as if neglecting the previous question and discussion, to urge them to avoid discord. And this can happen if you love one another in the Spirit, not in the flesh or for the works of the flesh or in natural observances. For he who loves another feels no envy, nor steals from another nor despises or abuses him. *Epistle to the Galatians 2.5.14.*

The Spirit Abides As the Strength of Love. CHRYSOSTOM: See how he also shows a better way. It makes virtue uncomplicated and rightly accomplishes what he has previously said—a way that brings forth love and is sustained by love. For nothing, *nothing* makes people so lovable as to be formed by the Spirit. And nothing so causes the Spirit to abide in us as the strength of love. . . . After having stated the cause of the illness he also shows the remedy that bestows health. *Homily on Galatians 5.16.*

Against the Flesh. JOHN CASSIAN: An inward war is being waged every day within us. The desires of the flesh and of the spirit are within one and the same person. The lust of the flesh rushes headlong into vice, delights in the worldly enjoyments that seem to satisfy. By contrast the opposed desire of the spirit is so eager to cleave entirely to spiritual pursuits that it in an exaggerated way chooses even to exclude the necessary uses of the flesh. By wishing to be so inseparably attached to spiritual things it refuses to take care of its own bodily fragility. *Conference 4.11.2.*

⛪ GOSPEL READING: *Luke 9:51-62*

REFLECTIONS FROM THE CHURCH FATHERS

The Disciples Benefit from Preaching the Gospel and Experiencing Rejection. CYRIL OF ALEXANDRIA: It also benefited them in another way. They were to be the instructors of the whole world and to travel through the cities and villages, proclaiming everywhere the good tidings of salvation. Of necessity, while seeking to fulfill their mission, they must fall in with wicked people who would reject the divine tidings and not receive Jesus to stay with them. . . . Christ rebuked them for their own good when they were enraged beyond measure at the hatred of the Samaritans. He did this so they might learn that as ministers of the divine tidings, they must rather be full of longsuffering and gentleness, not revengeful. They must not be given to wrath or savagely attack those who offend them. *Commentary on Luke, Homily 56.*

Human Obligation Gives Way to Christian Discipleship. BASIL THE GREAT: The man said, "Allow me first to go and bury my father." The Lord replied, "Let the dead bury their dead; but go and preach the kingdom of God." Another man said, "Let me first arrange my affairs at home." He rebuked him with a stern threat, saying, "No man, putting his hand to the plow and looking back, is fit for the kingdom of God." A person who wishes to become the Lord's disciple must repudiate a human obligation, however honorable it may appear, if it slows us ever so slightly in giving the wholehearted obedience we owe to God. *Concerning Baptism.*

Do Not Return to the World. CYPRIAN: The Lord warns us of this in his gospel lest we return to the devil again and to the world, which we have renounced and from which we have escaped. He says, "No one, having put his hand to the plow and looking back, is fit for the kingdom of God." Again he says, "And let him who is the field not turn back. Remember Lot's wife." Lest anyone, either because of some desire for wealth or by his own charm, be persuaded from following Christ, he added, "He that does not renounce all that he possesses, cannot be my disciple." *Exhortation to Martyrdom 5.13.7.*

CLOSING PRAYER

Grant, almighty God, that the words, which we have heard this day with our outward ears, may through thy grace be so grafted inwardly in our hearts that they may bring forth in us the fruit of good living, to the honor and praise of thy name; through Jesus Christ our Lord. Amen. *Liturgy of St. James*

Bearing Each Other's Burdens

THEME

Because God is with us (Is 66:10-14), we rejoice and sing his praises (Ps 66:1-8). We are called to bear one another's burdens, to do good to others, to not grow weary in well-doing (Gal 6:1-16) and to spread the Good News (Lk 10:1-11, 16-20).

OPENING PRAYER: *Proper 9*

O God of love, who has given a new commandment through thine only-begotten Son, that we should love one another, even as thou did love us, the unworthy and the wandering, and gave thy beloved Son for our life and salvation; we pray thee, Lord, give to us, thy servants, in all time of our life on the earth, a mind forgetful of past ill will, a pure conscience and sincere thoughts and a heart to love our brethren; for the sake of Jesus Christ, thy Son, our Lord and only Savior. Amen. *Coptic Liturgy of St. Cyril*

OLD TESTAMENT READING: *Isaiah 66:10-14*

REFLECTIONS FROM THE CHURCH FATHERS

The Serpent Cannot Reach the Nest of Christians. JEROME: Those who write of the nature of animals say that all wild creatures, beasts of burden, and sheep and birds have an innate affection for their offspring and young but that the greatest love is found among eagles, who build their nests in very high and inaccessible locations so that no serpent can harm their chicks. Also to be found among newly hatched eagles is the *aetiten* stone, which overcomes all poisons. If this is true, then the eagle's affection is rightly compared with that of God for his creatures, who protects his children by taking every precaution to shatter the adversary's plot on the name of the stone that is placed in Zion's foundation, lest the dragon and ancient serpent, the devil and Satan, seize his newborns. And this Jerusalem, a mother by whom sons are consoled and caressed on her knees, is she of whom the apostle wrote: "But the Jerusalem above, who is the mother of us all, is free." *Commentary on Isaiah 18.26.*

The River of the Holy Spirit. AMBROSE: So, then, the Holy Spirit is the river, and the abundant river, which according to the Hebrews flowed from Jesus in the lands, as we have received it prophesied by the mouth of Isaiah. This is the great river that flows always and never fails. And not only a river but also one of the copious stream and overflowing greatness, as also David said, "The stream of the river makes glad the city of God." *On the Holy Spirit 1.16.177.*

The Father Draws Near to Those Who Seek His Aid. CLEMENT OF ALEXANDRIA: A mother draws her children near her; we seek our mother, the church. Whatever is weak and young has an appeal and sweetness and loveableness of its own, just because in its weakness it does stand in need of assistance. But God does not withhold assistance from such an age of life. Just as the male and female parent regard their young tenderly—whether it be horses their colts, or cows their calves, or lions their cubs, or deer their fawn or men and women their children—so too does the Father of all draw near to those who seek his aid, giving them a new birth and making them his own adopted children. He recognizes them as his little ones, he loves only them, and he comes to the aid of such as these and defends them. That is why he calls them his children. *Christ the Educator 1.5.21.*

PSALM OF RESPONSE: *Psalm 66:1-8*

NEW TESTAMENT READING: *Galatians 6:1-16*

REFLECTIONS FROM THE CHURCH FATHERS

The Test of the Spirit-Led Person. AUGUSTINE: There is no surer test of the spiritual person than his treatment of another's sin. Note how he takes care to deliver the sinner rather than triumph over him, to help him rather than punish him and, so far as lies in his capacity, to support him. *Epistle to the Galatians 56 [1B.6.1].*

In Amending Another's Wrongdoing, Think of What Might Befall You. JEROME: Maybe Paul is saying that you should identify with the sinner in order to do him good. This is not to imply, of course, that one should seemingly commit the same wrong and pretend that one is also subject to it. No, in another's wrongdoing one should think of what might befall oneself. Help the other with the same compassion that one would hope to receive from another. *Letter 116.29.2.*

Bearing the Burdens of the Poor. ORIGEN: By "burdens" he means the needs of the body. So to the extent that anyone is richer in resources, he is called to bear the poor person's burden and relieve poverty by his abundance. *Commentary on Romans 10.6.*

Stringent Self-Examination. CHRYSOSTOM: Here Paul shows that we must scrutinize our lives. We must test what we have done not cheaply but stringently. For example, suppose you have done something good. Consider whether it might have been through vanity or through necessity, or with animosity, or in hypocrisy, or through some other self-centered motive. *Homily on Galatians 6.4.*

On Not Growing Weary in Doing Good. MARIUS VICTORINUS: It is not enough that we do good; for our goodness will not be recognized straight away by God if we do good, but only if we "do not grow weary in doing good." Many begin, many in a way persevere, yet later they give up, either tired or led astray. He justly warns them that they should not grow weary in any way, lest by their weariness they leave off what they began when they began to do well. *Epistle to the Galatians 2.6.9.*

Christ's More Perfect Law and More Perfect Circumcision. EPIPHA-NIUS: The former circumcision was not inappropriate in its own time. But the law announced that Christ would come to dispense the law of freedom. Then the circumcision in the flesh would no longer be of service in the time of Christ. *Panarion* 42.12.3, *Eighth Refutation of Marcion.*

GOSPEL READING: *Luke 10:1-11, 16-20*

REFLECTIONS FROM THE CHURCH FATHERS

The Disciples Are to Be Dependent on the Lord of the Harvest. CYRIL OF ALEXANDRIA: When preaching to people everywhere the word that he spoke and calling the inhabitants of the whole earth to salvation, he requires them to travel about without purse, bag or shoes. They are to travel rapidly from city to city and from place to place. Let no one say that the object of his teaching was to make the holy apostles refuse the use of the ordinary articles of equipment. What good or what harm would it do them to have shoes on their feet or go without them? By this command, he does wish them to learn and to attempt to practice that they must lay all thought of their livelihood on him. They must call to mind the saint who said, "Cast your care on the Lord, and he will feed you." He gives what is needful for life to the saints. *Commentary on Luke, Homily 62.*

The Victory of the Cross Crushes Satan. EPHREM THE SYRIAN: "I was looking at Satan, who fell like lightning from the heavens." It was not that he was actually in the heavens. He was not in them when he said, "I will place my throne above the stars," but he fell from his greatness and his dominion. "I was looking at Satan, who fell like lightning from the heavens." He did not fall from heaven, because lightning does not fall from heaven, since the clouds create it. Why then did he say "from the heavens"? This was because it was as though it was from the heavens, as if lightning which comes suddenly. In one second, Satan fell beneath the victory of the cross. *Commentary on Tatian's Diatessaron 10.13.*

Christ Heals Us Through the Cross. **MAXIMUS OF TURIN:** Since we possess the Lord Jesus who has freed us by his suffering, let us always look on him and hope for medicine for our wounds from his sign. That is to say, if perhaps the poison of greed spreads in us, we should look to him, and he will heal us. If the malicious desire of the scorpion stings us, we should beg him, and he will cure us. If bites of worldly thoughts tear us, we should ask him, and we will live. These are the spiritual serpents of our souls. The Lord was crucified in order to crush them. He says concerning them, "You will tread on serpents and scorpions, and they will do no harm to you." *Sermon 37.5.*

☙ CLOSING PRAYER

Almighty God, bestow on us the meaning of words, the light of understanding, the nobility of diction and the faith of the true nature. And grant that what we believe we may also speak. *Hilary of Poitiers*

The Worthy Life

THEME

We are called to obey God with all our heart and soul (Deut 30:9-14),
to trust him and learn his ways (Ps 25:1-9). We strive to lead a life worthy of God, bearing fruit in good works, increasing our knowledge (Col
1:1-14; Lk 10:25-37), and showing mercy to strangers.

OPENING PRAYER: *Proper 10*

Almighty God, who resists the proud and gives grace to the humble:
send thy Holy Spirit and let that mind be in us, which was also in
Christ Jesus, that we may be meek and lowly of heart and never by
our foolish pride provoke thine indignation, but, receiving into
humble and thankful hearts the gifts of thy providence and of thy
grace, may thereby be continually refreshed. Teach us not to think
of ourselves more highly than we ought to think; to be modest in
speech, just and merciful in action and benevolent to all. Let us prefer nothing to him, who preferred nothing to our salvation; but
grant us that adhering inseparably to his kingdom and standing
bravely by his cross, we may be found faithful to death, and at the
end may be admitted into the joy of his most blessed presence.
Amen. *Cyprian*

OLD TESTAMENT READING: *Deuteronomy 30:9-14*

REFLECTIONS FROM THE CHURCH FATHERS

Three Instruments. CLEMENT OF ALEXANDRIA: "Anyone who tries to act high-handedly annoys God," says Scripture. For bombast is a spiritual vice. Scripture tells us to repent from it as from the other vices by turning from disharmony and by linking ourselves to a change for the better through the three instruments of mouth, heart and hands. *Stromata 2.19.97.3.*

We Pray for the Kingdom in Ourselves. ORIGEN: The "kingdom of God," according to the word of our Lord and Savior, "comes not with observation"; and "neither shall they say: Behold here, or behold there"—but "the kingdom of God is within us" (for "the Word is very nigh unto" us, "in our mouth and in our heart"). So it is clear that he who prays for the coming of the kingdom of God rightly prays that the kingdom of God might be established and bear fruit and be perfected in himself. *On Prayer 25.1.*

PSALM OF RESPONSE: *Psalm 25:1-9*

NEW TESTAMENT READING: *Colossians 1:1-14*

REFLECTIONS FROM THE CHURCH FATHERS

By Free Choice. PELAGIUS: That man walks worthily of God who pleases him in all things: that is, that he may bear fruit in good work with the knowledge of God. At the same time Paul has expressed something here that is obscure elsewhere, namely, how God gives the power to will and helps and strengthens us by teaching wisdom and granting the grace of understanding, and not by taking away freedom of choice. This is why he prays that they may be filled with the knowledge of God's will in all wisdom and spiritual knowledge, so that they may walk worthily of God in all things. *Pelagius's Commentary on Colossians.*

The Heavenly Spectators. ORIGEN: A great theater is filled with spectators to watch your contests and your summons to martyrdom, just as if we were to speak of a great crowd gathered to watch the contests of athletes supposed to be champions. . . . Thus, the whole world and all of the angels of the right and the left, and all men, those from God's portion and those from the other portions, will serve as spectators when we contest for Christianity. Indeed, either the angels in heaven will cheer us on, and the floods will clap their hands together . . . or, may it not happen, the powers from below, which rejoice in evil, will cheer. *Exhortation to Martyrdom 18.*

Not Through Angels. SEVERIAN OF GABALA: Before the law and in the law the angels served God for our salvation, but God did not bring us to the kingdom through them. But now through our Lord, his only-begotten Son, the kingdom is given to you. *Pauline Commentary from the Greek Church.*

Only Through Christ. AMBROSIASTER: Freed thus from the condition of darkness, that is, plucked from the infernal place, in which we were held by the devil both because of our own and because of Adam's transgression, who is the father of sinners, we were translated by faith into the heavenly kingdom of the Son of God. This was so that he might show us by what love God loved us, when, raising us from deepest hell, he led us into heaven with his true Son. *Commentary on Colossians.*

GOSPEL READING: *Luke 10:25-37*

REFLECTIONS FROM THE CHURCH FATHERS

The Lawyer Misses His Prey. CYRIL OF ALEXANDRIA: He says, "What is written in the law? How do you read?" The lawyer repeated what is in the law. As if to punish his wickedness and reprove his malicious purpose, Christ, knowing all things, says, "You have answered correctly; do this, and you will live." The lawyer missed his prey. He shot off the mark. His wickedness is unsuccessful. The sting of envy ceased. The net of deceit is torn. His sowing bears no fruit, and his toil gains no profit. As some ship overwhelmed by misfortune, he has suffered a bitter shipwreck. *Commentary on Luke, Homily 69.*

All People Are Our Neighbors. JEROME: Some think that their neighbor is their brother, family, relative or their kinsman. Our Lord teaches who our neighbor is in the Gospel parable of a certain man going down from Jerusalem to Jericho. . . . Everyone is our neighbor, and we should not harm anyone. If, on the contrary, we understand our fellow human beings to be only our brother and relatives, is it then permissible to do evil to strangers? God forbid such a belief! We are neighbors, all people to all people, for we have one Father. *Homily on Psalm 14 (15).*

An Allegorical Interpretation of the Good Samaritan. ORIGEN: According to the passage that says, "Be imitators of me, as I too am of Christ," it is possible for us to imitate Christ and to pity those who "have fallen among thieves." We can go to them, bind their wounds, pour in oil and wine, put them on our own animals and bear their burdens. The Son of God encourages us to do things like this. He is speaking not so much to the teacher of the law as to us and to everyone when he says, "Go and do likewise." If we do, we will receive eternal life in Christ Jesus, to whom is glory and power for ages of ages. Amen. *Homilies on the Gospel of Luke 34.3, 9.*

God's Mercy Found in the Sacraments of the Church. AUGUSTINE: Robbers left you half-dead on the road, but you have been found lying there by the passing and kindly Samaritan. Wine and oil have been poured on you. You have received the sacrament of the only-begotten Son. You have been lifted onto his mule. You have believed that Christ became flesh. You have been brought to the inn, and you are being cured in the church. That is where and why I am speaking. This is what I too, what all of us are doing. We are performing the duties of the innkeeper. He was told, "If you spend any more, I will pay you when I return." If only we spent at least as much as we have received! However much we spend, brothers and sisters, it is the Lord's money. *Sermon 179A.7-8.*

The Physician Has Many Remedies. AMBROSE: "And bound up his wounds, pouring in oil and wine." That Physician has many remedies with which he is accustomed to cure. His speech is a remedy. One of his sayings binds up wounds, another treats with oil, another pours in wine. He binds wounds with a stricter rule. He treats with the forgiveness of sins. He stings with the rebuke of judgment as if with wine. *Exposition of the Gospel of Luke 7.75.*

CLOSING PRAYER

I am spent, O my Christ, breath of my life. Perpetual stress and surge, in league together, make long, O long, this life, this business of living. Grappling with foes within and foes without, my soul has lost its beauty, blurred your image. Did ever oak such buffeting from winds or ship receive from waves as I do now? Labor to labor, task succeeds to task. . . . Friendship has bowed and illness wasted me. . . . Do not forsake me, my Strength, I beseech you. When the storms beat hard I may have betrayed you, but let me return to you now. *Gregory of Nazianzus*

Good Works

⊰ THEME

Abraham's hospitality to strangers shows that we should do likewise, never knowing when we are entertaining angels unaware (Gen 18:1-10a). As we try to walk blamelessly, be truthful and do what is right (Ps 15), we acknowledge that we do everything through Jesus Christ (Col 1:15-28). We look to the acts of Mary and Martha and remember that Jesus calls us not only to good works but also to spending time listening and being with Him (Lk 10:38-42).

⊰ OPENING PRAYER: *Proper 11*

It is good that faith comes before reason so that we do not appear to demand our proofs from human beings but rather from the Lord our God. How unfitting it is for us to believe human testimony concerning others and not to believe God's oracles concerning himself! Therefore, let us imitate Abraham so that we may be heirs of the land through the justice of faith, through which he was made an heir of the world. *Ambrose*

⊰ OLD TESTAMENT READING: *Genesis 18:1-10a*

REFLECTIONS FROM THE CHURCH FATHERS

The Lord Appeared in One of the Three. EPHREM THE SYRIAN: Although Abraham ran from the tent toward them as if toward strangers, he ran to receive those strangers with love. His love for strangers was thus proved by the haste with which he ran to meet those strangers. Therefore the Lord, who had just appeared to him at the door of the tent, now appeared to Abraham clearly in one of the three. Abraham then fell down and worshiped him, seeking from him in whom majesty dwells that he condescend to enter his house and bless his dwelling. "If I have found favor in your sight, do not pass by your servant." God did not oppose him, for he said, "Do as you have said." Then Abraham ran to Sarah, telling her to make three measures of wheat, and then he ran to the herd to get a fatted calf. *Commentary on Genesis 15.1.*

Hospitality Has Its Recompense. AMBROSE: Hospitality is a good thing, and it has its recompense: first of all the recompense of human gratitude and then, more importantly, the divine reward. In this earthly abode we are all guests; here we have only a temporary dwelling place. We depart from it in haste. Let us be careful not to be discourteous or neglectful in receiving guests, lest we be denied entrance into the dwelling place of the saints at the end of our life. For this reason, the Savior said in the Gospel, "Make friends for yourselves by means of unrighteous mammon, so that when it fails they may receive you into the eternal habitations." Moreover, while we are in this body, there often arises the necessity of traveling. Therefore that which you will have denied to others, you will have decided against yourself. You must show yourself worthy of that which you will have offered to others. If all decided not to receive guests, where would those who are traveling find rest? Then we would have to abandon human habitations and seek out the dens of the wild beasts. *On Abraham 1.5.34.*

The Mystery of the Trinity. CAESARIUS OF ARLES: He received the three men and served them loaves out of three measures. Why is this, brothers, unless it means the mystery of the Trinity? He also served a calf; not a tough one, but a "good, tender one." Now what is so good and tender as he who humbled himself for us even to death? He himself is that fatted calf which the father killed on receiving his repentant son.

"For God so loved the world that he gave his only-begotten Son." For this reason Abraham went to meet the three men and adored them as one. In the fact that he saw three, as was already said, he understood the mystery of the Trinity; but since he adored them as one, he recognized that there is one God in the three persons. *Sermon 83.4.*

⌐ PSALM OF RESPONSE: *Psalm 15*

⌐ NEW TESTAMENT READING: *Colossians 1:15-28*

REFLECTIONS FROM THE CHURCH FATHERS

The Agent of the Father's Providence. THEODORET OF CYR: Paul did not say, "he was made before all things," but "he is before all things." He is not only the maker of all, but also he manages the care of what he has made and governs the creature, which exists by his wisdom and power. *Interpretation of the Letter to the Romans.*

On Earth and in Heaven, Between Earth and Heaven. BASIL THE GREAT: For the true peace is above. Yet, as long as we were bound to the flesh, we were yoked to many things which troubled us. Seek, then, after peace, a release from the troubles of this world. Possess a calm mind, a tranquil and unconfused state of soul, which is neither agitated by the passions nor drawn aside by false doctrines that challenge by their persuasiveness to an assent, in order that you may obtain "the peace of God which surpasses all understanding and guards your heart." He who seeks after peace, seeks Christ, because "he himself is our peace," who has made two men into one new man, making peace, and "making peace through the blood of his cross, whether on earth or in the heavens." *Homilies 16.10.*

What Is Lacking? CHRYSOSTOM: It seems indeed to be a great thing Paul has said, but it is not based on arrogance, far be it. Rather, Paul's words come from his deep love toward Christ. For he will not have the sufferings to be his own, but his, through the desire to reconcile these persons to him. And what things I suffer, I suffer, he says, on his account. Therefore, don't thank me, but express your gratitude to Christ, for it is he himself who suffers. *Homilies on Colossians 4.*

GOSPEL READING: *Luke 10:38-42*

REFLECTIONS FROM THE CHURCH FATHERS

The Body of Christ Needs Hearers and Doers of the Word. AM-BROSE: Virtue does not have a single form. In the example of Martha and Mary, there is added the busy devotion of the one and the pious attention of the other to the Word of God, which, if it agrees with faith, is preferred even to the very works, as it is written: "Mary has chosen the good portion, which shall not be taken away from her." So let us also strive to have what no one can take away from us, so that not careless but diligent hearing may be granted to us. For even the seeds of the heavenly Word itself are likely to be taken away if they are sowed by the wayside. Let the desire for wisdom lead you as it did Mary. It is a greater and more perfect work. Do not let service divert the knowledge of the heavenly Word. . . . Nor is Martha rebuked in her good serving, but Mary is preferred because she has chosen the better part for herself, for Jesus abounds with many blessings and bestows many gifts. And therefore the wiser chooses what she perceives as foremost. *Exposition of the Gospel of Luke 7.85-86.*

To Listen to the Word Is Eternal. JOHN CASSIAN: To cling always to God and to the things of God—this must be our major effort, this must be the road that the heart follows unswervingly. Any diversion, however impressive, must be regarded as secondary, low-grade and certainly dangerous. Martha and Mary provide a most beautiful scriptural paradigm of this outlook and of this mode of activity. In looking after the Lord and his disciples, Martha did a very holy service. Mary, however, was intent on the spiritual teaching of Jesus, and she stayed by his feet, which she kissed and anointed with the oil of her good faith. . . . In saying "Mary chose the good portion," he was saying nothing about Martha, and in no way was he giving the appearance of criticizing her. Still, by praising Mary he was saying that the other was a step below her. Again, by saying "it will not be taken away from her," he was showing that Martha's role could be taken away from her, since the service of the body can only last as long as the human being is there, whereas the zeal of Mary can never end. *Conference 1.8.*

Mary Sings Alleluias. AUGUSTINE: At present alleluia is for us a traveler's song, but this tiresome journey brings us closer to home and rest where, all our busy activities over and done with, the only thing that will remain will be alleluia. That is the delightful part that Mary chose for herself, as she sat doing nothing but learning and praising, while her sister, Martha, was busy with all sorts of things. Indeed, what she was doing was necessary, but it wasn't going to last. *Sermon 255.1-2.*

☙ CLOSING PRAYER

Eternal God, the refuge of all your children, in our weakness you are our strength, in our darkness our light, in our sorrow our comfort and peace. May we always live in your presence and serve you in our daily lives; through Jesus Christ our Lord. *Boniface*

Petitions

⊰ THEME

God listens to our petitions and prayers (Gen 18:20-32) and he answers (Ps 138). Through his son Jesus Christ we have fullness of life (Col 2:6-19). We offer him our prayers, asking, seeking and knocking (Lk 11:1-13), knowing that he wants only the best for us.

⊰ OPENING PRAYER: *Proper 12*

What more need be said on the duty of prayer? Even the Lord himself prayed. To him be honor and power forever and ever. *Tertullian*

⊰ OLD TESTAMENT READING: *Genesis 18:20-32*

REFLECTIONS FROM THE CHURCH FATHERS

An Example Not to Prejudge. EPHREM THE SYRIAN: It was not that God, who had just said, "their sins were very grave," did not know that they had sinned. This was an example to judges not to prejudge a case, even based on very reliable hearsay. For if he who knows all set aside his knowledge lest he exact vengeance without full knowledge before the trial, how much more should they set aside their ignorance and not effect judgment before the case is heard. *Commentary on Genesis 16.1.*

No Sentence Without Proof. CHRYSOSTOM: Then, to teach the whole human race that even if their sins are exceedingly great and confessed to be such, he does not pronounce sentence before proof is manifest, he says, "I am going down to see if their deeds correspond to the outcry reaching me, so as to know if it is true or not." What is meant by the deliberation of the expression? "I am going down to see if their deeds correspond to the outcry reaching me, so as to know if it is true or not." What is meant by the considerateness of the expression? "I am going down to see." I mean, does the God of all move from place to place? No indeed! It doesn't mean this; instead, as I have often remarked, he wants to teach us by the concreteness of the expression that there is need to apply precision and that sinners are not condemned on hearsay nor is sentence pronounced without proof. *Homilies on Genesis 42.12.*

The Lord Went His Way. ORIGEN: Finally, because no one besides Lot is found who would repent, no one would be converted. He alone is known; he alone is delivered from the conflagration. Neither his children, having been admonished, nor his neighbors nor his next of kin followed him. No one wished to know the mercy of God; no one wished to take refuge in his compassion. Consequently also no one is known. These things indeed have been said against those who "speak iniquity on high." But let us give attention to make our acts such, our manner of life such, that we may be held worthy of knowledge of God; that he may see fit to know us; that we may be held worthy of knowledge of his Son Jesus Christ and knowledge of the Holy Spirit; that we, known by the Trinity, might also deserve to know the mystery of the Trinity fully, completely and perfectly, the Lord Jesus Christ revealing it to us. "His is the glory and sovereignty forever and ever. Amen." *Homilies on Genesis 4.6.*

⁜ PSALM OF RESPONSE: *Psalm 138*

⁜ NEW TESTAMENT READING: *Colossians 2:6-19*

REFLECTIONS FROM THE CHURCH FATHERS

The Nature of the Bond and the Means of Release. AMBROSE: But Christ was sold because he took our condition on himself, not our sins themselves; he is not held to the price of sin, because he himself did not commit sin. And so he made a contract at a price for our debt, not for money for himself; he took away the debtor's bond, set aside the moneylender, freed the debtor. He alone paid what was owed by all. We ourselves were not permitted to escape from bondage. He undertook this on our behalf, so that he might drive away the slavery of the world, restore the liberty of paradise and grant new grace through the honor we received by his sharing of our nature. This is by way of mystery. *Joseph 4.19.*

PELAGIUS: Some say that the bond was, as it were, a written memorial before God of sins. This, then, was destroyed on the cross, when, sins being forgiven, the memorial of transgressions was abolished. *Pelagius's Commentary on the Letter to the Colossians.*

Stripping Off the Demonic Powers. AUGUSTINE: And where the devil could do something, there he met with defeat on every side. While from the cross he received the power to slay the Lord's body outwardly, it was also from the cross that the inward power, by which he held us fast, was put to death. For it came to pass that the chains of many sins in many deaths were broken by the one death of the One who himself had no previous sin that would merit death. And, therefore, for our sake the Lord paid the tribute to death which was not his due, in order that the death which was due might not injure us. For he was not stripped of the flesh by any obligation to any power whatsoever, but he willed his own death, for he who could not die unless he willed doubtless died because he willed; and therefore he openly exposed the principalities and the powers, confidently triumphing over them in himself. *On the Trinity 4.13.17.*

GOSPEL READING: *Luke 11:1-13*

REFLECTIONS FROM THE CHURCH FATHERS

The Privilege and Responsibility of Calling God Father. CYRIL OF ALEXANDRIA: For the Savior said, "When you pray, say, 'Our Father.'" And another of the holy Evangelists adds, "who art in heaven.". . . He commands us, therefore, to take boldness and say in our prayers, "Our Father." We, who are children of earth and slaves and subject by the law of nature to him who created us, call him who is in heaven "Father." Most fittingly, he enables those who pray to understand this also. Since we call God "Father" and have been counted worthy of such a distinguished honor, we must lead holy and thoroughly blameless lives. We must behave as is pleasing to our Father and not think or say anything unworthy or unfit for the freedom that has been bestowed on us. . . . The Savior of all very wisely grants us to call God "Father," that we, knowing well that we are sons of God, may behave in a manner worthy of him who has honored us. He will then receive the supplications that we offer in Christ. *Commentary on Luke, Homily 71.*

Daily Bread Is Spiritual and Physical. JOHN CASSIAN: With "daily" the Evangelist shows that without this bread we cannot live a spiritual life for even a day. When he says "this day," he shows that the bread must be eaten each day. It will not be enough to have eaten yesterday unless we eat similarly today. May our daily poverty encourage us to pour out this prayer at all times, for there is no day on which it is unnecessary for us to eat this bread to strengthen the heart of the person within us. "Daily" can also be understood as referring to our present life. That is, "give us this bread while we linger in this present world." We know that in the time to come you will give it to whoever deserves it, but we ask that you give it to us today. He who has not received it in this life will not be able to partake of it in that next life. *Conference 9.21.*

Seek the Kingdom of God and His Justice. BEDE: If we look into the words of our Lord and Savior that he encourages us to ask God our Father after the example of an earthly parent, we quickly recognize what is the righteousness that can open for us the way to the heavenly kingdom. "Which one of you," he says, "if his son asks his father for bread, will give him a stone? Or if he asks for a fish, will give him a serpent in place of the fish? Or if he asks for an egg, will hand him a scorpion?" This is truly a clear comparison, easy for all hearers to understand. Any human, mortal, weak and still burdened with sinful flesh, does not refuse to give the good things which he possesses, although they are earthly and weak, to the children whom he loves. Our heavenly Father, even more than this man, lavishes the good things of heaven, which do not perish, on those who ask of him and are endowed with fear and love of him. *Homilies on the Gospels 2.14.*

CLOSING PRAYER

Almighty God, who has given us grace at this time with one accord to make our common supplication to thee and has promised that when two or three are gathered together in thy name thou will grant their requests: Fulfill now, O Lord, the desires and petitions of thy humble servants, as may be most expedient for them, granting us in this world knowledge of thy truth, and in the world to come, life everlasting. Amen. *Liturgy of St. John Chrysostom*

True Riches

⊰ THEME

The pleasures and acquisitions we have on earth are fleeting (Eccles 1:2, 12-14, 2:18-23); wisdom and understanding are without price (Ps 49:1-11). With this in mind, we put away our old natures and put on the new (Col 3:1-11), knowing that our time here is also fleeting and our worldly treasures empty of true meaning (Lk 12:13-21).

⊰ OPENING PRAYER: *Proper 13*

O God, who declares thy almighty power most chiefly in showing mercy and pity, mercifully grant to us such a measure of thy grace that we, running the way of thy commandments, may obtain thy gracious promises and be made partakers of thy heavenly treasure; through Jesus Christ our Lord. Amen. *The Gelasian Sacramentary*

⊰ OLD TESTAMENT READING: *Ecclesiastes 1:2, 12-14, 2:18-23*

REFLECTIONS FROM THE CHURCH FATHERS

Vanity Means Futility. GREGORY OF NYSSA: The insubstantial is deemed "futile," that which has existence only in the utterance of the word. No substantial object is simultaneously indicated when the term is used, but it is a kind of idle and empty sound, expressed by syllables in the form of a word, striking the ear at random without meaning, the sort of word people make up for a joke but which means nothing. This then is one sort of futility. Another sense of "futility" is the pointlessness of things done earnestly to no purpose, like the sandcastles children build, and shooting arrows at stars, and chasing the winds, and racing against one's own shadow and trying to step on its head, and anything else of the same kind which we find done pointlessly. All these activities are included in the meaning of "futility." . . . And so also "futility of futilities" indicates the absolute extreme of what is futile. *Homilies on Ecclesiastes 1.*

Rejection of Vanity. JOHN OF DAMASCUS: So, following the teachings of these blessed saints, we utterly renounce these corruptible and perishable things of life, wherein may be found nothing stable or constant, or that continues in one stay. But all things are vanity and vexation of spirit, and many are the changes that they bring in a moment, for they are slighter than dreams and a shadow or the breeze that blows the air. Small and short-lived is their charm, that is after all no charm, but illusion and deception of the wickedness of the world. *Barlaam and Joseph 12.109-10.*

Wealth Perishable and Eternal. ATHANASIUS: If the whole earth is not worth the kingdom of heaven, surely he who has left a few fields leaves nothing, as it were; even if he has given up a house or much gold, he ought not to boast nor grow weary. Moreover, we should consider that if we do not relinquish these things for virtue's sake, we leave them behind later when we die and often, as Ecclesiastes reminds us, to those to whom we do not wish to leave them. Why, then, do we not relinquish them for the sake of virtue, so that we may inherit a kingdom? *Life of St. Anthony 17.*

PSALM OF RESPONSE: *Psalm 49:1-11*

NEW TESTAMENT READING: *Colossians 3:1-11*

REFLECTIONS FROM THE CHURCH FATHERS

A Matter of Focus. BABAI: You should realize that you are walking on the edge of a sharp sword, that you are standing on the edge of a precipice with a ravine on either side. Do not let your thoughts be upset by things here on earth, but keep your mind's gaze on "Jerusalem which is above." "Think of what is above, and not of what is on earth." Ensure that you let go of everything which belongs to this world. *Letter to Cyriacus 55.*

Stripping Off the Old. BASIL THE GREAT: Seek nothing with exterior gold and bodily adornment; but consider the garment as one worthy to adorn him who is according to the image of his Creator, as the apostle says: "Stripping off the old man, and putting on the new, one that is being renewed to perfect knowledge 'according to the image of his Creator.'" And he who has put on "the heart of mercy, kindness, humility, patience and meekness" is clothed within and has adorned the inner man. *Homilies 17.11.*

Reclaim the Image. AMBROSE: Therefore, as on the cross it was not the fullness of the Godhead but our weakness that was brought into subjection, so also will the Son hereafter become subject to the Father in his participation in our nature. This is so that when the lusts of the flesh are brought into subjection the heart may have no concern for riches or ambition or pleasures. The intention is that God may be all to us, if we live after his image and likeness, as far as we can attain to it, through all. The benefit has passed, then, from the individual to the community; for in his flesh he has tamed the nature of all human flesh. . . . Therefore, "laying aside all these," that is those things we read of: "anger, malice, blasphemy, filthy communication"; as he also says below: "Let us, having put off the old man with his deeds, put on the new man, which is renewed in knowledge after the image of him that created him." *Of the Christian Faith 5.14.175-76.*

GOSPEL READING: *Luke 12:13-21*

REFLECTIONS FROM THE CHURCH FATHERS

Surrounded by Wealth, Blind to Charity. CYRIL OF ALEXANDRIA: What does the rich man do, surrounded by a great supply of many blessings beyond all numbering? In distress and anxiety, he speaks the words of poverty. He says, "What should I do?" . . . He does not look to the future. He does not raise his eyes to God. He does not count it worth his while to gain for the mind those treasures that are above in heaven. He does not cherish love for the poor or desire the esteem it gains. He does not sympathize with suffering. It gives him no pain nor awakens his pity. Still more irrational, he settles for himself the length of his life, as if he would also reap this from the ground. He says, "I will say to myself, 'Self, you have goods laid up for many years. Eat, drink, and enjoy yourself.' " "O rich man," one may say, "you have storehouses for your fruits, but where will you receive your many years? By the decree of God, your life is shortened."

"God," it tells us, said to him, "You fool, this night they will require of you your soul. Whose will these things be that you have prepared?" *Commentary on Luke, Homily 89.*

The Bellies of the Poor Are Safer Storehouses Than Our Barns. AUGUSTINE: "The redemption of a man's soul is his riches." This silly fool of a man did not have that kind of riches. Obviously he was not redeeming his soul by giving relief to the poor. He was hoarding perishable crops. I repeat, he was hoarding perishable crops, while he was on the point of perishing because he had handed out nothing to the Lord before whom he was due to appear. How will he know where to look, when at that trial he starts hearing the words "I was hungry and you did not give me food to eat"? He was planning to fill his soul with excessive and unnecessary feasting and was proudly disregarding all those empty bellies of the poor. He did not realize that the bellies of the poor were much safer storerooms than his barns. What he was stowing away in those barns was perhaps even then being stolen away by thieves. But if he stowed it away in the bellies of the poor, it would of course be digested on earth, but in heaven it would be kept all the more safely. The redemption of a man's soul is his riches. *Sermon 36.9.*

The Habit of Good Works. LEO THE GREAT: The devil, even in the midst of our efforts, does not relax his schemes. At certain periods of time, we must take care of the reenergizing of our strength. The mind, concerned with the goods of the present, can rejoice in the temperate weather and the fertile fields. When the fruits are gathered into great barns, it can say to its soul, "You have many good things; eat." It may receive a kind of rebuke from the divine voice and may hear it saying, "Fool, this very night they demand your soul from you. The things you have prepared, whose will they be?" This should be the careful consideration of wise people, that since the days of this life are short and the time uncertain, death should never be unexpected for those who are to die. Those who know that they are mortal should not come to an unprepared end. *Sermon 90.4.1.*

⌘ CLOSING PRAYER

O Lord, who though you were rich yet for our sakes became poor, and has promised in your holy gospel that whatever is done for the least of your brethren you will receive as done to you: give us grace, we humbly beseech you, to be always willing and ready to minister, as you enable us, to the needs of others and to extend the blessings of your kingdom over all the world; to your praise and glory, who are God over all, blessed forever. *Augustine*

By Faith

THEME

God watches over us (Ps 33:12-22) and keeps his promises (Gen 15:1-6). By faith, we trust him for the things we cannot see, just as Abraham did (Heb 11:1-3, 8-16), and anticipate the time when Jesus will come again (Lk 12:32-40).

OPENING PRAYER: *Proper 14*

O God, who has prepared for them that love thee such good things as pass human understanding; pour into our hearts such love toward thee, that we, loving thee above all things, may obtain thy promises, which exceed all that we can desire; through Jesus Christ our Lord. Amen. *The Gelasian Sacramentary*

OLD TESTAMENT READING: *Genesis 15:1-6*

REFLECTIONS FROM THE CHURCH FATHERS

Fear Not, Abraham. CHRYSOSTOM: God said to him, "Don't be afraid, Abram." Notice the extraordinary degree of his care. Why did he say, "Don't be afraid"? Since Abraham had scorned so much wealth by giving little importance to the offerings of the king, God said to him, Have no fear for despising gifts of such value. Do not be distressed on the score of your diminished prosperity. "Don't be afraid." Then to cheer his spirit further, he adds his name to the encouragement by saying, "Don't be afraid, Abram." It proves to be no little help in encouraging a person to invoke the name of the person we are addressing. Then he said, "I am your shield." This phrase is also rich in meaning: I summoned you from the Chaldeans. I led you to this point. I rescued you from the perils of Egypt. I promised once and again to give this land to your descendants. It is I who will be your shield. After daily making you acclaimed by all, I will be your shield—that is, I will struggle in your place. I will be your shield. *Homilies on Genesis 36.10.*

He Desired the Progeny of the Church. AMBROSE: But the holy and prophetic mind is more concerned with an eternal posterity. What Abraham desires is in fact the offspring of wisdom and the inheritance of faith. This is why he says, "What will you give me, since I am about to depart without children?" What he desired was the progeny of the church. What he was requesting was a descendancy that would be not servile but free, not according to the flesh but according to grace. *On Abraham 2.8.48.*

Righteousness from Faith. CHRYSOSTOM: Accordingly let us learn, I beseech you, a lesson for ourselves as well from the patriarch: Let us believe in the words of God and trust in his promise. Let us not apply the yardstick of our own reasoning but give evidence of deep gratitude. This, you see, will succeed in making us also be seen to be righteous and will quickly cause us to attain to the promise made by him. In Abraham's case, however, the promise was made that a complete multitude would develop from his descendants. The effect of the promise was beyond the limits of nature and human logic. Hence faith in God won righteousness for him. In our case, . . . if we are alert enough to see it, he promised much more. We are able in great measure to transcend human reasoning, provided we believe in the power of the One who promises, in order that we may gain also righteousness from faith and attain to the good things promised. *Homilies on Genesis 36.15.*

⁋ PSALM OF RESPONSE: *Psalm 33:12-22*

⁋ NEW TESTAMENT READING: *Hebrews 11:1-3, 8-16*

REFLECTIONS FROM THE CHURCH FATHERS

The Delay of Salvation Strengthened Faith. LEO THE GREAT: Rejoice that whatever the shadows of the Old Testament used to veil beneath the testimonies of prophets has been brought out into the open through the mystery of the Lord's passion. As a result, the various kinds of sacrifices and the different means of purification have come to a halt. Thus, the precept of circumcision, the distinction between foods, the Sabbath rest and the killing of the paschal lamb have ceased, since "the law was given through Moses, but grace and truth came through Jesus Christ." *Sermon 69.2.*

Arouse the Reason in Your Heart. AUGUSTINE: If they are not seen, how can you be convinced that they exist? Well, where do these things that you see come from, if not from one whom you cannot see? Yes, of course you see something in order to believe something, and from what you can see to believe what you cannot see. Please do not be ungrateful to the one who made you able to see; this is why you are able to believe what you are not yet able to see. God gave you eyes in your head, reason in your heart. Arouse the reason in your heart, get the inner inhabitant behind your inner eyes on his feet, let him take to his windows, let him inspect God's creation. *Sermon 126.3.*

Our Mutual Faith. CHRYSOSTOM: Faith needs a generous and vigorous soul, one rising above all things of sense and passing beyond the weakness of human reasonings. For it is not possible to become a believer otherwise than by raising one's self above the common customs of the world. Inasmuch then as the souls of the Hebrews were thoroughly weakened—though they had begun from faith, yet from circumstance, I mean sufferings, affliction, they had afterwards become faint-hearted and of little spirit and were shaken from their position—he encouraged them first indeed from these very things, saying "Recall the former days"; next from the Scripture, saying, "But the righteous shall live by faith"; afterwards from arguments, saying, "But faith is the substance of things hoped for, the evidence of things not seen." And now again from their forefathers, those great and admirable people, as much as saying, "If, where the good things were close at hand, all were saved by faith, much more are we." For when a soul finds one that shares its same sufferings, it is refreshed and recovers breath. This we may see both in the case of faith and in the case of affliction, "that we may be mutually encouraged by each other's faith." For people are very distrustful, cannot place confidence in themselves, are fearful about whatever things they think they possess and have great regard for the opinion of the many. *On the Epistle to the Hebrews 22.1-2.*

GOSPEL READING: *Luke 12:32-40*

REFLECTIONS FROM THE CHURCH FATHERS

Almsgiving Raises Our Hearts into Heaven. PETER CHRYSOLOGUS: All this is what that treasure brings about. Either through almsgiving it raises the heart of a man into heaven, or through greed it buries it in the earth. That is why he said, "For where your treasure is, there your heart will be also." O man, send your treasure on, send it ahead into heaven, or else your God-given soul will be buried in the earth. Gold comes from the depth of the earth—the soul, from the highest heaven. Clearly it is better to carry the gold to where the soul resides than to bury the soul in the mine of the gold. That is why God orders those who will serve in his army here below to fight as men stripped of concern for riches and unencumbered by anything. To these he has granted the privilege of reigning in heaven. *Sermon 22.*

The True Meaning of Loins Girded and Lamps Burning. CYRIL OF

ALEXANDRIA: The girding of our loins signifies the readiness of the mind to work hard in everything praiseworthy. Those who apply themselves to bodily labors and are engaged in strenuous toil have their loins girded. The lamp apparently represents the wakefulness of the mind and intellectual cheerfulness. We say that the human mind is awake when it repels any tendency to slumber off into that carelessness that often is the means of bringing it into subjection to every kind of wickedness. When sunk in stupor, the heavenly light within the mind is liable to be endangered, or even already is in danger from a violent and impetuous blast of wind. Christ commands us to be awake. To this, his disciple also arouses us by saying, "Be awake. Be watchful." Further on, the very wise Paul also says, "Awake, O sleeper, and arise from the dead: and Christ shall give you light." *Commentary on Luke, Homily 92.*

Preparedness the Mark of a Christian. BASIL THE GREAT: What is the mark of a Christian? It is to watch daily and hourly and to stand prepared in that state of total responsiveness pleasing to God, knowing that the Lord will come at an hour that he does not expect. *The Morals 22.*

CLOSING PRAYER

We beseech thee, almighty God, let our souls enjoy this their desire, to be enkindled by thy Spirit, that being filled, as lamps, by the divine gift, we may shine like blazing lights before the presence of thy Son Christ at his coming; through the same Jesus Christ our Lord. Amen. *The Gelasian Sacramentary*

God's Watchful Care

◁ THEME

Wherever we are, God is (Jer 23:23-29). He rescues the weak and the
needy (Ps 82) and helps us to put away our sins (Heb 11:29–12:2) in
anticipation of his coming (Lk 12:49-56).

◁ OPENING PRAYER: *Proper 15*

Alone with none but thee, my God, I journey on my way. What need I
fear, when thou are near, O King of night and day? More safe am I
within thy hand than if a host did round me stand. *Columba*

◁ OLD TESTAMENT READING: *Jeremiah 23:23-29*

REFLECTIONS FROM THE CHURCH FATHERS

Make Your Journey to Jesus. CHRYSOSTOM: From this time on, bid
everything farewell for these five days and begin to observe the feast.
Away with the business of the law courts! Away with the business of
the city council! Away with daily affairs together with their contracts
and business deals! I wish to save my soul. "What does it profit a person if he gains the whole world but suffers the loss of his soul?" The
magi went forth from Persia. You go forth from the affairs of daily
life. Make your journey to Jesus. It is not far to travel if we are willing
to make the trip. We need not cross the sea or climb the mountain
crests. If you prove your piety and full compunction, you can see

him without leaving home, you can tear down the whole wall, remove every obstacle and shorten the length of the journey. As the prophet said, "I am a God near at hand and not a God afar off," and, "The Lord is close to all who call on him in truth." *Against the Anomoeans 6.34.*

God Sees What Is Secret. CYPRIAN: He sees the heart and mind of every person, and he will not judge our deeds alone, but even our words and thoughts. He looks into the minds and the wills and conceptions of all people, in the very lurking places of the heart that are still closed up. *The Lapsed 27.*

The Fullness of God Is Everywhere. AMBROSE: Since we are in his image and likeness, as Scripture says, let us presume to speak, just as he expresses himself in the fullness of his majesty and sees all things—sky, air, earth, sea—embracing all and penetrating each one, so that nothing passes his notice and nothing exists unless it exists in him and depends on him and is full of him, as he says: "I fill heaven and earth, declares the Lord." *Letter 43.*

Come to Christ. AUGUSTINE: Listen to him: "Come to me, all you who labor." You do not put an end to your labor by running away. You prefer to run away from him, do you, not to him? Find somewhere, and run away there. But if you cannot run away from him, for the good reason that he is present everywhere, the next thing to do is to run away to God, who is present right where you are standing. Run away, then. So, you see, you have run away beyond the heavens, he is there. You have gone right down to hell, he is there. Whatever solitary places of the earth you may choose, there he is, the one who said, "I fill heaven and earth." So if he fills heaven and earth and there is nowhere you can run away to from him, do not go on laboring with all that trouble. Run away to him where he is present right beside you, to avoid experiencing him as he comes to judge you. *Sermon 69.4.*

⁌ PSALM OF RESPONSE: *Psalm 82*

⁌ NEW TESTAMENT READING: *Hebrews 11:29–12:2*

REFLECTIONS FROM THE CHURCH FATHERS

The Blood of Christ. JUSTIN MARTYR: The red rope, which the spies sent by Joshua, son of Nun, gave to Rahab the harlot in Jericho, instructing her to tie it to the same window through which he lowered them down to escape their enemies, was a symbol of the blood of Christ. By this blood those of every nationality who were once fornicators and sinful are redeemed, receiving pardon of their past sin and avoiding all sin in the future. *Dialogue with Trypho 111.*

Following After Unseen Rewards. AUGUSTINE: Now this would be no praise for faith, nor would it be faith at all, if people were in believing to follow after rewards that they could see—in other words, if the reward of immortality were bestowed on believers in this present world. *On the Merits and Forgiveness of Sins and On Infant Baptism 2.50.*

An Arena of Struggle and Endurance. JEROME: God has entered us as contestants in a racecourse where it is our lot to be always striving. This place, then, a valley of tears, is not a condition of peace, not a state of security, but an arena of struggle and of endurance. *Homilies on the Psalms 16 (Psalm 83).*

What Is Superfluous, Do Without. CHRYSOSTOM: Why do I trifle in saying these things to people who do not even choose to disregard riches but hold fast to them as though they were immortal, and, if they give a little out of much, think they have done all? This is not almsgiving, for almsgiving is that of the widow, who emptied out "her whole living." But if you do not go on to contribute so much as the widow, at least contribute the whole of your superfluity. *On the Epistle to the Hebrews 28.9-10.*

GOSPEL READING: *Luke 12:49-56*

REFLECTIONS FROM THE CHURCH FATHERS

The Fire of the Gospel and Holy Spirit at Baptism. CYRIL OF ALEXANDRIA: We affirm that the fire that Christ sent out is for humanity's salvation and profit. May God grant that all our hearts be full of this. The fire is the saving message of the gospel and the power of its commandments. We were cold and dead because of sin and in ignorance of him who by nature is truly God. The gospel ignites all of us on earth to a life of piety and makes us fervent in spirit, according to the expression of blessed Paul. Besides this, we are also made partakers of the Holy Spirit, who is like fire within us. We have been baptized with fire and the Holy Spirit. We have learned the way from what Christ says to us. Listen to his words: "Truly I say to you, that except a man be born of water and spirit, he cannot see the kingdom of God." It is the divinely inspired Scripture's custom to give the name of fire sometimes to the divine and sacred words and to the efficacy and power which is by the Holy Spirit by which we are made fervent in spirit. *Commentary on Luke, Homily 94.*

Jesus' Baptism in Blood a Climax of Biblical Baptisms. JOHN OF DAMASCUS: We also are baptized with the perfect baptism of the Lord, which is by water and the Spirit. It is said that Christ baptizes in fire because he poured out the grace of the Spirit on the holy apostles in the form of tongues of fire. The Lord says, "John indeed baptized with water, but you will be baptized with the Holy Spirit and fire, not many days from now." It may also be that he is said to baptize with fire because of the chastising baptism of the fire to come. *Orthodox Faith 4.9.*

Parents Are Not to Be Loved More Than God. AMBROSE: Spiritual understanding is at work in every passage of the Gospels. In the present case, fearing that the rigidity of a simple explanation may offend someone, the sequence of the sense is to be qualified by spiritual depth. . . .

We will believe that the Lord took care to advise reverence for the God-head at the same time as the grace of piety. He said, "You will love the Lord your God, and you will love your neighbor." Is the present so changed as to erase the names of close kin and set affections at variance? *Exposition of the Gospel of Luke 7.134-36.*

⸎ CLOSING PRAYER

Lord God, open my heart and illuminate it with the grace of your Holy Spirit. By this grace may I always seek to do what is pleasing to you; direct my thoughts and feelings so that I may at last come to the unending joys of heaven. Thus on earth may I keep your commandments, and so be worthy of your everlasting reward. *Bede*

Merciful and Just

THEME

When we call out to God, he answers (Is 58:9b-14). Our God is merciful and just, slow to anger, steadfast in love (Ps 103:1-8). God is a consuming fire; his kingdom cannot be shaken (Heb 12:18-29). Through his power, he heals all infirmities (Lk 13:10-17).

OPENING PRAYER: *Proper 16*

O most merciful God, incline thy loving ears to our prayers, and illuminate the hearts of those called by thee with the grace of the Holy Spirit, that they may be enabled worthily to minister to thy mysteries, and to love thee with an everlasting love and to attain everlasting joys, through Jesus Christ our Lord. Amen. *Charlemagne, Gallican Collect*

OLD TESTAMENT READING: *Isaiah 58:9b-14*

REFLECTIONS FROM THE CHURCH FATHERS

God Hears Us the Moment We Call. CHRYSOSTOM: Were he distant from us in place, you might well doubt, but if God is present everywhere, to him that strives and is in earnest he is near. . . . What father would ever be thus obedient to his offspring? What mother is there, so ready and continually standing, in case her children call her? There is not one, no father, no mother, but God stands continually waiting . . .

and never, when we have called as we ought, has he refused to hear. *Homilies on the Gospel of Matthew 54.8.*

We Are Only Stewards. GREGORY OF NAZIANZUS: My father actually treated his own property as if it were another's, of which he was but the steward, relieving poverty as far as he could and expending not only his superfluities but his necessities—a manifest proof of love for the poor. . . . For he thought it much better to be generous even to the undeserving for the sake of the deserving than from fear of the undeserving to deprive those who were deserving. *On the Death of His Father, Oration 18.20-21.*

The Soul as a City. CYRIL OF ALEXANDRIA: The prophetic word comes to us through two further metaphors, and the beautiful form of hidden ideas is displayed. For it is about a deserted town and its defenseless state that a form of words is molded. It declares, your deserts will be lived in perpetually, that is, you will not be naked of good thoughts indwelling your heart, nor will you be defenseless or unguarded and insecure. For Christ will be your enduring foundation and support, and like a city you will have countless people dwelling there. For the souls of the saints are full of holy words and thoughts. And many will come to it as the level of perfection, running up and down, declaring it to be full of good things. And you will be called a builder of walls. . . . You must know that there are evil and contrary powers invading the vulnerable soul, giving rise to awful desires and in a despotic way carrying off whatever they want and strolling round the barren garden. But they will stop this interference when a wall is erected, that is, the divine fear set up within the soul. *Commentary on Isaiah 5.4.58.12.*

✦ **PSALM OF RESPONSE:** *Psalm 103:1-8*

✦ **NEW TESTAMENT READING:** *Hebrews 12:18-29*

REFLECTIONS FROM THE CHURCH FATHERS

Jesus Came to Raise Adam. AMBROSE: The Lord Jesus came to raise up Adam; Abel also was raised up, for his offerings were pleasing to God. The Lord Jesus offered his own self, that is, the firstlings of his own body, in the sprinkling of blood that speaks better than the blood of Abel spoke on the earth. *The Prayer of Job and David 5.9.32.*

Mercy Speaks a Better Word Than the Blood of Abel. CHRYSOS-TOM: The work of mercy is, as it were, a most excellent art and a protector of those who labor at it. For it is dear to God and ever stands near God, readily asking favor for whomsoever it will, if only it be not wronged by us. . . . So, if it is pure, it gives great confidence to those who offer it up. It intercedes even for those who have offended, so great is its power, even for those who have sinned. It breaks the chains, disperses the darkness, quenches the fire, kills the worm, drives away the gnashing of teeth. Nothing is so characteristic of a Christian as mercy. There is nothing that both unbelievers and all people so admire as when we are merciful. For often we are ourselves also in need of this mercy and say to God, "Have mercy on us, according to your steadfast love." Let us begin first ourselves, or rather it is not we that begin first, for God has already shown his mercy toward us. At least let us follow second. For if people have mercy on a merciful person, even if that person has done innumerable wrong, so much more does God. *On the Epistle to the Hebrews 32.7.*

The Steadfastness to Come. THEODORE OF MOPSUESTIA: Quite rightly on the basis of the prophetic verse does he establish the instability of the present order and the steadfastness of the things which shall be later. For the "shaking" shows that he is proclaiming the alteration of the present order exactly as it will be. And by adding the word *once* he shows that what will be afterwards cannot be changed. *Commentary on Hebrews 12.26.*

GOSPEL READING: *Luke 13:10-17*

REFLECTIONS FROM THE CHURCH FATHERS

The Infirm Woman Like a Vine. AMBROSE: The members of the church are similar to this vine. They are planted with the root of faith and held in check by the shoots of humility. . . . He placed in the church a tower of apostles, prophets and doctors who are ready to defend the peace of the church. He dug around it when he had freed it from the burden of earthly anxieties. Nothing burdens the mind more than concern for the world and lust for either wealth or power. An example of this is in the Gospel. We can read the story of the woman "who had sickness caused by a spirit, and she was bent over so that she was unable to look upwards." In fact, her soul was bent over. It inclined to earthly rewards and did not possess heavenly grace. Jesus saw her and addressed her. She immediately laid aside her earthly burdens. These people also were burdened with lusts. He addressed them in these words, "Come to me, all you who labor and are burdened, and I will give you rest." The soul of that woman breathed once more and stood up like a vine around which the soil has been dug and cleared. *Six Days of Creation 3.50.*

Jesus Overcomes Death and Destruction. CYRIL OF ALEXANDRIA: The incarnation of the Word and his assumption of human nature took place for the overthrow of death, destruction and the envy harbored against us by the wicked Serpent, who was the first cause of evil. This plainly is proved to us by facts themselves. He set free the daughter of Abraham from her protracted sickness, calling out and saying, "Woman, you are loosed from your infirmity." A speech most worthy of God, and full of supernatural power! With the royal inclination of his will, he drives away the disease. He also lays his hands on her. It says that she immediately was made straight. It is now also possible to see that his holy flesh bore in it the power and activity of God. It was his own flesh, and not that of some other Son beside him, distinct and separate from him, as some most impiously imagine. *Commentary on Luke, Homily 96.*

The Synagogue Leader Took the Sabbath Literally. AUGUSTINE: The whole human race, like this woman, was bent over and bowed down to the ground. Someone already understands these enemies. He cries out against them and says to God, "They have bowed my soul down." The devil and his angels have bowed the souls of men and women down to the ground. He has bent them forward to be intent on temporary and earthly things and has stopped them from seeking the things that are above. Since that is what the Lord says about the woman whom Satan had bound for eighteen years, it was now time for her to be released from her bondage on the sabbath day. Quite unjustly, they criticized him for straightening her up. Who were these, except people bent over themselves? Since they quite failed to understand the very things God had commanded, they regarded them with earthbound hearts. They used to celebrate the sacrament of the sabbath in a literal, material manner and did not notice its spiritual meaning. *Sermon 162B.*

CLOSING PRAYER

O Lord, give us we beseech you in the name of Jesus Christ your Son our Lord, that love which can never cease, that will kindle our lamps but not extinguish them, that they may burn in us and enlighten others. Do you, O Christ, our dearest Savior, yourself kindle our lamps that they may evermore shine in your temple and receive unquenchable light from you that will enlighten our darkness and lessen the darkness of the world. *Columba*

Right Paths

⊣ THEME

God wants us to follow him and be united with other believers (Jer 2:4-13). He also wants for us to be generous and just (Ps 112), free from the love of money, full of hospitality, good works (Heb 13:1-8, 15-16) and humility (Lk 14:1, 7-14).

⊣ OPENING PRAYER: *Proper 17*

Be present, O Lord, to our supplications, nor let thy merciful pity be far from thy servants; heal our wounds, forgive our sins; that, not being severed from thee by our iniquities, we may evermore cleave to thee and have fellowship one with another; through Jesus Christ our Lord and Master. Amen. *The Gelasian Sacramentary*

⊣ OLD TESTAMENT READING: *Jeremiah 2:4-13*

REFLECTIONS FROM THE CHURCH FATHERS

Do Not Abandon the Assembly of the Faithful. DIDASCALIA: Those who are not saved always are taking care of those things that do not profit or benefit them in any way. So what kind of excuse is there for a Christian who withdraws from the assembly of the church? Such a person does not even imitate the Gentiles but by reason of his absence grows indifferent and careless. He stands aloof and does evil. The Lord said, . . . You have not walked in my statutes or kept my ordinances, and have not even acted according to the rules of the nations that are all around you, "you were more corrupt than they in all your ways." How, then, shall the indifferent excuse himself, since he has no zeal for the assembly of the church? If anyone takes the occasion of worldly business to withdraw, let him know this: the trades of the faithful are called works of surplus, for their true work is religion. Pursue your trades, therefore, as a work of surplus, for your sustenance, but let your true work be religion. *Didascalia 13 (2.60).*

The Church Has the Spirit of God. IRENAEUS: For where the church is, there is the Spirit of God. Where the Spirit of God is, there is the church and every kind of grace. The Spirit is truth. *Against Heresies 3.24.1.*

Self-Deception of Sin. AUGUSTINE: Iniquity lies to itself either by corrupting the nature you have made and ordained or by perverting it. It lies to itself when it practices an immoderate use of things permitted or when it burns for things forbidden to that use which is against nature. It lies to itself when convicted, raging with heart and voice against you as it kicks against the goads, or when—breaking through the pale of human society—they audaciously rejoice in private cliques or divisions on the basis of whether they have been pleased or offended. These things happen whenever you are abandoned and whenever, from a self-willed pride, they choose to align themselves instead with something false that they cherish instead of you, O Fountain of Life, the one, true Creator and Ruler of the universe. *Confessions 3.8.16.*

The Body Corrupted by Sin. JEROME: O blessed change! Once the body wept but now laughs forevermore. Once it desired the broken cisterns of which the prophet speaks, but now it has been satisfied in the Lord, the fountain of life. *Letter 108.*

The "Pit" and the "Well." BASIL THE GREAT: "He has opened a pit and dug it." We do not find the name of "pit" ever assigned in the divine

Scriptures to something good or a "well" of water to something bad. That into which Joseph was thrown by his brothers is a pit. There is a slaughter "from the firstborn of Pharaoh to the firstborn of the captive woman that was in prison." In the Psalms, "I am counted among those who go down to the pit." In Jeremiah it is said, "They have forsaken me, the fountain of living water, and have dug to themselves cisterns, broken cisterns that can hold no water." *Homilies on the Psalms 11.8.*

PSALM OF RESPONSE: *Psalm 112*

NEW TESTAMENT READING: *Hebrews 13:1-8, 15-16*

REFLECTIONS FROM THE CHURCH FATHERS

He Forbade Not Possessions. THEODORET OF CYR: He forbade not possessions but the love of money, from which greed springs. *Interpretation of Hebrews 13.*

Release Your Heart from Money. AUGUSTINE: So keep a moderate amount of money for temporal uses; treat it as journey money, with the end in view stated in the text. Notice above all what he put first: "Free from love of money," he says, put your hand in the purse in such a way that you release your heart from it. *Sermon 177.3.*

Remaining What He Was and Always Will Be. CYRIL OF ALEXANDRIA: The Son of God, assuming our likeness and becoming human, not taking up what he was but taking on what he was (i.e., the divine condition) effects our salvation. For he remains, as Paul put it, the same yesterday and today and forever, without undergoing any change in his divinity by reason of his incarnation but remaining what he was and will always be. *Easter Homily 1.6.*

Bear All Things Thankfully. CHRYSOSTOM: Let us bear all things thankfully, be it poverty, be it disease, be it anything else whatever, for

God alone knows the things expedient for us, "for we do not know how to pray as we ought." We, then, who do not know even how to ask for what is fitting unless we have received of the Spirit, let us take care to offer up thanksgiving for all things, and let us bear all things nobly. Are we in poverty? Let us give thanks. Are we falsely accused? Let us give thanks. When we suffer affliction, let us give thanks. This brings us near to God. *On the Epistle to the Hebrews 33.8.*

GOSPEL READING: *Luke 14:1, 7-14*

REFLECTIONS FROM THE CHURCH FATHERS

Jesus Calls Us to Be Humble, Modest and Praiseworthy. CYRIL OF ALEXANDRIA: "When," he says, "a man more honorable than you comes, he that invited you and him will say, 'Provide a place for this man.'" Oh, what great shame is there in having to do this! It is like a theft, so to speak, and the restitution of the stolen goods. He must restore what he has seized because he had no right to take it. The modest and praiseworthy person, who without fear of blame might have claimed the dignity of sitting among the foremost, does not seek it. He yields to others what might be called his own, that he may not even seem to be overcome by empty pride. Such a one shall receive honor as his due. He says, "He shall hear him who invited him say, 'Come up here.'" . . . If anyone among you wants to be set above others, let him win it by the decree of heaven and be crowned by those honors that God bestows. Let him surpass the many by having the testimony of glorious virtues. The rule of virtue is a lowly mind that does not love boasting. It is humility. The blessed Paul also counted this worthy of all esteem. He writes to those who eagerly desire saintly pursuits, "Love humility." *Commentary on Luke, Homily 102.*

The Humble and the Proud. AUGUSTINE: There are humble religious, and there are proud religious. The proud ones should not promise themselves the kingdom of God. The place to which dedicated chastity leads is certainly higher, but the one who exalts himself will be humbled. Why seek the higher place with an appetite for the heights, when you can make it simply by holding on to lowliness? If you exalt yourself, God throws you down. If you cast yourself down, God lifts you up. One may not add to or subtract from the Lord's pronouncement. *Sermon 354.8.*

Jacob's Ladder the Place of Exaltation or Humiliation. **BENEDICT OF NURSIA:** The Scripture asserts that "everyone that exalts himself will be humbled, and he that humbles himself will be exalted." . . . If we want to attain to true humility and come quickly to the top of that heavenly ascent to which we can only mount by lowliness in this present life, we must ascend by good works. We must erect the mystical ladder of Jacob, where angels ascending and descending appeared to him. Ascent and descent mean that we go downward when we exalt ourselves and rise when we are humbled. The ladder represents our life in this world, which our Lord erects to heaven when our heart is humbled. The sides of the ladder represent our soul and body, sides between which God has placed several rungs of humility and discipline, whereby we are to ascend if we would answer his call. *Rule of St. Benedict 7.*

ᛞ CLOSING PRAYER

O God, who resists the proud and gives grace to the humble: grant us the virtue of true humility which your only-begotten Son himself gave us the perfect example; that we may never offend you by our pride and be rejected by our self-assertion; through Jesus Christ our Lord. *The Leonine Sacramentary*

Called to Obedience

⌘ THEME

The Lord calls us to obedience (Deut 30:15-20), to delight in his laws and to meditate on them day and night (Ps 1). Even when it is difficult (Philem 1-21), we are to put Christ above all else (Lk 14:25-33).

⌘ OPENING PRAYER: *Proper 18*

Grant thy servants, O God, to be set on fire with thy Spirit, strengthened by thy power, illuminated by thy splendor, filled with thy grace, and to go forward by thine aid. Give them, O Lord, a right faith, perfect love, true humility. Grant, O Lord, that there may be in us simple affection, brave patience, preserving obedience, perpetual peace, a pure mind, a right and honest heart, a good will, a holy conscience, spiritual strength, a life unspotted and unblameable; and after having manfully finished our course, may we be enabled happily to enter thy kingdom; through Jesus Christ our Lord. Amen. *The Gallican Sacramentary*

⌘ OLD TESTAMENT READING: *Deuteronomy 30:15-20*

REFLECTIONS FROM THE CHURCH FATHERS

Interior Balance. **BASIL THE GREAT:** There is a certain balance constructed in the interior of each of us by our Creator, on which it is possible to judge the nature of things. "I have set before you life and death, good and evil," two natures contrary to each other. Balance them against each other in your own tribunal. *Homily on Psalm 61.4.*

The Nature of Life and Death. AMBROSE: Let us ponder the nature of life and of death. Life is the enjoyment of the gift of breath, death the deprivation of it. Further, this gift of breath is considered by most people as a good. And so life is this, the enjoyment of goods, but death is the divestiture of them. And Scripture says, "Behold, I have set before your face life and death, good and evil," for it calls life good and death evil and attributes to each its proper deserts. *Death as a Good 1.2.*

Make the Right Choice. CAESARIUS OF ARLES: Behold, man, you have before you "water and fire, life and death, good and evil," heaven and hell, the legitimate king and a cruel tyrant, the false sweetness of the world and the true blessedness of paradise. Power is given to you through the grace of Christ: "Stretch forth your hand to whichever you choose." "Choose life, that you may live"; leave the broad way on the left which drags you to death and cling to the narrow path on the right which happily leads you to life. Do not allow the wideness of that road on the left to keep you or give you pleasure. *Sermon 151.5.*

What You Grasp You Have Forever. SALVIAN THE PRESBYTER: For since, as it is written, man is confronted equally with life and death and stretches out his hand toward what he wants, it is necessary that whatever a man grasps with his hands in time he must possess forever in eternity. What here he cleaves to in affection, he must in the future cleave to forever, with his will and mind wholly fixed on it. *Four Books of Timothy to the Church 1.1.7.*

⁙ PSALM OF RESPONSE: *Psalm 1*

⁙ NEW TESTAMENT READING: *Philemon 1-21*

REFLECTIONS FROM THE CHURCH FATHERS

Speaking from Love. AMBROSIASTER: Though Paul is writing to a layman, he nonetheless does not exert his apostolic authority in order to issue orders but respects Philemon as a faithful Christian and of the same age, one who is bound to Christ as he is. *Commentary on Paul's Epistles.*

The Gospel First. JEROME: I must stand in awe of the apostle's greatness of soul here, as a man whose mind burns for Christ. He is held in prison, he is constrained by chains, in physical misery, separated from dear ones, plunged into prison darkness, yet he does not feel the injury, he is not crucified with sadness. Rather, he knows nothing else than to ponder the gospel of Christ. *Commentary on Philemon.*

Careful Groundwork. THEODORET OF CYR: The idea that Paul could have kept Onesimus with him to minister to him in Philemon's place shows the great power of the gospel: that the servant is made equal to the master. *Interpretation of the Letter to Philemon.*

Two Good Effects. AUGUSTINE: And addressing himself to Philemon, Paul says: "that your kindness may not be as it were of necessity, but voluntary." . . . Now wherever there is the express statement not to do this or that, and whenever the performance of the will is required to do or refrain from some action, in keeping with God's commandments, that is sufficient proof of the free choice of the will. Let no one, therefore, blame God in his heart whenever he sins, but let him impute the sin to himself. *Grace and Free Will 2.4.*

Spiritual Grace. CHRYSOSTOM: Paul writes at once movingly and with subtle spiritual grace. The idea is that since Paul did not refuse to extend his credit, how ironic it would be if Philemon should refuse to receive Onesimus! The mention of this deserved favor would both shame Philemon into compliance and bring Onesimus out of trouble. *Homilies on Philemon 3.*

GOSPEL READING: *Luke 14:25-33*

REFLECTIONS FROM THE CHURCH FATHERS

Jesus Permits Us to Love Family but Not More Than God. CYRIL OF ALEXANDRIA: He says, "He that loves father or mother more than me is not worthy of me. He that loves son or daughter more than me is not worthy of me." By adding "more than me," it is plain that he permits us to love, but not more than we love him. He demands our highest affection for himself and that very correctly. The love of God in those who are perfect in mind has something in it superior both to the honor due to parents and to the natural affection felt for children. *Commentary on Luke, Homily 105.*

The Form of Martyrdom Amid Civil Peace Is the Death of Self-Will. SYMEON THE NEW THEOLOGIAN: I heard his holy voice speaking to all without distinction. "He who does not leave father and mother and brothers and all that he possesses and take up his cross and follow me is not worthy of me." I learned from Scripture and from experience itself that the cross comes at the end for no other reason than that we must endure trials and tribulations and finally voluntary death itself. In times past, when heresies prevailed, many chose death through martyrdom and various tortures. Now, when we through the grace of Christ live in a time of profound and perfect peace, we learn for sure that cross and death consist in nothing else than the complete putting to death of self-will. He who pursues his own will, however slightly, will never be able to observe the law of Christ the Savior. *Discourses 20.1.*

Virtue Built on the Foundations of the Tower. GREGORY OF NYSSA: The Gospel somewhere says that a person who begins to build a tower but stops with the foundations and never completes it is ridiculous. What do we learn from this parable? We learn that we should work to bring every aspiration to a conclusion, completing the work of God by an elaborate building up of his commandments. One stone does not make a complete tower, nor does one commandment bring the perfection of the soul to its desired measure. It is necessary to both erect the foundation and, as the apostle says, "to lay on it a foundation of gold and precious stones." That is what the products of the commandments are called by the prophet when he says, "I have loved your commandment more than gold and much precious stone." *On Virginity 18.*

CLOSING PRAYER

The chief service I owe you in my life, as I well know, O God, all-powerful Father, is that every word and thought of mind should speak of you. The power of speech that you have bestowed on me can give me no greater pleasure than to serve you by preaching and to show an ignorant world . . . what you are: the Father, the Father whose only Son is God. But in saying this, I am merely saying what I want to do. If I am actually to do it, I must ask you for your help and mercy, ask you to fill with wind the sails I have hoisted for you and to carry me forward on my course—to breathe, that is, your Spirit into my faith and my confession of it. *Hilary of Poitiers*

Precious to Him

⁌ THEME

Like Moses, we should be persistent in prayer (Ex 32:7-14), asking God to cleanse us from sin and teach us wisdom (Ps 51:1-11). Jesus Christ came into the world to forgive sinners; praise and thank God for his mercy and grace (1 Tim 1:12-17). Each of us is precious to him (Lk 15:1-10).

⁌ OPENING PRAYER: *Proper 19*

O Lord, the helper of the helpless, the hope of those who are past hope, the savior of the tempest-tossed, the harbor of the voyagers, the physician of the sick; you know each soul and our prayer, each home and its need; become to each one of us what we most dearly require, receiving us all into your kingdom, making us children of light; and pour on us your peace and love, O Lord our God. Amen. *Liturgy of St. Basil the Great*

⁌ OLD TESTAMENT READING: *Exodus 32:7-14*

REFLECTIONS FROM THE CHURCH FATHERS

The Power of Intercession. **EPHREM THE SYRIAN:** When he wished that the fig tree be uprooted, the event was similar to that earlier one, when the Father said to Moses, "Permit me to destroy the people." He thus gave him a reason to intercede with him. Here too he showed the vinedresser that he wished to uproot it. The vinedresser made known his plea, and the merciful one showed his pity, that if, in a further year, the fig tree did not yield fruit, it would be uprooted. *Commentary on Tatian's Diatessaron 14.27.*

Persistence in Prayer. JEROME: Moses resisted God and prevented him from destroying his people when God said to him, "Let me alone, that I may strike this people." Just see the power of Moses! What does God say to him? Let me alone; you are compelling me, your prayers, as it were, restrain me; your prayers hold back my hand. I shoot an arrow; I hurl a javelin; and your prayers are the shield of the people. Let me alone that I might strike down this people. Along with this, consider the compassionate kindness of God. When he says, "Let me alone," he shows that if Moses will continue to importune him, he will not strike. If you, too, will not let me alone, I shall not strike; let me alone, and I shall strike. In other words, what does he say? Do not cease your persistent entreaty, and I shall not strike. *Homilies on the Psalms 26.*

Does God Change His Mind? AUGUSTINE: Though we sometimes hear the expression "God changed his mind" or even read in the figurative language of Scripture that "God repented," we interpret these sayings not in reference to the decisions determined on by almighty God but in reference to the expectations of man or to the order of natural causes. *City of God 14.11.*

⁂ PSALM OF RESPONSE: *Psalm 51:1-11*

⁂ NEW TESTAMENT READING: *1 Timothy 1:12-17*

REFLECTIONS FROM THE CHURCH FATHERS

Let Your Life Be Openly Exposed. CHRYSOSTOM: If you have sinned and God has pardoned your sin, receive your pardon and give thanks. But do not be forgetful of your sin. It is not that you should fret over the thought of it, but that you may school your soul not to grow lax or relapse again into the same snares. *Homilies Concerning the Statues 12.1.*

Free to Fall, Helpless to Rise. AUGUSTINE: It is by the grace of God, you see, that we are saved from our sins, in which we are languishing. God alone is the medicine that cures the soul. The soul was well able to injure itself but quite unable to cure itself. In the body, too, after all, people have it in their power to get sick, but not equally in their power to get better. I mean, if they exceed the proper limits, and live self-indulgent lives and do all the things that undermine the constitution and are injurious to health, the day comes, if that's what they want, when they fall sick. When they've so fallen, though, they don't get better. In order to fall sick, you see, they apply themselves to self-indulgence. But in order to get better, they must apply the doctor's services to their health. . . . And so it goes with the soul. *Sermon 278.1-2.*

A Great Invalid. AUGUSTINE: There was no reason for Christ the Lord to come, except to save sinners. Eliminate diseases, eliminate wounds, and there is no call for medicine. If a great doctor has come down from heaven, a great invalid must have been lying very sick throughout the whole wide world. This invalid is the whole human race. *Sermon 175.1.*

Still Making a Beginning. ISAAC OF NINEVEH: We bring to mind how the holy apostle Paul recounts his transgressions and puts his soul in the last and nethermost place, saying, "Jesus Christ came into the world to save sinners, of whom I am chief." . . . When and at what time did he say this? After great struggles, after mighty works, after the preaching of the gospel of Christ which he proclaimed throughout the whole world, after continual deaths and manifold tribulations which he suffered from the Jews and from the heathen. Even then he saw himself as only making a beginning. He was of the opinion not merely that he had not yet attained to purity of soul but that he would not even number himself among the disciples of Christ, as was fitting. *An Epistle to Abba Symeon of Caesarea.*

GOSPEL READING: *Luke 15:1-10*

REFLECTIONS FROM THE CHURCH FATHERS

The Lord's Patience for the Lost. TERTULLIAN: There is a breadth of patience in our Lord's parables, the patience of the shepherd that makes him seek and find the straying sheep. Impatience would readily take no account of a single sheep, but patience undertakes the wearisome search. He carries it on his shoulders as a patient bearer of a forsaken sinner. In the case of the prodigal son, it is the patience of his father that welcomes, clothes, feeds and finds an excuse for him in the face of the impatience of his angry brother. The one who perished is rescued, because he embraced repentance. Repentance is not wasted because it meets up with patience! *On Patience 12.*

The Sheep Restored to Verdant Fields. PRUDENTIUS:
When one ailing sheep lags behind the others
And loses itself in the sylvan mazes,
Tearing its white fleece on the thorns and briars,
Sharp in the brambles,
Unwearied the Shepherd, that lost one seeking,
Drives away the wolves and on his strong shoulders
Brings it home again to the fold's safekeeping,
Healed and unsullied.
He brings it back to the green fields and meadows,
Where no thorn bush waves with its cruel prickles,
Where no shaggy thistle arms trembling branches
With its tough briars.
But where palm trees grow in the open woodland,
Where the lush grass bends its green leaves, and laurels

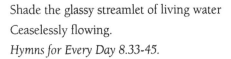

Shade the glassy streamlet of living water
Ceaselessly flowing.
Hymns for Every Day 8.33-45.

The Father Confers on Us the Wealth of the Kingdom. AMBROSE: The woman did not idly rejoice to find her coin. The coin, having the image of the emperor, is not ordinary. The image of the King is the register of the church. We are sheep. Let us pray that he would be pleased to place us beside the water of rest. We are sheep. Let us seek pastures. We are coins. Let us have a price. We are sons. Let us hurry to the Father. Let us not fear because we have squandered the inheritance of spiritual dignity that we received on earthly pleasures. Since the Father conferred on the Son the treasure that he had, the wealth of faith is never made void. Although he has given all, he possesses all and does not lose what he has bestowed. Do not fear that perhaps he will not receive you, for the Lord has no pleasure in the destruction of the living. Already meeting you on the way, he falls on your neck, "for the Lord sets the fallen right." He will give you a kiss, that is, the pledge of piety and love. He will order the robe, ring and the shoes to be brought. You still dread harshness, but he has restored dignity. You are terrified of punishment, but he offers a kiss. You fear reproach, but he prepares a banquet. *Exposition of the Gospel of Luke 7.211-12.*

CLOSING PRAYER

Keep us, O Lord, from the vain strife of words, and grant to us a constant profession of the truth. Preserve us in the faith, true and undefiled, so that we may ever hold fast that which we professed when we were baptized into the name of the Father, and of the Son and of the Holy Spirit; that we may have you for our Father, that we may abide in your Son and in the fellowship of the Holy Spirit; through the same Jesus Christ our Lord. Amen. *Hilary of Poitiers*

God Draws Us Near

⊰ THEME

Even in the depths of grief (Jer 8:18–9:1) we can trust the Lord to draw
near to us (Ps 113). Jesus gave himself as a ransom for many (1 Tim
2:1-7); in return, we are to be thankful for the forgiveness of sins, great
and small, and serve him faithfully (Lk 16:1-13).

⊰ OPENING PRAYER: *Proper 20*

O God, forasmuch as without thee we are not able to please thee, mercifully grant that thy Holy Spirit may in all things direct and rule our
hearts; through Jesus Christ our Lord. Amen. *The Gelasian Sacramentary*

⊰ OLD TESTAMENT READING: *Jeremiah 8:18–9:1*

REFLECTIONS FROM THE CHURCH FATHERS

The Healing Balm of the Law and Gospel. BASIL THE GREAT: Jesus
Christ came into the world to save sinners. "O come, let us worship and
fall down; let us weep before him." The Word who invited us to repentance calls aloud, "Come to me, all you who labor and are heavy laden,
and I will give you rest." There is, then, a way of salvation, if we want
it. "Death in his might has swallowed up, but again the Lord has wiped
away tears from off all faces" of those who repent. The Lord is faithful
in all his words. He does not lie when he says, "Though your sins are
scarlet, they shall be as white as snow. Though they are red like crim-

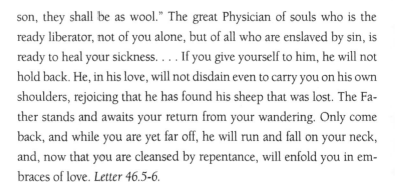

son, they shall be as wool." The great Physician of souls who is the ready liberator, not of you alone, but of all who are enslaved by sin, is ready to heal your sickness. . . . If you give yourself to him, he will not hold back. He, in his love, will not disdain even to carry you on his own shoulders, rejoicing that he has found his sheep that was lost. The Father stands and awaits your return from your wandering. Only come back, and while you are yet far off, he will run and fall on your neck, and, now that you are cleansed by repentance, will enfold you in embraces of love. *Letter 46.5-6.*

Let Us Confess Our Sins. HORSIESI: What should we do? Let us allow a spring of tears to flow every day, day and night. Let us, too, say with the weeping Jeremiah, the great prophet, "Who will give some water to my head, and a spring of tears to my eyes? I would weep for my sins day and night." Let us first of all confess our sins before this . . . which is full of terror and trembling tears. Let us invoke the goodness and mercy of our God, while we are in this exile of tears, before death overtakes us. *Instructions 1.3.*

An Appropriate Time for Lamentation. CHRYSOSTOM: Let us collect ourselves, I exhort you. There are daily wars, submersions of towns, innumerable destructions all around us. . . . We all make our hands ready for unjust gains and not for helping others. We are all ready to plunder, but no one is ready to protect. Each one of us has much anxiety over how he may add to his wealth. No one has anxiety over how he may save his own soul. One fear possesses all, that we should not become poor. No one is in anguish and trembling out of fear that we should fall into hell. These things call for lamentation, these call for accusation, for eternal damnation. I do not wish to speak of these things, but I am constrained by my grief. Forgive me. I am forced by sorrow to utter many things, even those that I do not wish to say. I see that our wound is grievous, that our calamity is beyond comfort, that woes have overtaken us that exceed the consolation. We are undone. "O that my head were waters and my eyes a fountain of tears," that I might lament. Let us weep, beloved, let us groan. *On the Epistle to the Hebrews 23.8-9.*

PSALM OF RESPONSE: *Psalm 113*

NEW TESTAMENT READING: *1 Timothy 2:1-7*

REFLECTIONS FROM THE CHURCH FATHERS

Distinguishing Various Types of Prayer. THEODORE OF MOPSUESTIA: Here *supplications* express the desire for good things from God. *Prayers* express the desire to be released from various evils. *Intercessions* ask for freedom from undeserved consequences. And *thanksgivings* express gratitude for blessings. *Commentary on 1 Timothy.*

God Gives Lavishly. JOHN OF DAMASCUS: The third kind of absolute worship is thanksgiving for all the good things he has created for us. All things owe a debt of thanks to God and must offer him ceaseless worship, because all things have their existence from him, and in him all things hold together. He gives lavishly of his gifts to all, without being asked. He desires all men to be saved and to partake of his goodness. He is long-suffering with us sinners, for he makes his sun rise on the evil and on the good and sends rain on the just and the unjust. He is the Son of God, yet he became one of us for our sake and made us participants of his divine nature, so that "we shall be like him," as John the Theologian says in his catholic epistle. *On Divine Images 3.30.*

Overflowing Kindness. LETTER TO DIOGNETUS: O the overflowing kindness and love of God toward man! God did not hate us, or drive us away or bear us ill will. Rather, he was long-suffering and forbearing. In his mercy, he took up the burden of our sins. He himself gave up his own Son as a ransom for us—the holy one for the unjust, the innocent for the guilty, the righteous one for the unrighteous, the incorruptible for the corruptible, the immortal for the mortal. *Letter to Diognetus 9.1-2.*

GOSPEL READING: *Luke 16:1-13*

REFLECTIONS FROM THE CHURCH FATHERS

Jesus Recommends the Foresight, Prudence and Ingenuity of the Steward. AUGUSTINE: Why did the Lord Jesus Christ present this parable to us? He surely did not approve of that cheat of a servant who cheated his master, stole from him and did not make it up from his own pocket. On top of that, he also did some extra pilfering. He caused his master further loss, in order to prepare a little nest of quiet and security for himself after he lost his job. Why did the Lord set this before us? It is not because that servant cheated but because he exercised foresight for the future. When even a cheat is praised for his ingenuity, Christians who make no such provision blush. I mean, this is what he added, "Behold, the children of this age are more prudent than the children of light." They perpetrate frauds in order to secure their future. In what life, after all, did that steward insure himself like that? What one was he going to quit when he bowed to his master's decision? He was insuring himself for a life that was going to end. Would you not insure yourself for eternal life? *Sermon 359A.10.*

Riches Are a Loan from God Not to Be Left Idle. CHRYSOSTOM: You know that many high-standing people renege on repayment of a loan. They are either resistant with a bad attitude or unable to pay because of poverty, as it often happens. In the case of the Lord of all, there is no room for thinking this. On the contrary, the loan is proof against loss. He guarantees to return in good time one hundred percent of what was deposited, and he keeps life everlasting in reserve for us. In the future, what excuse will we have if we are negligent and fail to gain a hundredfold in place of the little we have, the future in place of the present, the eternal in place of the temporary? What excuse will we have if we heedlessly lock our money behind doors and barricades, and we prefer to leave it lying idle? Instead, we should make it available to the needy now, so that in the future we may count on support from them. Remember that Scripture says, "Make friends with ill-gotten gains so that, when you go down in the world, they may welcome you into their eternal dwellings." *Homilies on Genesis 3.21.*

If Unfaithful in What Is Another's, Who Will Give You What Is Your Own? CYRIL OF ALEXANDRIA: Let those of us who possess earthly wealth open our hearts to those who are in need. Let us show ourselves faithful and obedient to the laws of God. Let us be followers of our Lord's will in those things that are from the outside and not our own. Let us do this so that we may receive what is our own, that holy and admirable beauty that God forms in people's souls, making them like himself, according to what we originally were. *Commentary on Luke, Homily 109.*

CLOSING PRAYER

Grant to us, Lord, we beseech thee, the spirit to think and do always such things as are rightful, that we, who cannot do anything that is good without thee, may by thee be enabled to live according to thy will; through Jesus Christ our Lord. Amen. *The Leonine Sacramentary*

Heavenly Treasure

⁙ THEME

We should not put our confidence in earthly wealth (Amos 6:1a, 4-7);
rather, we should put our trust in the Lord who made heaven and earth
(Ps 146). Desiring to be rich often causes us to fall into temptation;
contentment comes when we realize we have brought nothing into the
world and can take nothing out of it (1 Tim 6:6-19). In Jesus' parable
of the poor man Lazarus, we see that in light of eternity, wealth means
nothing (Lk 16:19-31).

⁙ OPENING PRAYER: *Proper 21*

Gracious and holy Father, give us wisdom to perceive you, intelligence
to understand you, diligence to seek you, patience to wait for you, eyes
to behold you, a heart to meditate on you, and a life to proclaim you;
through the power of the Spirit of Jesus Christ our Lord. Amen. *Benedict of Nursia*

⁙ OLD TESTAMENT READING: *Amos 6:1a, 4-7*

REFLECTIONS FROM THE CHURCH FATHERS

Luxurious Living Condemned. CHRYSOSTOM: Let us not be careless,
dearly beloved, in dealing with matters concerning our salvation; recognizing instead the troubles that could come from that evil source, let us
avoid the harm it produces. After all, we are warned against intemper-

ance not only in the new dispensation by its greater attention to right thinking, its more frequent struggles and greater effort, its many rewards and ineffable consolations. Not even people living under the old law were permitted to indulge themselves in that way, even though they were sitting in the dark dependent on tapers and were brought forward gradually into the light, like children being weaned off milk. Lest you think I am idly finding fault with intemperance in what I say, listen to what the prophet says: "Woe to those who fall on evil days in sleeping on beds of ivory, luxuriating on their couches, living on a diet of goats picked from the flocks and suckling calves from the herds, and drinking strained wines, anointed with precious unguents—like men treating this as a lasting city, and not seeking one to come." *Homilies on Genesis 1.10.*

Modesty in Serving Guests. BASIL THE GREAT: Just as it is not proper to provide ourselves with worldly trappings like a silver vessel, or a curtain edged with purple, or a downy couch or transparent draperies, so we act unfittingly in contriving menus that deviate in any important way from our usual diet. That we should run about searching for anything not demanded by real necessity but calculated to provide a wretched delight and ruinous vainglory is not only shameful and out of keeping with our avowed purpose; it also causes harm of no mean gravity when they who spend their lives in sensual gratification and measure happiness in terms of pleasure for the appetite see us also taken up with the same preoccupations that keep them enthralled. . . . Has a guest arrived? If he is a brother and follows a way of life aiming at the same objective as ours, he will recognize the fare we provide as properly his own. What he has left at home, he will find with us. Suppose he is weary from his journey. We then provide as much extra nourishment as is required to relieve his weariness. *The Long Rules, Question 20.*

Woe to Those Who Do Not Grieve Over the Ruin of Joseph. JOHN OF ANTIOCH: There is nothing else to see happening everywhere in the world except disorder, unheralded war, unrestrained wrath and savagery exceeding all barbaric inhumanity, and there is no one suffering "by the collapse of Joseph." We bite and we devour one another, and then we have been destroyed by one another, providing pleasure to the enemies of piety. *Letter to Cyril of Alexandria 6.*

PSALM OF RESPONSE: *Psalm 146*

NEW TESTAMENT READING: *1 Timothy 6:6-19*

REFLECTIONS FROM THE CHURCH FATHERS

The Paradox of Faith. CYRIL OF JERUSALEM: For those who in appearance are rich, though they have many possessions, are yet poor in soul. The more they amass, the more they pine with longing for what they lack. But the believer, paradoxically, is rich even when poor. Knowing that we have need only of raiment and food and being content with these, he has trampled riches underfoot. *Catechetical Lecture 5.2.*

Moderation. BASIL THE GREAT: But, if a man would also have mercy on his body as being a possession necessary to the soul and its co-operator in carrying on life on earth, he will occupy himself with its needs only so far as is required to preserve it and keep it vigorous by moderate care in the service of the soul. He will by no means allow it to become unmanageable through satiety. *On Detachment, Homily 21.*

GOSPEL READING: *Luke 16:19-31*

REFLECTIONS FROM THE CHURCH FATHERS

Anxious Fear. CYPRIAN: You are afraid that your wealth may fail. You may have begun to do some good generously from it, yet you do not know, in your wretchedness, that your life itself may fail, and your salvation as well. While you are anxious lest any of your possessions be diminished, you do not take notice that you yourself, a lover of mammon rather than of your soul, are being diminished. While you are afraid lest for your own sake you lose your estate, you yourself are perishing for the sake of your estate. *Works and Almsgiving 10.*

Do Not Be Diverted. AMBROSE: Let godliness move you to justice, continence, gentleness, that you may avoid childish acts, and that rooted and grounded in grace you may fight the good fight of faith. Do not entangle yourself in the affairs of this life, for you are fighting for God. *Duties of the Clergy 1.36.184.*

The Cost of the Kingdom. LEO THE GREAT: Let those who want Christ to spare them have compassion for the poor. Let those who desire a bond with the fellowship of the blessed be "readily disposed" toward nourishing the wretched. No human being should be considered worthless by another. The nature which the Creator of the universe made his own should not be looked down on in anyone. *Sermon 9.2.*

GOSPEL READING: *Luke 16:19-31*

REFLECTIONS FROM THE CHURCH FATHERS

The Dogs and the Rich Man Compared. CYRIL OF ALEXANDRIA: Cut off from compassion and care, he would have gladly gathered the worthless morsels that fell from the rich man's table to satisfy his hunger. A severe and incurable disease also tormented him. Yes, it says that even the dogs licked his sores and did not injure him yet sympathized with him and cared for him. Animals relieve their own sufferings with their tongues, as they remove what pains them and gently soothe the sores. The rich man was crueler than the dogs, because he felt no sympathy or compassion for him but was completely unmerciful. *Commentary on Luke, Homily 111.*

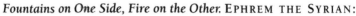
Fountains on One Side, Fire on the Other. EPHREM THE SYRIAN:
This place, despised and spurned
By the denizens of paradise,
Those who burn in Gehenna
hungrily desire;
Their torment doubles
At the sight of its fountains,
They quiver violently
As they stand on the opposite side;
The rich man, too, begs for succor
But there is no one to wet his tongue,
For fire is within them,
While the water is opposite them.
Hymns on Paradise 1.17.

The Rich Man Did Not Make Friends with His Unrighteous Mammon.
AUGUSTINE: Why then, rich man, do you desire too late in hell what
you never hoped for while you were enjoying your luxuries? Are you not
the one who ignored the person lying at your gate? Are you not the one
who in your disdain for the poor man made fun of Moses and the prophets? You refused to hold faith with a neighbor in his poverty; now you do
not enjoy his good times. . . . We should not hold faith with a poor neighbor in such a way that we hope riches are coming to him in due course,
and so we keep faith with him in order to hold them with him. That is
not the way at all. "Whoever receives a prophet in the name of a prophet
will receive a prophet's reward. Whoever gives one of my little ones a cup
of cold water simply in the name of a disciple, truly, I say to you, he will
not lose his reward." He holds faith with a neighbor in his poverty, and
therefore he will enjoy his good things. *Sermon 41.5-6.19.*

CLOSING PRAYER

O good Jesus, word of the Father, the brightness of the Father's glory, whom angels desire to behold; teach us to do your will, that guided by your good spirit, we may come to that blessed city where there is everlasting day and all are of one spirit; where there is certain security and secure eternity and eternal tranquility and quiet felicity and happy sweetness and sweet pleasantness; where you, with the Father and the Holy Spirit, are alive and reign, one God forever and ever. Amen. *Gregory the Great*

Delight in the Lord

THEME

The righteous are told to live by faith (Hab 1:1-4; 2:1-4). Scripture promises that when we delight in the Lord, he will give us the desires of our heart. Don't fret over evil ones who prosper (Ps 37:1-10). Rather, focus on your holy calling, with love and self-control (2 Tim 1:1-14), carrying out Jesus' commandments (Lk 17:5-10).

OPENING PRAYER: *Proper 22*

God, the origin of creation, open our eyes to know you and place our hope in you, the highest and the holiest. You put down the insolence of the proud, and scatter the plotting of the nations; you lift up the humble and lay low the mighty; you make some rich and make others poor, kill some and bring others to life; the God of the spiritual and the material worlds; you see everything that happens; you are the helper of those who are in trouble and the Savior of those in despair; creator and overseer of every spirit; you cause nations to grow, and you have chosen from all the world those who love you through Jesus Christ, your beloved Son, through whom you taught us, made us holy and honored us. Lord and Master, help us and rescue all those who are in trouble; have mercy on the lowly; lift up those who have fallen; reveal yourself to the needy; heal the ungodly; convert those of your people who have gone astray; feed the hungry; release those of our number who are in prison; give power to the weak; encourage the faint-hearted. Let all the nations know that you are God alone, and Jesus Christ is your Son, and we are your people and the sheep of your pasture. *Clement of Rome*

OLD TESTAMENT READING: *Habakkuk 1:1-4; 2:1-4*

REFLECTIONS FROM THE CHURCH FATHERS

Habakkuk's Indignation Is Not Against God. THEODORE OF MOP-SUESTIA: It is not as though bringing a censure against God that the prophet says this. Rather, he speaks this way as it is the custom with people who are in some sort of trouble or who are righteously indignant with those responsible to present the injustice of what is being done under the guise of censure. Blessed David also says in like manner, "Why, O Lord, do you keep your distance? Why do you look down on us in good times and in bad? When the godless act disdainfully, the poor person is inflamed," and so on, saying this not to censure God but to express indignation with those responsible for it and at a loss as to how they are not quickly called to account. *Commentary on Habakkuk 1.2.*

Hearing God's Voice. AUGUSTINE: All seek counsel concerning what they wish, but they do not always hear what they wish. He serves you best who does not so much expect to hear the thing from you that he himself desires, but rather to desire what he hears from you. *Confessions 10.26.*

Help in Trials Foretold. BASIL THE GREAT: And, if in all this there is sorrow to be borne, I trust in the Lord that it will not be without its use to you. Therefore, the more have been your trials, look for a more perfect reward from your last judge. Do not take your present troubles ill. Do not lose hope. Yet a little while and your helper will come to you and will not tarry. *Letter 238.*

Care for the Poor Gives Life to Faith. LEO THE GREAT: And hence Tobias also, while instructing his son in the precepts of godliness, says,

"Give alms of your substance, and turn not your face from any poor man. So shall it come to pass that the face of God shall not be turned from you." This virtue makes all virtues profitable, for by its precepts it gives life to that very faith by which "the just lives" and which is said to be "dead without works." As the reason for works consists in faith, so the strength of faith consists in works. *Sermon 10.4.*

PSALM OF RESPONSE: *Psalm 37:1-10*

NEW TESTAMENT READING: *2 Timothy 1:1-14*

REFLECTIONS FROM THE CHURCH FATHERS

A Son by Faith. CASSIODORUS: When writing to Timothy he put at the head of the letter, "To my dearly beloved son," for he had begotten him, not in body but in faith. *Explanation of the Psalms 101.29.*

No Longer Dying. AUGUSTINE: "From Adam to Moses death reigned"; but the presence of the Word abolished death. No longer in Adam are we all dying. In Christ we are all reviving. *Against the Arians 1.59.8.*

An Impressed Image. CHRYSOSTOM: After the manner of artists, Paul is saying, I have impressed on you the image of virtue, fixing in your soul a sort of rule and model and outline of all things pleasing to God. Hold fast to these things, whether you are meditating on any matter of faith or love or of a sound mind. Form your ideas from this pattern in the future. *Homilies on 2 Timothy 3.*

Preserve the Heavenly Seed. JOHN OF DAMASCUS: Before all things, keep that truth which is committed to your trust, the holy Word of faith by which you have been taught and instructed. And let no weeds of heresy grow up among you, but preserve the heavenly seed pure and sincere, that it may yield a great harvest to the master, when he comes to demand account of our lives. He shall reward us according to our deeds, when the righteous shall shine forth as the sun, but darkness and everlasting shame shall cover the sinners. *Barlaam and Joseph 36.335.*

GOSPEL READING: *Luke 17:5-10*

REFLECTIONS FROM THE CHURCH FATHERS

To Increase Faith Is to Strengthen It by the Holy Spirit. CYRIL OF ALEXANDRIA: They ask, "Add faith to us." They do not ask simply for faith, for perhaps you might imagine them to be without faith. They rather ask Christ for an addition to their faith and to be strengthened in faith. Faith partly depends on us and partly is the gift of the divine grace. The beginning of faith depends on us and our maintaining confidence and faith in God with all our power. The confirmation and strength necessary for this comes from the divine grace. For that reason, since all things are possible with God, the Lord says that all things are possible for him who believes. The power that comes to us through faith is of God. Knowing this, blessed Paul also says in the first epistle to the Corinthians, "For to one is given through the Spirit the word of wisdom, to another the word of knowledge according to the same Spirit, and to another faith in the same Spirit." You see that he has placed faith also in the catalogue of spiritual graces. The disciples requested that they might receive this from the Savior, contributing also what was of themselves. By the descent on them of the Holy Spirit, he granted it to them after the fulfillment of the dispensation. Before the resurrection, their faith was so feeble that they were liable even to the charge of being "little of faith." *Commentary on Luke, Homilies 113-16.*

The Great Faith of the Church. AUGUSTINE: A mustard seed looks small. Nothing is less noteworthy to the sight, but nothing is stronger to the taste. What does that signify but the very great fervor and inner strength of faith in the church? *Sermon 246.3.*

The Faithful Are Called to Humble Service. **AMBROSE:** You do not say to your servant, "Sit down," but require more service from him and do not thank him. The Lord also does not allow only one work or labor for you, because so long as we live we must always work. *Exposition of the Gospel of Luke 8.31-32.*

CLOSING PRAYER

While morn awakes with wondrous light
    We come to thee, O Lord, in prayer;
Guard thou and guide our steps aright
    And keep us in thy holy care.
Lord, let our tongues be free from blame,
    Nor utter words of guilt or strife;
Lift up our eyes from deeds of shame,
    And all the vanities of life.
Our hearts be purged and purified
    That naught of evil shall remain;
From worldly vice and fleshly pride
    Our souls by temperance restrain.
So keep us, Lord, from evil free,
    Till fades in dusk the sunset flame,
That we unstained may come to thee
    And sing the glories of thy name.
Ambrose

Trust and Obey

THEME

We are to trust and obey (2 Kings 5:1-3, 7-15c), giving thanks to the Lord for his power and mercy (Ps 111). He is faithful, even when we are faithless (2 Tim 2:8-15). Just as the leper returned to thank God for healing, so also we should thank God for cleansing us from all sin (Lk 17:11-19).

OPENING PRAYER: *Proper 23*

O Lord my God, my one hope, hear me, that weariness may not lessen my will to seek you, that I may seek your face ever more with eager heart. Lord, give me strength to seek you, as you have made me to find you, and give hope of finding you ever more and more. My strength and my weakness are in your hands: Preserve the one, and remedy the other. In your hands are my knowledge and my ignorance. When you have opened to me, receive my entering in. Where you have shut, open to my knocking. Let me remember you, understand you, love you. Increase in me all these until you restore me to your perfect pattern. *Augustine*

OLD TESTAMENT READING: *2 Kings 5:1-3, 7-15c*

REFLECTIONS FROM THE CHURCH FATHERS

Elisha's Order to Wash in the Jordan Prefigures Baptism. EPHREM THE SYRIAN: Therefore Naaman was sent to the Jordan as to the remedy capable to heal a human being. Indeed, sin is the leprosy of the soul, which is not perceived by the senses, but intelligence has the proof of it, and human nature must be delivered from this disease by Christ's power which is hidden in baptism. It was necessary that Naaman, in order to be purified from two diseases, that of the soul and that of the body, might represent in his own person the purification of all the nations through the bath or regeneration, whose beginning was in the river Jordan, the mother and originator of baptism. *On the Second Book of Kings 5.10-11.*

The Regeneration of the Gentiles Through the Baptism of Christ.
CAESARIUS OF ARLES: Holy Elisha, as we said, typified our Lord and Savior, while Naaman prefigured the Gentiles. The fact that Naaman believed he would recover his health as the result of his own rivers indicates that the human race presumed on its free will and its own merits; but without the grace of Christ their own merits cannot possess health, although they can have leprosy. For this reason, if the human race had not followed the example of Naaman and listened to the advice of Elisha, with humility receiving the gift of baptism through the grace of Christ, they could not be freed from the leprosy of the original and actual sins. "Wash seven times," he said, because of the sevenfold grace of the Holy Spirit, which reposed in Christ our Lord. Moreover, when our Lord was baptized in this river, the Holy Spirit came on him in the form of a dove. When Naaman descended into the river as a figure of baptism, "his flesh became like the flesh of a little child." Notice, beloved brothers, that this likeness was perfected in the Christian people, for you know that all who are baptized are still called infants, whether they are old or young. *Sermon 129.4-5.*

⌾ PSALM OF RESPONSE: *Psalm 111*

NEW TESTAMENT READING: *2 Timothy 2:8-15*

REFLECTIONS FROM THE CHURCH FATHERS

The Soldier of Virtue. CHRYSOSTOM: You are a spiritual soldier. This kind of soldier does not sleep on an ivory bed but on the ground. He is not anointed with perfumed oils. These are the concern of those corrupt men who dally with courtesans, of those who act on the stage, of those who live carelessly. You must not smell of perfumes but of virtue. *On Lazarus and the Rich Man 1.*

The Centrality of Resurrection. AUGUSTINE: Let us believe in Christ crucified; but in him as the one who rose again on the third day. That's the faith that distinguishes us from them, distinguishes us from the pagans, distinguishes us from the Jews—the faith by which we believe that Jesus Christ has risen from the dead. The apostle says to Timothy, "Remember that Jesus Christ has risen from the dead, of the seed of David, according to my gospel." And again the same apostle, "Because if you believe in your heart," he says, "that Jesus is Lord, and confess with your lips that God raised him from the dead, you will be saved." This is the salvation, the well-being, the safety and the soundness, which I discussed yesterday. Whoever believes and is baptized will be saved. I know that you believe; you will be saved. Hold firmly in your hearts, profess it with your lips, that Christ has risen from the dead. *Sermon 234.3.*

Light Amid Storms. CHRYSOSTOM: Any cloud passing over our skies may from time to time make us gloomy. But Paul's heart had no such storms sweeping over it. Or better, there did sweep over him, and often, many storms, but his day was not darkened. Rather, in the midst of the temptations and dangers the light shone out. Thus when bound with his chain he kept exclaiming, "The word of God is not bound." Thus continually by means of that tongue the Word was sending forth its rays. *Homilies on First Corinthians 13.4.*

His Sign on Our Bodies. **APHRAHAT:** Let us honor the spirit of Christ, that we may receive grace from him. Let us be strangers to the world, even as Christ was not of it. Let us be humble and mild, that we may inherit the land of life. Let us be unflagging in his service, that he may cause us to serve in the abode of the saints. Let us pray his prayer in purity, that it may have access to the Lord of majesty. Let us be partakers in his suffering, so that we may also rise up in his resurrection. Let us bear his sign on our bodies, that we may be delivered from the wrath to come. *Select Demonstrations 6.1.*

Plow Straight Furrows. **THEODORET OF CYR:** Good teachers are like farmers who plow straight furrows, thus presenting the rule of Scripture in a correct manner. *Interpretation of the Second Letter to Timothy 9.*

GOSPEL READING: *Luke 17:11-19*

REFLECTIONS FROM THE CHURCH FATHERS

Bless the Helper for Benefits Received. **ATHANASIUS:** Today, the Lord rebukes those who keep the Passover the way the Jews did, just as he rebuked certain lepers he had cleansed. You recall that he loved the one who was thankful, but he was angry with the ungrateful ones, because they did not acknowledge their Deliverer. They thought more highly of their cure from leprosy than of him who had healed them. . . . Actually, this one was given much more than the rest. Besides being healed of his leprosy, he was told by the Lord, "Stand up and go on your way. Your faith has saved you." You see, those who give thanks and those who glorify have the same kind of feelings. They bless their helper for the benefits they have received. That is why Paul urged everybody to "glorify God with your body." Isaiah also commanded, "Give glory to God." *Festal Letter 6.*

The Thankfulness of the Samaritan. **CYRIL OF ALEXANDRIA:** Falling into a thankless forgetfulness, the nine lepers that were Jews did not return to give glory to God. By this, he shows that Israel was hard of heart and utterly unthankful. The stranger, a Samaritan, was of foreign race brought from Assyria. The phrase "in the middle of Samaria and Galilee" has meaning. "He returned with a loud voice to glorify God." It shows that the Samaritans were grateful but that the Jews, even when they benefited, were ungrateful. *Commentary on Luke, Homilies 113-16.*

CLOSING PRAYER

O God of infinite mercy and boundless majesty, whom no distance can part from those for whom thou care, be present to thy servants who everywhere confide in thee, and through all the way in which they are to go be pleased to be their guide and companion. May no adversity harm them, no difficulty oppose them; may all things turn out happily and prosperously for them, that by the aid of thy right hand, whatsoever they have asked for with reasonable desire they may speedily find brought to good effect, through Jesus Christ our Lord. Amen. *The Gelasian Sacramentary*

Persistence

☙ THEME

Just as Jacob did, we seek a blessing from God (Gen 32:22-31) from whom our help comes. He keeps us from stumbling into wrongdoing and from all evil (Ps 121). We continue to learn from God's Word (2 Tim 3:14–4:5) and petition him for help day and night (Lk 18:1-8).

☙ OPENING PRAYER: *Proper 24*

O God, whose nature and property is ever to have mercy and to forgive, receive our humble petitions, and though we are tied and bound with the chain of our sins, yet let the pitifulness of thy great mercy loose us; for the honor of Jesus Christ, our mediator and advocate. Amen. *The Gregorian Sacramentary*

☙ OLD TESTAMENT READING: *Genesis 32:22-31*

REFLECTIONS FROM THE CHURCH FATHERS

Jacob Held On Bravely. AUGUSTINE: "Let me go, because it is already morning." "Morning" we understand as the light of truth and wisdom, through whom all things were made. You will enjoy the morning when this night has gone, that is, the iniquity of this world. That's when it will be morning, when the Lord comes, in order to be seen by us as he is already seen by the angels. Because "now we see through a mirror in a riddle, but then it will be face to face." So let us hold fast to this saying, brothers, "Let me go; behold, it is already morning." But what did *he* say? "I will not let you go, unless you bless me." The Lord, you see, does bless us first through the flesh. The faithful know what they receive, that they are blessed through the flesh. And they know that they would not be blessed unless that flesh had been crucified and given for the life of the world. But how is Jacob blessed? In that he got the upper hand with God, in that he held on bravely and persevered and did not lose from his grasp what Adam lost. So let us, the faithful, hold on to what we receive, in order that we may deserve to be blessed. *Sermon 5.7.*

You Behold God Face to Face. HILARY OF POITIERS: What is this that you are asking from one who is weak? What do you expect from one who is feeble? This one for whose blessing you pray is the one whom you, as the more powerful, weaken by your embrace. The activity of your soul is not in harmony with the deeds of your body, for you think differently from the way you act. By your bodily motions during this struggle you keep this man helpless, but this man is for you the true God, not in name but in nature. You do not ask to be sanctified by adoptive but by true blessings. You struggle with a man, but you behold God face to face. You do not see with your bodily eyes what you perceive with the glance of your faith. In comparison with you he is a feeble man, but your soul has been saved by the vision of God. During this struggle you are Jacob, but after your faith in the blessing for which you prayed you are Israel. The man is subject to you according to the flesh in anticipation of the sufferings in the flesh. You recognize God in the weakness of his flesh in order to foreshadow the mystery of his blessing in the spirit. His appearance does not prevent you from remaining steadfast in the fight, nor does his weakness deter you from seeking his blessing. Nor does the man bring it about that he is not God who is man, nor is he who is God not the true God, because he who is God cannot but be the true God by the blessing, the transfer and the name. *On the Trinity 5.19.*

PSALM OF RESPONSE: *Psalm 121*

NEW TESTAMENT READING: *2 Timothy 3:14–4:5*

REFLECTIONS FROM THE CHURCH FATHERS

Profitable for Correction. CHRYSOSTOM: By Scripture we may disprove what is false, be corrected, be brought to a right understanding and be comforted and consoled. *Homilies on 2 Timothy 9.*

A Judicious Timing. BENEDICT OF NURSIA: In his teaching the abbot is ever to observe this rule of the apostle: "Reprove, beseech, correct." This consists in a judicious timing: to mix gentleness with sternness—at one time to show the severity of a master, at another the tenderness of a father. Use rigor with the irregular and the turbulent, but win to better things the obedient, mild and patient. *Rule of St. Benedict 2.23-25.*

The Golden Mean. GREGORY THE GREAT: Pastoral guides must also see to it with careful concern that not only should nothing evil proceed from their lips but that not even what is proper be said in excess or in a slovenly manner. Often the force of what is said is wasted when it is enfeebled in the hearts of the hearers by a careless and offensive torrent of words. Indeed, this sort of loquacity defiles the speaker himself, inasmuch as it takes no notice of the practical needs of the hearer. . . . Thus Paul also, admonishing his disciple to be constant in preaching, said, I charge you before God and Jesus Christ, who shall judge the living and the dead, by his coming and his kingdom: preach the word, be instant in season, out of season. When he was about to say "out of season," he premised it with "in season," for if being in season is not combined with being out of season, the preaching destroys itself in the mind of the hearer by its worthlessness. *Pastoral Care 2.4.*

GOSPEL READING: *Luke 18:1-8*

REFLECTIONS FROM THE CHURCH FATHERS

The Persistence of the Widow. CYRIL OF ALEXANDRIA: The present parable assures us God will bend his ear to those who offer him their prayers, not carelessly or negligently but with earnestness and constancy. The constant coming of the oppressed widow conquered the unjust judge that did not fear God or have any shame. Even against his will, he granted her request. How will not he who loves mercy and hates iniquity, and who always gives his helping hand to those that love him, accept those who draw near to him day and night and avenge them as his elect? *Commentary on Luke, Homily 119.*

Not an Allegorical Representation of God. AUGUSTINE: These examples now are proposed so that important things may be suggested from things of less importance. They are like the example of the judge who feared neither God nor people and who nevertheless yielded to the widow bothering him to judge her case. He yielded not through piety or kindness but through fear of suffering annoyance. By no means does that unjust judge furnish an allegorical representation of God. The example is of an unjust man who, although he yields for the mere sake of avoiding annoyance, nevertheless cannot disregard those who bother him with continual pleadings. By this the Lord wishes us to infer how much care God bestows on those who beseech him, for God is both just and good. *Sermon on the Mount 15.*

God Vindicates Us Against Satan's Attacks. MARTYRIUS: As our Savior pointed out, even the cruel and wicked judge eventually looked into the poor widow's case because she had wearied him with her insistence. It is quite clear that God does not neglect us. Even if he makes us wait, he will nonetheless answer us and see to our case all of a sudden. When we pray all the time, we should not weary. We should eagerly cry out to him day and night, begging him with a broken heart and a humble spirit. "A humble spirit is a sacrifice to God, and God will not reject a broken heart." *Book of Perfection 75.*

CLOSING PRAYER

Prayer, to speak somewhat boldly, is converse with God. Even if we address him in a whisper, without opening our lips or uttering a sound, still we cry to him in our heart. For God never ceases to listen to the inward converse of the heart. For this reason also we raise our head and lift the hands toward heaven and stand on tiptoe as we join in the closing outburst of prayer, following the eternal flight of the spirit into the intelligible world. And while we thus endeavor to detach the body from the earth by lifting it upwards along with the uttered words, we spurn the fetters of the flesh and constrain the soul, winged with desire of better things, to ascend into the holy place. *Clement of Alexandria*

God's Help

THEME

We are prone to wander away from God (Jer 14:7-10, 19-22). Blessed are those who dwell with him and long for him (Ps 84:1-6) and humbly offer him prayers (Lk 18:9-14). The Lord stands by us, rescues us from every evil and gives us strength (2 Tim 4:6-8, 16-18).

OPENING PRAYER: *Proper 25*

Lord, teach us to seek you, and reveal yourself to us when we seek you. For we cannot seek you unless you first teach us or find you except you reveal yourself to us. Let us seek you in longing and long for you in seeking; let us find you in love and love you in finding, O Jesus Christ our Lord. Amen. *Ambrose*

OLD TESTAMENT READING: *Jeremiah 14:7-10, 19-22*

REFLECTIONS FROM THE CHURCH FATHERS

Enemies of Nicaea Love to Wander. ATHANASIUS: Hence it is that they are always writing and always altering their own previous statements, and thus they show an uncertain faith, or rather a manifest unbelief and perverseness. And this, it appears to me, must be the case with them. Since they have fallen away from the truth and desire to overthrow that sound confession of faith that was drawn up at Nicaea, they have, in the language of Scripture, "loved to wander and have not

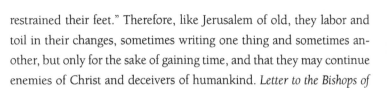

restrained their feet." Therefore, like Jerusalem of old, they labor and toil in their changes, sometimes writing one thing and sometimes another, but only for the sake of gaining time, and that they may continue enemies of Christ and deceivers of humankind. *Letter to the Bishops of Egypt 1.6.*

The Penitent Is God's Throne. JEROME: We should not think that the glorious throne of God is only the throne of the temple, which was repeatedly destroyed, but that it is also every saint who is cast down and destroyed when he offends God by his multitude of sins, according to what is written: "You have cast his throne to the ground." Nevertheless, the one who perishes from his own guilt is sustained by the clemency of the Lord, whereby the severity of the sentence is altered, lest the Lord invalidate his covenant in which he promised to be our coming salvation. *Six Books on Jeremiah 3.40.1.*

How Tragic to Abandon Christ for Idols. ORIGEN: What a state the person is in who has deserted the easy yoke and the light burden of Christ to subject himself once again to the yoke of demons and to bear the burden of the heaviest sin! How can this be after we have known that the heart of those who worship idols is ashes and their life more worthless than clay, and after we have said, "Our ancestors possessed false idols, and none of them can bring rain"? *Exhortation to Martyrdom 32.*

🔹 **PSALM OF RESPONSE:** *Psalm 84:1-6*

🔹 **NEW TESTAMENT READING:** *2 Timothy 4:6-8, 16-18*

REFLECTIONS FROM THE CHURCH FATHERS

Only by Hope. BASIL THE GREAT: "Turn, O my soul, into your rest: for the Lord has been bountiful to you." The brave contestant applies to himself the consoling words, very much like to Paul, when he says, "I have fought the good fight, I have finished the course, I have kept the faith. For the rest, there is laid up for me a crown of justice." These things the prophet also says to himself: Since you have fulfilled sufficiently the course of this life, turn then to your rest, "for the Lord has been bountiful to you." For, eternal rest lies before those who have struggled through the present life observant of the laws, a rest not given in payment for a debt owed for their works but provided as a grace of the munificent God for those who have hoped in him. *Homilies 22.*

Prayer the Primary Arena. CASSIODORUS: As someone has said, you will scarcely ever find that when a person prays, some empty and external reflection does not impede him, causing the attention which the mind directs on God to be sidetracked and interrupted. So it is a great and most wholesome struggle to concentrate on prayer once begun, and with God's help to show lively resistance to the temptations of the enemy, so that our minds may with unflagging attention strain to be ever fastened on God. Then we can deservedly recite Paul's words: I have fought a good fight, I have finished my course, I have kept the faith. *Explanation of the Psalms 101.1.*

Written from Nero's Prison. EUSEBIUS: Story has it that the apostle, after defending himself, was again sent on the ministry of preaching and coming a second time to the same city met death by martyrdom under Nero. While he was being held in prison, he composed the second epistle to Timothy, at the same time indicating that his first defense had taken place and that martyrdom was at hand. *Ecclesiastical History 2.22.*

GOSPEL READING: *Luke 18:9-14*

REFLECTIONS FROM THE CHURCH FATHERS

The Infirmity of Others Is Not a Fit Subject for Praise for Those in Good Health. CYRIL OF ALEXANDRIA: He says, "I am not as the rest of humankind." Moderate yourself, O Pharisee. Put a door and lock on your tongue. You speak to God who knows all things. Wait for the decree of the judge. No one who is skilled in wrestling ever crowns himself. No one also receives the crown from himself but waits for the summons of the referee. . . . Lower your pride, because arrogance is accursed and hated by God. It is foreign to the mind that fears God. Christ even said, "Do not judge, and you shall not be judged. Do not condemn, and you will not be condemned." One of his disciples also said, "There is one lawgiver and judge. Why then do you judge your neighbor?" No one who is in good health ridicules one who is sick for being laid up and bedridden. He is rather afraid, for perhaps he may become the victim of similar sufferings. A person in battle, because another has fallen, does not praise himself for having escaped from misfortune. The weakness of others is not a suitable subject for praise for those who are in health. *Commentary on Luke, Homily 120.*

On Reporting One's Own Symptoms, Not Another's, to a Doctor. AUGUSTINE: How useful and necessary a medicine is repentance! People who remember that they are only human will readily understand this. It is written, "God resists the proud but gives grace to the humble." . . . The Pharisee was not rejoicing so much in his own clean bill of health as in comparing it with the diseases of others. He came to the doctor. It would have been more worthwhile to inform him by confession of the things that were wrong with himself instead of keeping his wounds secret and having the nerve to crow over the scars of others. It is not surprising that the tax collector went away cured, since he had not been ashamed of showing where he felt pain. *Sermon 351.1.*

Humility Is the Mark of a Sinner. BASIL THE GREAT: The stern Pharisee, who in his overweening pride not only boasted of himself but also discredited the tax collector in the presence of God, made his justice void by being guilty of pride. Instead of the Pharisee, the tax collector went down justified, because he had given glory to God, the holy One. He did not dare lift his eyes but sought only to plead for mercy.

He accused himself by his posture, by striking his breast and by entertaining no other motive except propitiation. Be on your guard, therefore, and bear in mind this example of severe loss sustained through arrogance. The one guilty of insolent behavior suffered the loss of his justice and forfeited his reward by his bold self-reliance. He was judged inferior to a humble man and a sinner because in his self-exaltation he did not await the judgment of God but pronounced it himself. Never place yourself above anyone, not even great sinners. Humility often saves a sinner who has committed many terrible transgressions. *On Humility.*

CLOSING PRAYER

Now may the God and Father of our Lord Jesus Christ, and may Jesus Christ himself also, the eternal high priest and Son of God, build you up in faith and truth, and in gentleness, avoidance of anger, forbearance, longsuffering, patient endurance and purity; and may he grant you to inherit a place among his saints; may he grant this to us also so that we can be with you, and to everyone under heaven who will believe in our Lord Jesus Christ and in his Father who raised him from the dead. *Polycarp*

Cultivating Character

☙ THEME

The prophets tell of mysterious future events (Dan 7:1-3, 15-18). Until Christ comes again, we praise God's name, acknowledging his power (Ps 149), asking for wisdom and comprehension of things we do not understand (Eph 1:11-23) and the strength to follow Christ's teachings (Lk 6:20-31).

☙ OPENING PRAYER: *All Saints' Day*

Glory to you, Lord Jesus Christ! You built your cross as a bridge over death, so that departed souls might pass from the realm of death to the realm of life. Glory to you! You put on the body of a mortal man and made it the source of life for all mortal human beings. You are alive! Your murderers handled your life like farmers: they sowed it like grain deep in the earth, for it to spring up and raise with itself a multitude of people. We offer you the great, universal sacrifice of our love, and pour out before you our richest hymns and prayers. For you offered your cross to God as a sacrifice in order to make us all rich. *Ephrem the Syrian*

☙ OLD TESTAMENT READING: *Daniel 7:1-3, 15-18*

REFLECTIONS FROM THE CHURCH FATHERS

Four Kingdoms. JEROME: But as for the four beasts who came up out of the sea and were differentiated from one another, we may identify them from the angel's discourse. "These four great beasts," he says, "are four kingdoms that shall rise up from the earth." And as for the winds that strove in the great sea, they are called winds of heaven because each one of the angels does for his realm the duty entrusted to him. This too should be noted, that the fierceness and cruelty of the kingdoms concerned are indicated by the term "beasts." *Commentary on Daniel 7.2-3.*

Visibly Shaken. CHRYSOSTOM: Quite understandably, given what things he had seen. He is the first and only one to see the Father and the Son as in a vision. . . . When the advent of our Lord was soon drawing near, quite appropriately marvelous visions also appeared. *Commentary on Daniel 7.7.*

The Kingdoms Count for Nothing. THEODORET OF CYR: These kingdoms will be wiped out and the true, eternal kingdom will be handed over to the saints of the Almighty. Thus, while waiting for that eternal kingdom, count the kingdoms of this present age to be as nothing, which will soon enough come to their end. *Commentary on Daniel 7.17-18.*

PSALM OF RESPONSE: *Psalm 149*

NEW TESTAMENT READING: *Ephesians 1:11-23*

REFLECTIONS FROM THE CHURCH FATHERS

***God's Foreknowledge Sees All Things Before They Occur.* CHRYSOSTOM:** Since inheritance is a matter of fortune, not of choice or virtue, it often depends on obscure or fortuitous circumstance, overlooking virtue. It may bring to the fore those who are of no account. But notice how Paul qualifies this statement. . . . He says "have been destined," that is, God has set us apart for himself. It is as if to say God saw us before we became heirs. The foreknowledge of God is wonderful and

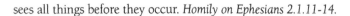

sees all things before they occur. *Homily on Ephesians 2.1.11-14.*

How the Spirit Seals Us. **DIDYMUS THE BLIND:** One who takes on discipline and virtue receives in his own character the seal and form of the knowledge that he puts on. So one who is made a partaker of the Holy Spirit becomes likewise spiritual and holy through disciplined fellowship with him. *On the Holy Spirit 20.*

Understanding Eschatological Metaphors. **JEROME:** He demonstrates the power of God through a human image. It is not that a material throne is set up and God the Father is physically seated on it and has the Son seated above with him. Rather, he communicates with this metaphor because we could not understand his role as incomparable governor and judge except in our own terms. . . . Being on the right or left of God is to be understood as meaning that saints are on his right but sinners on his left. . . . The very word *sits* denotes the power of kingship, through which God confers benefits on those above whom he is seated. He has reined them in and has them in his service, guiding those who had previously strayed. *Epistle to the Ephesians 1.1.21.*

That Name from Which All Naming Comes. **MARIUS VICTORINUS:** All names are secondary inventions. They primarily point to that which is in the created order, whether it is angels, human beings or temporal powers. By contrast, only that is eternal in essence which has existence without dependency on something else that exists, which lives by its own power. That which is eternal has no name in itself. Such "names" are added by us with our vocabulary and language. Christ receives these names from us (Son of God, divine, Spirit), yet he is still more than whatever these names convey. . . . Among names, the name that holds the chief place and that from which all names come is that which the Greeks call Being itself. But Christ is above this very being and is therefore above every name. *Epistle to the Ephesians 1.1.20-23.*

GOSPEL READING: *Luke 6:20-31*

REFLECTIONS FROM THE CHURCH FATHERS

Jesus, Though Rich, Became Poor for Us. AMBROSE: "Blessed," it says, "are the poor." Not all the poor are blessed, for poverty is neutral. The poor can be either good or evil, unless, perhaps, the blessed pauper is to be understood as he whom the prophet described, saying, "A righteous poor man is better than a rich liar." Blessed is the poor man who cried and whom the Lord heard. Blessed is the man poor in offense. Blessed is the man poor in vices. Blessed is the poor man in whom the prince of this world finds nothing. Blessed is the poor man who is like that poor Man who, although he was rich, became poor for our sake. Matthew fully revealed this when he said, "Blessed are the poor in spirit." One poor in spirit is not puffed up, is not exalted in the mind of his own flesh. This beatitude is first, when I have laid aside every sin, and I have taken off all malice, and I am content with simplicity, destitute of evils. All that remains is that I regulate my conduct. For what good does it do me to lack worldly goods, unless I am meek and gentle? *Exposition of the Gospel of Luke 5.53-54.*

To Turn the Other Cheek Requires Patience. AUGUSTINE: Temporal goods are to be despised in favor of eternal ones, as things on the left are to be despised in favor of those on the right. This has always been the aim of the holy martyrs. A final just vengeance is looked for, that is, the last supreme judgment, only when no chance of correction remains. But now we must be on our guard, more than anything else, not to lose patience in our eagerness to be justified, for patience is to be more highly prized than anything an enemy can take from us against our will. *Letter 138.*

Persecution Is Certainty of Heavenly Treasures. GREGORY OF NYSSA: The Christian who has advanced by means of good discipline and the gift of the Spirit to the measure of the age of reason experiences glory and pleasure and enjoyment that is greater than any human pleasure. These come to one after grace is given to him, after being hated because of Christ, being driven and enduring every insult and shame in behalf of his faith in God. For such a person, whose entire life centers on the resurrection and future blessings, every insult and scourging and persecution and the other sufferings leading up to the cross are all pleasure and refreshment and surety of heavenly treasures. For Jesus says, "Blessed are you when men reproach you and persecute you and, speaking falsely, say all manner of evil against you; for my sake rejoice and exult because your reward is great in heaven." *On the Christian Mode of Life.*

Virtuous Living Will Not Bring Praise from All People. CHRYSOS-TOM: "Woe to you when all people speak well of you." Notice how by the word *woe* he revealed to us the extent of the punishment awaiting such people. This word *woe,* after all, is an exclamation of lament, so that it is as if he is lamenting their fate when he says, "Woe to you when all people speak well of you." Notice too the precision in the expression: he didn't simply say "people" but "all people." You see, it is not possible for a virtuous person who travels by the straight and narrow path and follows Christ's commands to enjoy the praise and admiration of all people—so strong is the impulse of evil and the resistance to virtue. *Homilies on Genesis 23.8.*

The Custom of Christians Only. TERTULLIAN: To love friends is the custom for all people, but to love enemies is customary only for Christians. *To Scapula 1.*

⌘ CLOSING PRAYER

Remember, O Lord, the souls of those who have kept the faith, both those whom we remember and those whom we remember not, and grant them rest in the land of the living, in the joy of paradise, whence all pain and grief have fled away, where the light of your countenance shines forever; and guide in peace, O Lord, the end of our lives so as to be Christian and well-pleasing to you; gathering us around your throne, when you will and as you will, only without shame and sin; through your only-begotten Son our Lord and Savior Jesus Christ. Amen. *Liturgy of St. James*

Walking the Talk

⟩ THEME

We should do good, seek justice, defend the fatherless and care for the widow (Is 1:10-18). We confess our sins and give thanks that God forgives us (Ps 32:1-8), pray that we will be worthy of God's calling (2 Thess 1:1-4, 11-12) and are thankful that Christ came to save the lost (Lk 19:1-10).

⟩ OPENING PRAYER: *Proper 26*

Give us, O Lord, purity of lips, clean and innocent hearts and rectitude of action; give us humility, patience, self-control, prudence, justice and courage; give us the spirit of wisdom and understanding, the spirit of counsel and strength, the spirit of knowledge and godliness, and of thy fear; make us ever to seek thy face with all our heart, all our soul, all our mind; grant us to have a contrite and humbled heart in thy presence, to prefer nothing to thy love. Have mercy on us, we humbly beseech thee, through Jesus our Lord. Amen. *The Gallican Sacramentary*

⟩ OLD TESTAMENT READING: *Isaiah 1:10-18*

REFLECTIONS FROM THE CHURCH FATHERS

New Law of Christ. **EPISTLE OF BARNABAS:** The aids of our faith are fear and patience. Allies to us are endurance and self-control.

Where these things remain in purity in matters relating to the Lord, there wisdom, understanding, insight and knowledge are rejoicing with them. He has made it obvious to us through all the prophets that he does not require sacrifices, burnt offerings or oblations. . . . Therefore he has annulled these things, in order that the new law of our Lord Jesus Christ, which is free from the yoke of compulsion, might have an offering not made by humans. *Epistle of Barnabas* 2.2-6.

Purify the Conscience. CHRYSOSTOM: I say this, for in the prophet's words he does not mean bathing by water—the Jewish method of purification—but the purifying of the conscience. Let us also, then, be clean. *Homilies on the Gospel of John 70.*

Draw Near to Christ. JOHN OF DAMASCUS: Such therefore being the promises made by God to them that turn to him, don't delay . . . but draw near to Christ, our loving God, and be enlightened, and your face shall not be ashamed. For as soon as you go down into the bath of holy baptism, all the defilement of the old nature and all the burden of your many sins are buried in the water and pass into nothingness. And you come up from there a new person, pure from all pollution, with no spot or wrinkle of sin on you. *Barlaam and Joseph 32.*

PSALM OF RESPONSE: *Psalm 32:1-8*

NEW TESTAMENT READING: *2 Thessalonians 1:1-4, 11-12*

REFLECTIONS FROM THE CHURCH FATHERS

Thanksgiving Our Bounden Duty. THEODORE OF MOPSUESTIA: Paul seems to say here that the activity of grace has grown, for he does not say that "we give thanks" but that "we are bound to give thanks." In the same way we deserve to have a complaint lodged against us if we do not render to someone what is justly owed. This is the force of "as is fitting," where the point is that there has been an increase in the work of grace, such that what has happened in the Thessalonians is rightly referred to God as its source. *Commentary on 2 Thessalonians.*

How Can Faith Grow? CHRYSOSTOM: And how, you say, can faith increase? It does so when we suffer something horrible for the sake of faith. It is a great thing for faith to be solidly established and not to be carried away by some sophistry. But when the winds assail us, when the rains burst on us, when a violent storm is raised on every side and the waves follow on one another, that fact that we are not shaken is a proof that faith grows, grows abundantly and becomes more exalted. *Homilies on 2 Thessalonians 2.*

Only by Grace. AUGUSTINE: I said, "Salvation through this religion, through which alone true salvation is promised and truly promised, has never been lacking to anyone who was worthy of it, and the one to whom it was lacking was unworthy of it." I did not mean this as though anyone were worthy according to his own merits, but as the apostle says, "God's purpose in election" does not depend on deeds but is applied according to him who calls—Rebekah was told, "The elder shall serve the younger"—and he asserts that this call depends on the purpose of God. Hence Paul says, "Not according to our works, but according to his own purpose and grace." Similarly, he says, "We know that for those who love God all things work together for good, for those who are called according to his purpose." Concerning this call he says, "that he may consider you worthy of his calling." *Retractions 2.31.*

GOSPEL READING: *Luke 19:1-10*

REFLECTIONS FROM THE CHURCH FATHERS

Zacchaeus, Unable to See Jesus Through the Crowd, Was Unashamed to Climb the Tree of Folly. AUGUSTINE: Zacchaeus climbed away from the crowd and saw Jesus without the crowd getting in his way. The crowd laughs at the lowly, to people walking the way of humility, who leave the wrongs they suffer in God's hands and do not insist on getting back at their enemies. The crowd laughs at the lowly and says, "You helpless, miserable clod, you cannot even stick up for yourself and get back what is your own." The crowd gets in the way and prevents Jesus from being seen. The crowd boasts and crows when it is able to get back what it owns. It blocks the sight of the one who said as he hung on the cross, "Father, forgive them, because they do not know what they are doing." . . . He ignored the crowd that was getting in his way. He instead climbed a sycamore tree, a tree of "silly fruit." As the apostle says, "We preach Christ crucified, a stumbling block indeed to the Jews [now notice the sycamore], but folly to the Gentiles." Finally, the wise people of this world laugh at us about the cross of Christ and say, "What sort of minds do you people have, who worship a crucified God?" What sort of minds do we have? They are certainly not your kind of mind. "The wisdom of this world is folly with God." No, we do not have your kind of mind. You call our minds foolish. Say what you like, but for our part, let us climb the sycamore tree and see Jesus. The reason you cannot see Jesus is that you are ashamed to climb the sycamore tree. Let Zacchaeus grasp the sycamore tree, and let the humble person climb the cross. That is little enough, merely to climb it. We must not be ashamed of the cross of Christ. *Sermon 174.3.*

Zacchaeus Used His Property to Express Gratitude for His Salvation.
MAXIMUS OF TURIN: Zacchaeus must be praised. His riches were unable to keep him from the royal threshold. He should be greatly praised because his riches brought him to the threshold of the kingdom. From this, we understand that wealth is not a hindrance but a help to attaining the glory of Christ. While we possess it, we should not squander it on wild living but give it away for the sake of salvation. There is no crime in possessions, but there is crime in those who do not know how to use possessions. For the foolish, wealth is a temptation to vice, but for the wise, it is a help to virtue. Some receive an oppor-

tunity for salvation, but others acquire an obstacle of condemnation. *Sermons 95-96.*

Zacchaeus a True Son of Abraham. CYPRIAN: Finally, he also calls sons of Abraham those whom he perceives are active in helping and nourishing the poor. Zacchaeus said, "Behold, I give one half of my possessions to the poor, and if I have defrauded anyone of anything, I restore it fourfold." Jesus responded, "Today salvation has come to this house, since he too is a son of Abraham." If Abraham believed in God and it was accounted to him as righteousness, then he who gives alms according to the command of God certainly believes in God. He that possesses the true faith keeps the fear of God. Moreover, he keeps the fear of God by showing mercy to the poor. *Works and Almsgiving 8.*

⌐ CLOSING PRAYER

God grant that we may live our lives here without trouble and in security, and attain the joys of eternal life, by the grace of our Lord Jesus Christ and his love for us, to whom be glory and might, together with the Father and the Holy Spirit, now and always, and to the ages of ages. Amen. *Chrysostom*

Eternity

☧ THEME

We know that our Redeemer lives (Job 19:23-27a)! We walk in the paths of righteousness, always kept close by the Lord in "the shadow of [his] wings" (Ps 17:1-9). We give thanks to him (2 Thess 2:1-5, 13-17) and look forward to being resurrected and living with him in eternity in heaven (Lk 20:27-38).

☧ OPENING PRAYER: *November 9*

May all of us who call on the name of our Lord Jesus Christ be delivered from the present delights and the future afflictions of the evil one by participating in the reality of the blessings held in store and already revealed to us in Christ our Lord himself, who alone with the Father and the Holy Spirit is praised by all creation. Amen. *Maximus the Confessor*

☧ OLD TESTAMENT READING: *Job 19:23-27a*

REFLECTIONS FROM THE CHURCH FATHERS

Job Speaks Truly and Deliberately. JULIAN OF ECLANUM: We desire what we have said with a troubled mind not be confusedly relegated to oblivion as a cause of shame. On the contrary, we want what we have said seriously and carefully to be fixed in the memory and remain in the mouth of many people. Therefore also holy Job, intending to show that he had not poured out what he had said with a troubled mind but that his words were truthful and reasonable, wishes that his words are not only written on paper but also engraved on lead and stone, so that they may be preserved for a long time. *Exposition on the Book of Job 19.23-24.*

A Prophecy. EPHREM THE SYRIAN: "For I know that my Redeemer lives and that at last he will be revealed on the earth." Here the blessed Job predicts the future manifestation of Emmanuel in the flesh at the end of time. *Commentary on Job 19.25.*

⫷ PSALM OF RESPONSE: *Psalm 17:1-9*

⫷ NEW TESTAMENT READING: *2 Thessalonians 2:1-5, 13-17*

REFLECTIONS FROM THE CHURCH FATHERS

The Timing of the Resurrection Unknown. CHRYSOSTOM: When the resurrection will be, he has not said: "It will come in due order"; he has said: "And our assembling to meet him." This point is quite important. Observe how Paul's exhortation is accompanied by praise and encouragement, for he makes it clear that Jesus and all the saints will certainly appear at that time with us. *Homilies on 2 Thessalonians 3.*

The Benefit of Not Knowing. ATHANASIUS: And further, not to know when the end is, or when the day of the end will occur, is actually a good thing. If people knew the time of the end, they might begin to ignore the present time as they waited for the end days. They might well begin to argue that they should only focus on themselves. Therefore, God has also remained silent concerning the time of our death. If people knew the day of their death, they would immediately begin to neglect themselves for the greater part of their lifetime. The Word, then, has concealed both the end of all things and the time of our own death from us, for in the end of all is the end of each, and in the end of each the end of all is comprehended. This is so that, when things remain uncertain and always in prospect, we advance day by day as if summoned, reaching forward to the things before us and forgetting the things behind. . . . The Lord, then, knowing what is good for us beyond ourselves, thus stabilized the disciples in a correct understanding. They, being taught, set right those of Thessalonica, who were likely to err on the very same point. *Discourses Against the Arians 3.49-50.*

The Trial Is Transitory. BASIL THE GREAT: In truth, both of our ears rang on learning of the shameless and inhuman heresy of those who persecuted you. They had no regard for age, or for the labors of a life well spent or for the affection of the people. On the contrary, they tortured and dishonored bodies, handed them over to exile and plundered whatever property they were able to find, not fearing the censure of men or foreseeing the fearful requital of the just Judge. . . . But, along with these considerations, there came this thought also: The Lord has not entirely abandoned his churches, has he? And this is not the last hour, is it? Is apostasy finding an entrance through them, in order that now the impious one may be revealed, "the son of perdition, who opposes and is exalted above all that is called God, or that is worshiped"? But if the trial is transitory, bear it, noble champions of Christ. . . . For if all creation is destroyed and the scheme of the world is altered, what wonder is it if we also, being a part of creation, suffer the common evils and are given over to afflictions? . . . The crowns of martyrs await you, brothers; the choirs of confessors are ready to reach out to you their hands and to receive you into their own number. *Letter 139.*

Delivered Without Writing. CHRYSOSTOM: Paul did not instruct Timothy in his duty through letters alone, but also through the spoken word. He shows this, both in many other passages, as where he says, "whether by word or our epistle," and especially here. Let us not, therefore, suppose that Paul spoke anything imperfectly that was related to doctrine. For he delivered many things to Timothy without writing. He reminds him of these when he says, "Hold fast the form of sound

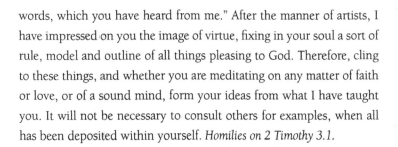

words, which you have heard from me." After the manner of artists, I have impressed on you the image of virtue, fixing in your soul a sort of rule, model and outline of all things pleasing to God. Therefore, cling to these things, and whether you are meditating on any matter of faith or love, or of a sound mind, form your ideas from what I have taught you. It will not be necessary to consult others for examples, when all has been deposited within yourself. *Homilies on 2 Timothy 3.1.*

⑊ GOSPEL READING: *Luke 20:27-38*

REFLECTIONS FROM THE CHURCH FATHERS

The Sadducees Consider Themselves Just. EPHREM THE SYRIAN: "The Sadducees came and were saying to him, 'There is no resurrection of the dead.'" They are called Sadducees, that is, "the just," because they say, "We do not serve God for the sake of reward." They do not await the resurrection, and for this reason they call themselves "the just," since they say, "We should love God without a reward." *Commentary on Tatian's Diatessaron 16.22.*

No Marriage in the Resurrection. AUGUSTINE: What did the Lord say to the Sadducees? He said, "You are mistaken, not knowing the Scriptures or the power of God. For in the resurrection they marry neither husbands nor wives; for neither do they start dying again, but they will be equal to the angels of God." The power of God is great. Why do they not marry husbands or wives? They will not start dying again. When one generation departs, another is required to succeed it. There will not be such liability to decay in that place. The Lord passed through the usual stages of growth, from infancy to adult manhood, because he was bearing the substance of flesh that still was mortal. After he had risen again at the age at which he was buried, are we to imagine that he is growing old in heaven? He says, "They will be equal to the angels of God." He eliminated the assumption of the Jews and refuted the objection of the Sadducees, because the Jews did indeed believe the dead would rise again, but they had crude, fleshly ideas about the state of humanity after resurrection. He said, "They will be equal to the angels of God." . . . It has already been stated that we are to rise again. We have heard from the Lord that we rise again to the life of the angels. In his own resurrection, he has shown us in what specific form we are to rise again. *Sermon 362.18-19.*

No Marriage and No Physical Desire in the Resurrection. CLEMENT OF ALEXANDRIA: If anyone ponders over this answer about the resurrection of the dead, he will find that the Lord is not rejecting marriage but is purging the expectation of physical desire in the resurrection. The words "the children of this age" were not spoken in contrast to the children of some other age. It is like saying, "those born in this generation," who are children by force of birth, being born and engendering themselves, since without the process of birth no one will pass into this life. This process of birth is balanced by a process of decay and is no longer in store for the person who has once been cut off from life here. *Stromata 3.87.2-3.*

CLOSING PRAYER

Father, I am seeking: I am hesitant and uncertain, but will you, O God, watch over each step of mine and guide me? *Augustine*

Faithfulness

⊰ THEME

We look toward Christ's second coming (Mal 4:1-2a), and with all creation, we sing praises to God for his marvelous works (Ps 98). In anticipation of his second coming, we work hard and look for the good that
we might do (2 Thess 3:6-13), knowing that God will protect and care
for us (Lk 21:5-19).

⊰ OPENING PRAYER: *Proper 28*

O Lord our God, under the shadow of your wings we will rest. Defend
us and support us, bear us up when we are little, and we know that
even down to our gray hairs, you will carry us. *Augustine*

⊰ OLD TESTAMENT READING: *Malachi 4:1-2a*

REFLECTIONS FROM THE CHURCH FATHERS

Jesus Guides the Ship, the Church. CHRYSOSTOM: A person who
has no knowledge of the sea could not sail in full daylight with such
confidence and ease as the helmsman sails in the middle of the night,
when the sea shows itself in a more formidable mood. Why is this? The
helmsman is wide awake and quite calm as he puts to practice his skill
in sailing. He keeps careful watch not only on the pathways of the sea
and the courses of the stars but also on the assaults of the winds. The
helmsman's wisdom and knowledge are great. So it is that many a time

when the blast of a more violent gale has struck his ship and is about to swamp it, he has the wisdom to make many a quick change in the angle of his sails. He runs before the wind and puts an end to all danger from the gale. By pitting his skill against the violence of the winds' blasts, he snatches his vessel from the storm. Those sailors voyage over waters we can see and hear and feel. Although they are searching for this world's goods, they continuously keep their minds watchful and alert. All the more must we keep ourselves prepared in the same way they do. Surely the careless person faces a greater danger, while the sober one is more secure. This ship of ours is not constructed of timbers but is joined fast together with the divine Scriptures. The stars in the sky do not guide us on our way, but the Sun of justice steers our ship on its course. As we sit at the tiller, we are not waiting for the blasts of wind. We are waiting for the gentle breath of the Spirit. *Against the Anomoeans, Homily 7.5-6.*

The Lord's Day Is the Day of the Sun of Justice. JEROME: "This is the day the Lord has made; let us be glad and rejoice in it." The Lord has made all days, of course, but other days may belong as well to the Jews, and heretics too; they may even belong to the heathens. The Lord's day, however, the day of the resurrection, the day of Christians, is our day. It is called the Lord's day because on this day the Lord ascended to the Father as victor. *Homily 94 (On Easter Sunday).*

A Sign of Christ's Two Comings. THEODORET OF CYR: This applies both to the first coming of our Savior and the second: in the first he rose like a kind of sun for us who were seated in darkness and shadow, freed us from sin, gave us a share in righteousness, covered us with spiritual gifts like wings and provided healing for our souls. In the second coming for those worn out in the present life he will appear either in accord with their will or against it, and as a just judge he will judge justly and provide the promised good things. *Commentary on Malachi 4.2.*

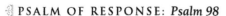

PSALM OF RESPONSE: *Psalm 98*

NEW TESTAMENT READING: *2 Thessalonians 3:6-13*

REFLECTIONS FROM THE CHURCH FATHERS

Avoid Controversy, Practice Charity. BASIL THE GREAT: Desist from curious inquiry and unseemly controversies. Think on those things that are worthy of your heavenly calling. Live in a manner befitting the gospel of Christ, relying on the hope of eternal life and the heavenly kingdom prepared for all those who keep the commandments of God the Father, according to the gospel of Jesus Christ our Lord in the Holy Spirit and in truth. *Concerning Faith.*

Watch for Those Who Traffic in Christ. DIDACHE: Let everyone who comes in the name of the Lord be received, and then, when you have taken stock of him, you will know—for you will have insight—what is right and false. If the person who comes is just passing through, help him as much as you can, but he shall not stay with you more than two or three days—if that is necessary. If he wants to settle in with you, though, and he is a craftsman, let him work and eat. If he has no craft, take care in your insight: no Christian should live with you in idleness. If he is unwilling to do what that calls for, he is using Christ to make a living. Be on your guard against people like this. *The Didache 12.1-5.*

Look at the Ant. APOSTOLIC CONSTITUTIONS: Let the young persons of the church endeavor to minister diligently in all essential matters. Mind your business with all suitable seriousness, that so you may always have enough to support yourselves and those who are needy, and not burden the church of God. For we ourselves, besides our attention to the word of the gospel, do not neglect our inferior vocations. For some of us are fishermen, some tentmakers, some farmers, that so we may never be idle. So says Solomon somewhere, "Go to the ant, you sluggard; consider her ways diligently, and become wiser than she. For she, having neither field, overseer nor ruler, prepares her food in the summer, and lays up a great store in the harvest. Or else go to the bee, and learn how laborious she is, and how valuable her work is, whose labors both kings and common men make use of for their health. The bee is desirable and glorious, though she is weak in strength, yet by honoring wisdom she is improved." . . . Labor therefore continually; for the blot of the slothful is not to be healed. But "if anyone among you does not work, let not such a one eat" among you. For the Lord our God hates the lazy. For no one of those who are dedicated to God ought to be idle. *Constitutions of the Holy Apostles 2.6.3.*

GOSPEL READING: *Luke 21:5-19*

REFLECTIONS FROM THE CHURCH FATHERS

Apostles Will Be Persecuted As a Sign of the Coming Consummation.
CYRIL OF ALEXANDRIA: Jesus gives them clear and evident signs of the time when the consummation of the world draws near. He says that there will be wars, turmoil, famines and epidemics everywhere. There will be terrors from heaven and great signs. As another Evangelist says, "All the stars shall fall, and the heaven be rolled up like a scroll, and its powers will be shaken." In the middle of this, the Savior places what refers to the capture of Jerusalem. He mixes the accounts together in both parts of the narrative. Before all these things, he says, "They will lay their hands on you and persecute you, delivering you up to synagogues and to prisons and bringing you before kings and rulers for my name's sake. This will be a witness to you." Before the times of consummation, the land of the Jews was taken captive, and the Roman armies overran it. They burned the temple, overthrew their national government and stopped the means for legal worship. They no longer had sacrifices, now that the temple was destroyed. The country of the Jews together with Jerusalem itself was totally laid waste. Before these things happened, they persecuted the blessed disciples. They imprisoned

them and had a part in unendurable trials. They brought the disciples before judges and sent them to kings. Paul was sent to Rome to Caesar. . . . Christ promises, however, that he will deliver them certainly and completely. He says that a hair of your head will not perish. *Commentary on Luke, Homily 139.*

The Faithful Christian Recognized by Belief in Resurrection of the Body. AUGUSTINE: We should have no doubt that our mortal flesh also will rise again at the end of the world. . . . Believe Christ when he says, "Not a hair of your head shall perish." Putting aside all unbelief, consider how valuable you are. How can our Redeemer despise any person when he cannot despise a hair of that person's head? How are we going to doubt that he intends to give eternal life to our soul and body? He took on a soul and body in which to die for us, which he laid down for us when he died and which he took up again that we might not fear death. *Sermon 214.11-12.*

⁙ CLOSING PRAYER

Be present, O merciful God, and protect us through the silent hours of the night, that we who are wearied by the changes and chances of this fleeting world may repose on thy eternal changelessness, through the everlasting Christ our Lord. *The Gelasian Sacramentary*

Our Refuge

⊰ THEME

Just as a shepherd gathers his flock, so God will gather us together and cause us to be fruitful and multiply (Jer 23:1-6). He is our refuge and strength, a very present help in trouble—why should we fear (Ps 46)? We acknowledge God's power and our deliverance from the darkness of sin (Col 1:11-20). Even as Jesus remembered the criminal who asked him for mercy at the crucifixion (Lk 23:33-43), so he will remember us.

⊰ OPENING PRAYER: *Proper 29, Christ the King*

O God, you divide the day from the night; separate our deeds from the darkness of sin, that we may continually live in your light and reflect in all our deeds your eternal beauty. Amen. *The Leonine Sacramentary*

⊰ OLD TESTAMENT READING: *Jeremiah 23:1-6*

REFLECTIONS FROM THE CHURCH FATHERS

Zerubbabel as a Type of Christ. THEODORET OF CYR: These things were fulfilled according to the type in the case of Zerubbabel and Jeshua, the son of Jozadak. However, this prophecy was not altogether fulfilled, for many would rise up against them—not only their neighbors but also later on the Macedonians and finally the Romans. But the prophecy proclaims the everlasting nature of grace. Therefore, it is clear that these things were not fulfilled during their lifetimes but during the lifetimes of the apostles, for they alone had the gift of the Holy Spirit. . . . The stupefied Jews shamelessly endeavor to apply this to Zerubbabel. But they need to understand that he was no king—just a popular leader—and he was not called Jozadak. Neither is the meaning of the name appropriate to him, the word meaning "the Lord our righteousness" or, in the Syriac rendering, "Lord, make us righteous"—neither of which applies to Zerubbabel. Since, however, he was a type of Christ the Lord and brought back the captives from Babylon to Judah, just as the Lord transferred those enslaved by the devil to truth, anyone applying this to him in the manner of a type would do nothing beyond reason. It is necessary that we understand, however, that it is the Lord Jesus Christ, a descendant of David according to the flesh, who is proclaimed by the prophets as "the righteous dawn," "the righteous king" and "the Lord of righteousness." *On Jeremiah 5.23.*

The Righteous Branch and the Fallen. LEO THE GREAT: There was only one remedy in the secret of the divine plan that could help the fallen living in the general ruin of the entire human race. This remedy was that one of the sons of Adam should be born free and innocent of original transgression, to prevail for the rest by his example and by his merits. This was not permitted by natural generation. There could be no clean offspring from our faulty stock by this seed. The Scripture says, "Who can make a clean thing conceived of an unclean seed? Isn't it you alone?" David's Lord was made David's Son, and from the fruit of the promised branch sprang. He is one without fault, the twofold nature coming together into one person. By this one and the same conception and birth sprung our Lord Jesus Christ, in whom was present both true Godhead for the performance of mighty works and true manhood for the endurance of sufferings. *Sermon 28.3.*

⌐ PSALM OF RESPONSE: *Psalm 46*

❧ NEW TESTAMENT READING: *Colossians 1:11-20*

REFLECTIONS FROM THE CHURCH FATHERS

Vessels Made Perfect. BASIL THE GREAT: For he himself has bound the strong man and stolen his goods, that is, humanity itself, whom our enemy had abused in every evil activity. God has created "vessels fit for the Master's use," that is, us who have been perfected for every work through the preparation of that part of us which is in our own control. Thus we gained our approach to the Father through him, being translated from "the power of darkness to be partakers of the inheritance of the saints in light." *On the Holy Spirit 8.18.*

From Him and Then from Us. CHRYSOSTOM: The whole is from him, the giving both of these things and of those; for no achievement finds its source in us. . . . Not then so as to deliver humankind from darkness only did he show his love toward him. It is a great thing indeed to have been delivered from darkness; but to have been brought into a kingdom too is far greater. *Homilies on Colossians 2.*

Sharers in His Kingdom. THEODORE OF MOPSUESTIA: Because we share a likeness of nature with the man whom Christ assumed in the incarnation, we also share in his kingdom of love when we do good works as his adopted sons. *Commentary on Colossians.*

Only Through Christ. AMBROSIASTER: Freed thus from the condition of darkness, that is, plucked from the infernal place, in which we were held by the devil both because of our own and because of Adam's transgression, who is the father of sinners, we were translated by faith into the heavenly kingdom of the Son of God. This was so that he might show us by what love God loved us, when, raising us from deepest hell, he led us into heaven with his true Son. *Commentary on Colossians.*

Live Your Baptism! LEO THE GREAT: "Snatched from the powers of darkness" at such a great "price" and by so great a "mystery," and loosed from the chains of the ancient captivity, make sure, dearly beloved, that the devil does not destroy the integrity of your souls with any stratagem. Whatever is forced on you contrary to the Christian faith, whatever is presented to you contrary to the commandments of God, it comes from the deceptions of the one who tries with many wiles to divert you from eternal life, and, by seizing certain occasions of human weakness, leads careless and negligent souls again into his snares of death. Let all those reborn through water and the Holy Spirit consider the one whom they have renounced. *Sermon 57.5.1-2.*

⸎ GOSPEL READING: *Luke 23:33-43*

REFLECTIONS FROM THE CHURCH FATHERS

Jesus Removes the Flaming Sword. ORIGEN: "Today you will be with me in paradise." Through saying this, he also gave to all those who believe and confess access to the entrance that Adam previously had closed by sinning. Who else could remove "the flaming turning sword which was placed to guard the tree of life" and the gates of paradise? What other sentinel was able to turn the "cherubim" from their incessant vigil, except only he to whom "was given all power in heaven and in earth"? No one else besides him could do these things. *Homilies on Leviticus 9.5.53.*

Humanity Again Permitted to Enter Paradise. PRUDENTIUS:
We believe in thy words, O Redeemer,
Which, when triumphing over death's darkness,
Thou did speak to thy robber companion,
Bidding him in thy footprints to follow.
Lo, now to the faithful is opened
The bright road to paradise leading;
Man again is permitted to enter
The garden he lost to the Serpent.

To that sacred abode, O great Leader,
Take, we pray thee, the soul of thy servant;
Let it rest in its native country,
Which it left, as an exile to wander.
Hymns for Every Day 10.157-68.

Through the Altar of the Cross the Thief Enters Paradise. LEO THE GREAT: This cross of Christ holds the mystery of its true and prophesied altar. There, through the saving victim, a sacrifice of human nature is celebrated. There the blood of a spotless lamb dissolved the pact of that ancient transgression. There the whole perversity of the devil's mastery was abolished, while humility triumphed as conqueror over boasting pride. The effect of faith was so swift that one of the two thieves crucified with Christ who believed in the Son of God entered paradise justified. Who could explain the mystery of such a great gift? Who could describe the power of such a marvelous transformation? In a brief moment of time, the guilt of a longstanding wickedness was abolished. In the middle of the harsh torments of a struggling soul, fastened to the gallows, that thief passes over to Christ, and the grace of Christ gives a crown to him, someone who incurred punishment for his own wickedness. *Sermon 55.3.*

CLOSING PRAYER

O Lord, you have given us your Word as a light to shine on our path; grant that we may so meditate on that Word and follow its teaching that we may find in it the light that shines more and more until the perfect day; through Jesus Christ our Lord. *Jerome*

Ancient Christian Commentary on Scripture
CITATIONS

The following volumes from the Ancient Christian Commentary on Scripture, Thomas C. Oden, General Editor, from InterVarsity Press, Downers Grove, Illinois, were cited in this book.

Genesis 1–11, ed. Andrew Louth, Old Testament volume 1, ©2001.

Genesis 12–50, ed. Mark Sheridan, Old Testament volume 2, ©2002.

Exodus, Leviticus, Numbers, Deuteronomy, ed. Joseph T. Lienhard, Old Testament volume 3, ©2001.

Joshua, Judges, Ruth, 1–2 Samuel, ed. John R. Franke, Old Testament volume 4, ©2005.

1–2 Kings, 1–2 Chronicles, Ezra, Nehemiah, Esther, ed. Mario Conti, Old Testament volume 5, ©2008.

Proverbs, Ecclesiastes, Song of Solomon, ed. J. Robert Wright, Old Testament volume 9, ©2005.

Isaiah 1–39, ed. Steven A. McKinion, Old Testament volume 10, ©2004.

Isaiah 40–66, ed. Mark W. Elliott, Old Testament volume 11, ©2007.

Jeremiah, Lamentations, ed. Dean O. Wenthe, Old Testament volume 12, ©2009.

Ezekiel, Daniel, ed. Kenneth Stevenson and Donald McCullough, Old Testament volume 13, ©2008.

The Twelve Prophets, ed. Alberto Ferreiro, Old Testament volume 14, ©2003.

Matthew 1–13, ed. Manlio Simonetti, New Testament volume 1a, ©2001.

Luke, ed. Arthur A. Just Jr., New Testament volume 3, ©2003.

John 1–10, ed. Joel C. Elowsky, New Testament volume 4a, ©2006.

John 11–21, ed. Joel C. Elowsky, New Testament volume 4b, ©2007.

Acts, ed. Francis Martin, New Testament volume 5, ©2006.

Romans, ed. Gerald Bray, New Testament volume 6, ©2005.

1–2 Corinthians, ed. Gerald Bray, New Testament volume 7, ©2006.

Galatians, Ephesians, Philippians, ed. Mark J. Edwards, New Testament volume 8, ©2005.

Colossians, 1–2 Thessalonians, 1–2 Timothy, Titus, Philemon, ed. Peter Gorday, New Testament volume 9, ©2000.

Hebrews, ed. Erik M. Heen and Philip D. W. Krey, New Testament volume 10, ©2005.

Revelation, ed. William C. Weinrich, New Testament volume 12, ©2005.

PRAYER CITATIONS

WEEK 1

Opening Prayer: The Gelasian Sacramentary, *A Chain of Prayer Across the Ages,* arr. Selina Fitzherbert Fox (New York: E. P. Dutton, 1943), p. 4.

Closing Prayer: The Leonine Sacramentary, *A Chain of Prayer Across the Ages,* p. 16.

WEEK 2

Opening Prayer: The Leonine Sacramentary, *Ancient Collects and Other Prayers,* comp. William Bright (Oxford: James Parker & Co., 1908), p. 137.

Closing Prayer: The Gelasian Sacramentary, *Ancient Collects and Other Prayers,* p. 87.

WEEK 3

Opening Prayer: Clement of Rome, *The Westminster Collection of Christian Prayers,* comp. Dorothy M. Stewart (Louisville, Ky.: Westminster John Knox Press, 2002), p. 266.

Closing Prayer: Augustine, *The Westminster Collection of Christian Prayers,* p. 267.

WEEK 4

Opening Prayer: Serapion, *Two Thousand Years of Prayer,* comp. Michael

Counsell (Harrisburg, Penn.: Morehouse Publishing, 1999), p. 24.

Closing Prayer: Cyprian, *Two Thousand Years of Prayer,* p. 17.

WEEK 5 *(CHRISTMAS)*

Opening Prayer: Leo the Great, *Readings for the Daily Office from the Early Church,* comp. J. Robert Wright (New York: Church Hymnal Corporation, 1991), p. 130.

Closing Prayer: Gregory of Nazianzus, *The Westminster Collection of Christian Prayers,* p. 18.

WEEK 6 *(EPIPHANY)*

Opening Prayer: The Gelasian Sacramentary, *The Westminster Collection of Christian Prayers,* p. 81.

Closing Prayer: Columbanus, *The Westminster Collection of Christian Prayers,* p. 199.

WEEK 7

Opening Prayer: The Leonine Sacramentary, *A Chain of Prayer Across the Ages,* p. 154.

Closing Prayer: Ambrose, excerpt from "Deus Creator Omnium," in *The Macmillan Book of Earliest Christian Hymns,* ed. F. Forrester Church and Terrence J. Mulry (New York: Macmillan, 1988), p. 203.

WEEK 8

Opening Prayer: The Gallican Sacramentary, *A Chain of Prayer Across the Ages,* p. 110.

Closing Prayer: Origen, *The Westminster Collection of Christian Prayers,* p. 16.

WEEK 9

Opening Prayer: Polycarp, *The Westminster Collection of Christian Prayers,* p. 33.

Closing Prayer: The Gelasian Sacramentary, *Two Thousand Years of Prayer,* p. 98.

WEEK 10

Opening Prayer: The Gregorian Sacramentary, *Two Thousand Years of Prayer,* p. 104.

Closing Prayer: The Leonine Sacramentary, *Two Thousand Years of Prayer,* p. 107.

WEEK 11

Opening Prayer: The Gelasian Sacramentary, *A Chain of Prayer Across the Ages,* p. 47.

Closing Prayer: Clement of Alexandria, *The Westminster Collection of Christian Prayers,* p. 330.

WEEK 12

Opening Prayer: The Gelasian Sacramentary, *Two Thousand Years of Prayer,* p. 100.

Closing Prayer: Augustine, *The Westminster Collection of Christian Prayers,* p. 162.

WEEK 13

Opening Prayer: The Gelasian Sacramentary, *Prayers for Public Worship,* comp. and ed. James Ferguson (New York: Harper & Brothers, 1958), p. 222.

Closing Prayer: Liturgy of St. Mark, *A Chain of Prayer Across the Ages,* p. 53.

WEEK 14

Opening Prayer: Columbanus, *The Westminster Collection of Christian Prayers,* p. 187.

Closing Prayer: Apollonius, *The Westminster Collection of Christian Prayers,* p. 187.

WEEK 15

Opening Prayer: Patrick, *The Westminster Collection of Christian Prayers,* p. 339.

Closing Prayer: The Gregorian Sacramentary, *Book of English Collects,* no. 96, in Roger Geffen, *The Handbook of Public Prayer* (New York: Macmillan, 1963), p. 67.

WEEK 16

Opening Prayer: Jerome, *The Westminster Collection of Christian Prayers,* p. 335.

Closing Prayer: Hilary of Poitiers, *Two Thousand Years of Prayer,* p. 27.

WEEK 17

Opening Prayer: Columbanus, *Readings for the Daily Office from the Early Church,* p. 441.

Closing Prayer: Ambrose, *Readings for the Daily Office from the Early Church,* p. 181.

WEEK 18

Opening Prayer: Augustine, *The Westminster Collection of Christian Prayers,* p. 336.

Closing Prayer: The Leonine Sacramentary, *A Chain of Prayer Across the Ages,* p. 194.

WEEK 19 *(EASTER)*

Opening Prayer: The Gelasian Sacramentary, *Ancient Collects and Other Prayers,* p. 54.

Closing Prayer: From an Ancient Collect, *A Chain of Prayer Across the Ages,* p, 198.

WEEK 20

Opening Prayer: Augustine, *The Westminster Collection of Christian Prayers,* p. 224.

Closing Prayer: Ephrem the Syrian, *Two Thousand Years of Prayer,* p. 58.

WEEK 21

Opening Prayer: The Gelasian Sacramentary, *A Chain of Prayer Across the Ages,* p. 90.

Closing Prayer: Clement of Rome, *The Westminster Collection of Christian Prayers,* p. 346.

WEEK 22

Opening Prayer: Liturgy of St. Mark, *A Chain of Prayer Across the Ages,* p. 71.

Closing Prayer: Jerome, *Two Thousand Years of Prayer,* p. 30.

WEEK 23

Opening Prayer: Augustine, *The Westminster Collection of Christian Prayers,* p. 282.

Closing Prayer: Patrick, *The Westminster Collection of Christian Prayers,* p. 137.

WEEK 24

Opening Prayer: The Gelasian Sacramentary, *Prayers for Public Worship,* p. 38.

Closing Prayer: Augustine, *The Westminster Collection of Christian Prayers,* p. 277.

WEEK 25

Opening Prayer: Attributed to Benedict of Nursia, *The Westminster Collection of Christian Prayers,* p. 369.

Closing Prayer: The Gelasian Sacramentary, *A Chain of Prayer Across the Ages,* p. 24.

WEEK 26 *(PENTECOST)*

Opening Prayer: The Leonine Sacramentary, *A Chain of Prayer Across the Ages,* p. 74.

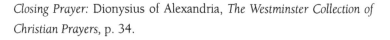

Closing Prayer: Dionysius of Alexandria, *The Westminster Collection of Christian Prayers*, p. 34.

WEEK 27

Opening Prayer: The Gregorian Sacramentary, *Two Thousand Years of Prayer*, p. 103.

Closing Prayer: Augustine, *The Westminster Collection of Christian Prayers*, p. 121.

WEEK 28

Opening Prayer: Andrew of Crete, *The Westminster Collection of Christian Prayers*, p. 303.

Closing Prayer: Gregory of Nazianzus, *The Westminster Collection of Christian Prayers*, p. 280.

WEEK 29

Opening Prayer: Augustine, *The Westminster Collection of Christian Prayers*, p. 308.

Closing Prayer: Jerome, *Two Thousand Years of Prayer*, p. 29.

WEEK 30

Opening Prayer: Cyril of Jerusalem, *The Westminster Collection of Christian Prayers*, p. 270.

Closing Prayer: Liturgy of St. James, *Two Thousand Years of Prayer*, p. 47.

WEEK 31

Opening Prayer: Coptic Liturgy of St. Cyril, *A Chain of Prayer Across the Ages*, p. 48.

Closing Prayer: Hilary of Poitiers, *The Westminster Collection of Christian Prayers*, p. 369.

WEEK 32

Opening Prayer: Cyprian, *Prayers for Public Worship*, p. 55.

Closing Prayer: Gregory of Nazianzus, *The Westminster Collection of Christian Prayers,* p. 341.

WEEK 33

Opening Prayer: Ambrose, *Readings for the Daily Office from the Early Church,* pp. 74-75.

Closing Prayer: Boniface, *The Westminster Collection of Christian Prayers,* p. 131.

WEEK 34

Opening Prayer: Tertullian, *Readings for the Daily Office from the Early Church,* p. 148.

Closing Prayer: Liturgy of St. John Chrysostom, *Two Thousand Years of Prayer,* pp. 48-49.

WEEK 35

Opening Prayer: The Gelasian Sacramentary, *A Chain of Prayer Across the Ages,* p. 55.

Closing Prayer: Augustine, *The Westminster Collection of Christian Prayers,* p. 317.

WEEK 36

Opening Prayer: The Gelasian Sacramentary, *A Chain of Prayer Across the Ages,* p. 33.

Closing Prayer: The Gelasian Sacramentary, *A Chain of Prayer Across the Ages,* p. 176.

WEEK 37

Opening Prayer: Columba, *The Westminster Collection of Christian Prayers,* p. 188.

Closing Prayer: Bede, *Two Thousand Years of Prayer,* p. 87.

WEEK 38

Opening Prayer: Charlemagne, Gallican Collect, *A Chain of Prayer Across the Ages*, p. 238.

Closing Prayer: Columba, *The Westminster Collection of Christian Prayers*, p. 199.

WEEK 39

Opening Prayer: The Gelasian Sacramentary, *Prayers for Public Worship*, p. 204.

Closing Prayer: The Leonine Sacramentary, *The Westminster Collection of Christian Prayers*, p. 164.

WEEK 40

Opening Prayer: The Gallican Sacramentary, *A Chain of Prayer Across the Ages,* p. 32.

Closing Prayer: Hilary of Poitiers, *The Westminster Collection of Christian Prayers*, p. 290.

WEEK 41

Opening Prayer: Liturgy of St. Basil the Great, *Two Thousand Years of Prayer,* pp. 47-48.

Closing Prayer: Hilary of Poitiers, *Two Thousand Years of Prayer,* p. 28.

WEEK 42

Opening Prayer: The Gelasian Sacramentary, *Two Thousand Years of Prayer,* p. 100.

Closing Prayer: The Leonine Sacramentary, *Two Thousand Years of Prayer,* p. 108.

WEEK 43

Opening Prayer: Benedict of Nursia, *Two Thousand Years of Prayer,* p. 35.

Closing Prayer: Gregory the Great, *Two Thousand Years of Prayer,* p. 108.

WEEK 44

Opening Prayer: Clement of Rome, *Two Thousand Years of Prayer,* pp. 7-8.

Closing Prayer: Ambrose, excerpt from "Jam Lucis Orto Sidera," *The Macmillan Book of Earliest Christian Hymns,* p. 205.

WEEK 45

Opening Prayer: Augustine, *The Westminster Collection of Christian Prayers,* p. 334.

Closing Prayer: The Gelasian Sacramentary, *A Chain of Prayer Across the Ages,* p. 61.

WEEK 46

Opening Prayer: The Gregorian Sacramentary, *Two Thousand Years of Prayer,* p. 105.

Closing Prayer: Clement of Alexandria, *Readings for the Daily Office from the Early Church,* p. 82.

WEEK 47

Opening Prayer: Ambrose, *Two Thousand Years of Prayer,* p. 28.

Closing Prayer: Polycarp, *Two Thousand Years of Prayer,* p. 10.

WEEK 48 *(ALL SAINTS' DAY)*

Opening Prayer: Ephrem the Syrian, *Two Thousand Years of Prayer,* p. 59.

Closing Prayer: Liturgy of St. James, *Two Thousand Years of Prayer,* p. 47.

WEEK 49

Opening Prayer: The Gallican Sacramentary, *A Chain of Prayer Across the Ages,* p. 142.

Closing Prayer: Chrysostom, *Two Thousand Years of Prayer,* p. 37.

WEEK 50

Opening Prayer: Maximus the Confessor, *Two Thousand Years of Prayer,* p. 43.

Closing Prayer: Augustine, *The Westminster Collection of Christian Prayers,* p. 333.

WEEK 51

Opening Prayer: Augustine, *The Westminster Collection of Christian Prayers,* p. 305.

Closing Prayer: The Gelasian Sacramentary, *The Westminster Collection of Christian Prayers,* p. 280.

WEEK 52

Opening Prayer: The Leonine Sacramentary, *Two Thousand Years of Prayer,* p. 108.

Closing Prayer: Jerome, *The Westminster Collection of Christian Prayers,* p. 16.

BIOGRAPHICAL
SKETCHES

Ambrose of Milan (c. 333 or 339-397; fl. 374-397). Bishop of Milan and teacher of Augustine who defended the divinity of the Holy Spirit and the perpetual virginity of Mary. He was known as a pastor of souls as well as a scholar, a good listener and counselor. Among his chief works are *On the Gospel of Luke, On the Holy Spirit* and *Mysteries.*

Ambrosiaster (fl. c. 366-384). Name given by Erasmus to the author of a work once thought to have been composed by Ambrose.

Ammonius (c. fifth century). An Aristotelian commentator and teacher in Alexandria, where he was born and of whose school he became head. Also an exegete of Plato, he enjoyed fame among his contemporaries and successors, although modern critics accuse him of pedantry and banality.

Andreas (c. seventh century). Monk who collected commentary from earlier writers to form a catena on various biblical books.

Andrew of Caesarea (early sixth century). Bishop of Caesarea in Cappadocia. He produced one of the earliest Greek commentaries on Revelation and defended the divine inspiration of its author.

Andrew of Crete (c. 660-740). Bishop of Crete, known for his hymns, especially for his "canons," a genre which supplanted the *kontakia* and is believed to have originated with him. A significant number of his

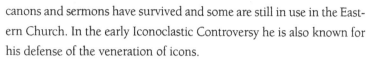

canons and sermons have survived and some are still in use in the Eastern Church. In the early Iconoclastic Controversy he is also known for his defense of the veneration of icons.

Aphrahat (c. 270-350; fl. 337-345). "The Persian Sage" and first major Syriac writer whose work survives. He is also known by his Greek name Aphraates.

Apollonius (d. c. 185-190). A Roman senator who was particularly well read in the philosophy of the pagans. He was forced to appear before the praetorian prefect Perennes and was eventually martyred.

Apostolic Constitutions (c. 381-394). Also known as *Constitutions of the Holy Apostles* and thought to be redacted by Julian of Neapolis. The work is divided into eight books and is primarily a collection of and expansion on previous works such as the *Didache* (c. 140) and the *Apostolic Traditions*. Book 8 ends with 85 canons from various sources and is elsewhere known as the Apostolic Canons.

Apringius of Beja (middle sixth century). Iberian bishop and exegete. Heavily influenced by Tyconius, he wrote a commentary on Revelation in Latin, of which two large fragments survive.

Arator (490-550). Latin poet and orator, perhaps of Milan. He is known for his epic *On the Acts of the Apostles*, which he composed in Rome for Pope Vigilius, who ordained him a subdeacon. It is the only Western writing on Acts before Bede. The epic, favored by Bede and popular during medieval times, is marked by Arator's allegorical and mystical exegesis.

Athanasius (c.295-373). A native of Alexandria and secretary/deacon to his bishop at the Council of Nicaea (325), Athanasius was elevated to the Episcopal See of Alexandria. He was exiled more than four times. He was a prolific writer whose works include *Three Discourses Against the Arians* and *Life of St. Anthony.*

Athenagoras (fl. 176-180). Early Christian philosopher and apologist from Athens, whose only authenticated writing, *A Plea Regarding Christians,* is addressed to the emperors Marcus Aurelius and Commodius, and defends Christians from the common accusations of atheism, incest and cannibalism.

Augustine of Hippo (354-430). Bishop of Hippo and a voluminous writer on philosophical, exegetical, theological and ecclesiological topics. He formulated the Western doctrines of predestination and original sin in his writings against the Pelagians. He was very involved in the theological controversies of the time period.

Babai the Great (d. 628). Syriac monk who founded a monastery and school in his region of Beth Zabday and later served as third superior at the Great Convent of Mount Izla during a period of crisis in the Nestorian church.

Basil the Great (b. c. 330; fl. 357-379). One of the Cappadocian fathers, bishop of Caesarea and champion of the teaching on the Trinity propounded at Nicaea in 325. He was a great administrator and founded a monastic rule. His devotion to the cause of the poor earned him the title of "Great."

Bede the Venerable (c. 672/673-735). Born in Northumbria, he was put under the care of Benedictine monks at the age of seven and received a broad classical education in the monastic tradition. Considered one of the most learned men of his age, he is the author of *An Ecclesiastical History of the English People.*

Benedict of Nursia (c. 480-547). Considered the most important figure in the history of Western monasticism. Benedict founded many monasteries, the most notable found at Montecassino, but his lasting influence lay in his famous Rule. The Rule outlines the theological and inspirational foundation of the monastic ideal while also legislating the shape and organization of the cenobitic life.

Boniface (c. 675-754). A monk who spent time teaching before leaving Wessex for the Netherlands to preach to the pagans of Europe. He also traveled as a missionary throughout central Germany before eventually being martyred.

Caesarius of Arles (c. 470-543). Bishop of Arles renowned for his at-

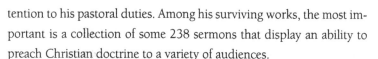

tention to his pastoral duties. Among his surviving works, the most important is a collection of some 238 sermons that display an ability to preach Christian doctrine to a variety of audiences.

Cassiodorus (c. 485-580). Founder of the monastery of Vivarium, Calabria, where monks transcribed classic sacred and profane texts, Greek and Latin, preserving them for the Western tradition.

Chromatius of Aquileia (fl. 400). Bishop of Aquileia, friend of Rufinus and Jerome, and author of tracts and sermons.

Chrysostom (John Chrysostom) (344/354-407; fl. 386-407). Bishop of Constantinople who was noted for his orthodoxy, his eloquence (hence his nickname Chrysostom = "Golden-tongued") and his attacks on Christian laxity in high places.

Clement of Alexandria (c. 150-215). Born to pagan parents, Clement is sometimes called "the first Christian scholar." A highly educated Christian convert from paganism, head of the catechetical school in Alexandria and pioneer of Christian scholarship. His major works, *Protrepticus, Paedagogus* and the *Stromata,* bring Christian doctrine face to face with the ideas and achievements of his time.

Clement of Rome (fl. c. 92-101). Pope whose *Epistle to the Corinthians* is one of the most important documents of subapostolic times.

Columbanus (Columban) (543-615). A teacher, missionary, and founder of monasteries who fought against corruption in the church. His Irish Latin poetry, rules and letters were formational for the culture of the time period.

Constitutions of the Holy Apostles. *See Apostolic Constitutions.*

Cyprian (fl. 248-258). Martyred bishop of Carthage who maintained that those baptized by schismatics and heretics had no share in the blessings of the church. He was generous with his wealth and dedicated to chastity.

Cyril of Alexandria (375-444; fl. 412-444). Patriarch of Alexandria whose extensive exegesis, characterized especially by a strong espousal of the unity of Christ, led to the condemnation of Nestorius in 431.

Cyril of Jerusalem (c. 315-386; fl. c. 348). Bishop of Jerusalem after

350 and author of Catechetical Homilies, which were important for
sacramental theology and baptism.

Didache (c. 140). Of unknown authorship, this text intertwines Jewish
ethics with Christian liturgical practice to form a whole discourse on
the "way of life." It exerted an enormous amount of influence in the patristic period and was especially used in the training of catechumen.

***Didascalia Apostolorum (Teaching of the Twelve Apostles and Holy
Disciples of Our Savior)*** (early third century). A Church Order composed for a community of Christian converts from paganism in the
northern part of Syria. This work forms the main source of the first six
books of the Apostolic Constitutions and provides an important window to view what early liturgical practice may have looked like.

Didymus the Blind (c. 313-398). Blind from the age of four or five,
this Alexandrian exegete was much influenced by Origen and admired
by Jerome, who considered him his master.

Dionysius of Alexandria (d. c. 264). Bishop of Alexandria and student of Origen. Dionysius actively engaged in the theological disputes
of his day, opposed Sabellianism, defended himself against accusations
of tritheism and wrote the earliest extant Christian refutation of Epicu-
reanism. His writings have survived mainly in extracts preserved by
other early Christian authors.

Ephrem the Syrian (b. c. 306; fl. 363-373). A Syrian writer of commentaries and devotional hymns that are sometimes regarded as the
greatest specimens of Christian poetry prior to Dante.

Epiphanius the Latin. Author of the late fifth century or early sixth-
century Latin text Interpretation of the Gospels, with constant references to early patristic commentators. He was possibly a bishop of Ben-
evento or Seville.

Epistle of Barnabas. An allegorical and typological interpretation of
the Old Testament with a decidedly anti-Jewish tone. It was included
with other New Testament works as a "Catholic epistle" at least until
Eusebius of Caesarea questioned its authenticity.

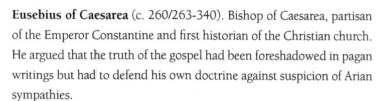

Eusebius of Caesarea (c. 260/263-340). Bishop of Caesarea, partisan of the Emperor Constantine and first historian of the Christian church. He argued that the truth of the gospel had been foreshadowed in pagan writings but had to defend his own doctrine against suspicion of Arian sympathies.

Fulgentius of Ruspe (c. 467-532). Bishop of Ruspe and author of many orthodox sermons and tracts under the influence of Augustine.

Gallican Litanies, Sacramentary, Old Gallican Missal. From the fifth century to the ninth century, these were chants of the ancient liturgies as practiced in French Gaul.

Gaudentius of Brescia (fl. 395). Successor of Filastrius as bishop of Brescia and author of twenty-one Eucharistic sermons.

Gelasian Sacramentary. The most complete and oldest extant manuscript of the Roman Sacramentary. Its ancestry is believed to date back to between 628 and 715. Trium Magorum ("Three Magi") refers to the prayers associated with the Feast of the Epiphany.

Gregorian Sacramentary. A service book with a complex history, whose date and authenticity are still debated. It has been suggested it dates back to 593. It received its definitive form under Gregory II.

Gregory of Elvira (fl. 359-385). Bishop of Elvira who wrote allegorical treatises in the style of Origen and defended the Nicene faith against the Arians.

Gregory of Nazianzus (b. 329/330; fl. 372-389). Cappadocian father, bishop of Constantinople, friend of Basil the Great and Gregory of Nyssa, and author of theological orations, sermons and poetry.

Gregory of Nyssa (c. 335-394). Bishop of Nyssa and brother of Basil the Great. A Cappadocian father and author of catechetical orations, he was a philosophical theologian of great originality.

Gregory the Great (c. 540-604). Pope from 590, the fourth and last of the Latin "Doctors of the Church." He was a prolific author and a powerful unifying force within the Latin Church, initiating the liturgical reform that brought about the Gregorian Sacramentary and Gregorian chant.

Hesychius of Jerusalem (fl. 412-450). Presbyter and exegete, thought to have commented on the whole of Scripture.

Hilary of Poitiers (c. 315-367). Bishop of Poitiers and called the "Athanasius of the West" because of his defense (against the Arians) of the common nature of Father and Son.

Horsiesi (c. 305-c. 390). Pachomius's second successor, after Petronius, as a leader of cenobitic monasticism in Southern Egypt.

Irenaeus (c. 135-c. 202). Bishop of Lyons who published the most famous and influential refutation of Gnostic thought.

Isaac of Nineveh (d. c. 700). Also known as Isaac the Syrian or Isaac Syrus, this monastic writer served for a short while as bishop of Nineveh before retiring to live a secluded monastic life. His writings on ascetic subjects survive in the form of numerous homilies.

Isho'dad of Merv (fl. c. 850). Nestorian bishop of Hedatta. He wrote commentaries on parts of the Old Testament and all of the New Testament, frequently quoting Syriac fathers.

Jerome (c. 347-420). Gifted exegete and exponent of a classical Latin style, now best known as the translator of the Latin Vulgate. He defended the perpetual virginity of Mary, attacked Origen and Pelagius, and supported extreme ascetic practices.

John Cassian (360-432). Author of the *Institutes* and the *Conferences*, works purporting to relay the teachings of the Egyptian monastic fathers on the nature of the spiritual life which were highly influential in the development of Western monasticism.

John of Antioch (d. 441/42). Bishop of Antioch, commencing in 428. He received his education together with Nestorius and Theodore of Mopsuestia in a monastery near Antioch. A supporter of Nestorius, he condemned Cyril of Alexandria, but later reached a compromise with him.

John of Damascus (c. 650-750). Arab monastic and theologian whose writings enjoyed great influence in both the Eastern and Western Churches. His most influential writing was the *Orthodox Faith*.

John the Monk. Traditional name found in *The Festal Menaion*, believed to refer to John of Damascus. *See* John of Damascus.

Julian of Eclanum (c. 385-450). Bishop of Eclanum in 416/417 who was removed from office and exiled in 419 for not officially opposing Pelagianism. In exile, he was accepted by Theodore of Mopsuestia, whose Antiochene exegetical style he followed. Although he was never able to regain his ecclesiastical position, Julian taught in Sicily until his death. His works include commentaries on Job and parts of the Minor Prophets, a translation of Theodore of Mopsuestia's commentary on the Psalms, and various letters. Sympathetic to Pelagius, Julian applied his intellectual acumen and rhetorical training to argue against Augustine on matters such as free will, desire and the locus of evil.

Justin Martyr (c. 100/110-165; fl. c. 148-161). Palestinian philosopher who was converted to Christianity, "the only sure and worthy philosophy." He traveled to Rome where he wrote several apologies against both pagans and Jews, combining Greek philosophy and Christian theology; he was eventually martyred.

Leo the Great (regn. 440-461). Bishop of Rome whose Tome to Flavian helped to strike a balance between Nestorian and Cyrilline positions at the Council of Chalcedon in 451.

Leonine (Sacramentary). Mass prayer formularies with a Roman origin, which have been variously attributed, including to Leo I. It was likely written in the seventh century.

Letter to Diognetus (c. third century). A refutation of paganism and an exposition of the Christian life and faith. The author of this letter is unknown, and the exact identity of its recipient, Diognetus, continues to elude patristic scholars.

Liturgy of St. James. Considered by some to be the oldest surviving liturgy for general church use. Some date it around A.D. 60.

Liturgy of St. Mark. The traditional main liturgy of the Orthodox Church of Alexandria.

Macarius of Egypt (c. 300-c. 390). One of the Desert Fathers. Accused of supporting Athanasius, Macarius was exiled c. 374 to an island in

the Nile by Lucius, the Arian successor of Athanasius. Macarius continued his teaching of monastic theology at Wadi Natrun.

Marius Victorinus (b. c. 280/285; fl. c. 355-363). Grammarian of Af-
rican origin who taught rhetoric at Rome and translated works of Pla-
tonists. After his conversion (c. 355), he wrote against the Arians, and
also wrote commentaries on Paul's letters.

Martyrius. See Sahdona.

Maximus of Turin (d. 408/423). Bishop of Turin. Over one hundred
of his sermons survive on Christian festivals, saints and martyrs.

Maximus the Confessor (c. 580-662). Palestinian-born theologian
and ascetic writer. Fleeing the Arab invasion of Jerusalem in 614, he
took refuge in Constantinople and later Africa. He died near the Black
Sea after imprisonment and severe suffering, having his tongue cut off
and his right hand mutilated. He taught total preference for God and
detachment from all things.

Methodius (d. 311). Bishop of Olympus who celebrated virginity in a
Symposium partly modeled on Plato's dialogue of that name.

Novatian (fl. 235-258). Roman theologian, otherwise orthodox, who
formed a schismatic church after failing to become pope. His treatise
on the Trinity states the classic Western doctrine.

Oecumenius (sixth century). Called the Rhetor or the Philosopher,
Oecumenius wrote the earliest extant Greek commentary on Revelation. Scholia by Oecumenius on some of John Chrysostom's commentaries on the Pauline Epistles are still extant.

Origen (b. 185; fl. c. 200-254). Influential exegete and systematic theologian. He was condemned (perhaps unfairly) for maintaining the preex-
istence of souls while purportedly denying the resurrection of the body.
His extensive works of exegesis focus on the spiritual meaning of the text.

Pacian of Barcelona (c. fourth century). Bishop of Barcelona whose
writings polemicize against popular pagan festivals as well as Novatian
schismatics.

Patrick (Breastplate of). This beautiful prayer is attributed to St.

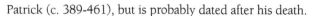

Patrick (c. 389-461), but is probably dated after his death.

Pelagius (c. 354-c. 420). Contemporary of Augustine whose followers were condemned in 418 and 431 for maintaining that even before Christ there were people who lived wholly without sin and that salvation depended on free will.

Peter Chrysologus (c. 380-450). Latin archbishop of Ravenna whose teachings included arguments for adherence in matters of faith to the Roman see, and the relationship between grace and Christian living.

Photius (c. 820-891). An important Byzantine churchman and university professor of philosophy, mathematics and theology. He was twice the patriarch of Constantinople. First he succeeded Ignatius in 858, but was deposed in 863 when Ignatius was reinstated. Again he followed Ignatius in 878 and remained the patriarch until 886, at which time he was removed by Leo VI. His most important theological work is Address on the Mystagogy of the Holy Spirit, in which he articulates his opposition to the Western filioque, i.e., the procession of the Holy Spirit from the Father and the Son. He is also known for his Amphilochia and Library (Bibliotheca).

Polycarp of Smyrna (c. 69-155). Bishop of Smyrna who vigorously fought heretics such as the Marcionites and Valentinians. He was the leading Christian figure in Roman Asia in the middle of the second century.

Primasius (fl. 550-560). Bishop of Hadrumetum in North Africa (modern Tunisia) and one of the few Africans to support the condemnation of the Three Chapters. Drawing on Augustine and Tyconius, he wrote a commentary on the apocalypse, which in allegorizing fashion views the work as referring to the history of the church.

Procopius of Gaza (c. 465-c. 530). A Christian exegete educated in Alexandria. He wrote numerous theological works and commentaries on Scripture (particularly the Hebrew Bible), the latter marked by the allegorical exegesis for which the Alexandrian school was known.

Prudentius (c. 348-c. 410). Latin poet and hymn-writer who devoted his later life to Christian writing. He wrote didactic theological poetry.

Romanus the Melodist (fl. c. 536-556). A Jewish convert to Christianity, who may have written as many as eighty metrical sermons, which were sung rather than preached.

Sahdona (fl. 635-640). Known in Greek as Martyrius, this Syriac author was bishop of Beth Garmai. He studied in Nisibis and was exiled for his christological ideas. His most important work is the deeply scriptural "Book of Perfection," which ranks as one of the masterpieces of Syriac monastic literature.

Salvian the Presbyter of Marseilles (c. 400-c. 480). An important author for the history of his own time. He saw the fall of Roman civilization to the barbarians as a consequence of the reprehensible conduct of Roman Christians. In *The Governance of God* he developed the theme of divine providence.

Serapion Bishop of Thmuis and disciple of Anthony the Great. Serapion was a supporter of Athanasius in his struggle against Arianism.

Severian of Gabala (fl. c. 400). A contemporary of John Chrysostom, he was a highly regarded preacher in Constantinople, particularly at the imperial court, and ultimately sided with Chrysostom's accusers. He wrote homilies on Genesis.

Symeon the New Theologian (c. 949-1022). Compassionate spiritual leader known for his strict rule. He believed that the divine light could be perceived and received through the practice of mental prayer.

Tertullian of Carthage (c. 155/160-225/250; fl. c. 197-222). Brilliant Carthaginian apologist and polemicist who laid the foundations of Christology and trinitarian orthodoxy in the West, though he himself was later estranged from the catholic tradition due to its laxity.

Theodore of Heraclea (d. c. 355). An anti-Nicene bishop of Thrace. He was part of a team seeking reconciliation between Eastern and Western Christianity. In 343 he was excommunicated at the council of Sardica. His writings focus on literal interpretations of Scripture.

Theodore of Mopsuestia (c. 350-428). Bishop of Mopsuestia, founder of the Antiochene, or literalistic, school of exegesis. A great man in his

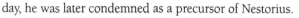

day, he was later condemned as a precursor of Nestorius.

Theodoret of Cyr (c. 393-466). Bishop of Cyr (Cyrrhus), he was an opponent of Cyril who commented extensively on Old Testament texts as a lucid exponent of Antiochene exegesis.

Tyconius (c. 330-390). A lay theologian and exegete of the Donatist church in North Africa who inf luenced Augustine. His *Book of Rules* is the first manual of scriptural interpretation in the Latin West. In 380 he was excommunicated by the Donatist council at Carthage.

Index of Names and Sources

Scripture Index